THE ATHEIST'S PRIMER

The
Atheist's
Primer

MALCOLM MURRAY

BROADVIEW GUIDES to PHILOSOPHY

© 2010 Malcolm Murray

All rights reserved. The use of any part of this publication reproduced, transmitted in any form or by any means, electronic, mechanical, photocopying, recording, or otherwise, or stored in a retrieval system, without prior written consent of the publisher—or in the case of photocopying, a licence from Access Copyright (Canadian Copyright Licensing Agency), One Yonge Street, Suite 1900, Toronto, Ontario M5E 1E5—is an infringement of the copyright law.

LIBRARY AND ARCHIVES CANADA CATALOGUING IN PUBLICATION

Murray, R. Malcolm (Robert Malcolm), 1959-
    The atheist's primer / Malcolm Murray.

(Broadview guides to philosophy)
Includes bibliographical references and index.
ISBN 978-1-55111-962-5

    1. Atheism. I. Title. II. Series: Broadview guides to philosophy

BL2747.3.M87 2010   211'.8   C2010-900827-8

BROADVIEW PRESS is an independent, international publishing house, incorporated in 1985. Broadview believes in shared ownership, both with its employees and with the general public; since the year 2000 Broadview shares have traded publicly on the Toronto Venture Exchange under the symbol BDP.

We welcome comments and suggestions regarding any aspect of our publications—please feel free to contact us at the addresses below or at broadview@broadviewpress.com / www.broadviewpress.com.

NORTH AMERICA
Post Office Box 1243
Peterborough, Ontario
Canada K9J 7H5

2215 Kenmore Ave.,
Buffalo, New York, USA 14207
TEL: (705) 743-8990
FAX: (705) 743-8353

customerservice@broadviewpress.com

UK, EUROPE, CENTRAL ASIA, MIDDLE EAST, AFRICA, INDIA, AND SOUTHEAST ASIA
Eurospan Group
3 Henrietta St., London WC2E 8LU
United Kingdom
TEL: 44 (0) 1767 604972
FAX: 44 (0) 1767 601640
eurospan@turpin-distribution.com

AUSTRALIA & NEW ZEALAND
NewSouth Books
c/o TL Distribution
15-23 Helles Avenue, Moorebank, NSW
Australia 2170
TEL: (02) 8778 9999
FAX: (02) 8778 9944
orders@tldistribution.com.au

Broadview Press acknowledges the financial support of the Government of Canada through the Book Publishing Industry Development Program (BPIDP) for our publishing activities.

Edited by John Burbidge
Designed and typeset by Em Dash Design

This book is printed on paper containing 100% post-consumer fibre.

Printed in Canada

CONTENTS

"Beware lest any man spoil you through philosophy."
Colossians *2:8*

ACKNOWLEDGEMENTS

Beyond the early — and lasting — influences of my brothers Cam and Doug, and my parents John and Joan, many others have helped me formulate this particular project over the years. I would like to thank, in alphabetical order, John Burbidge, Maxime Burke, Richard Carrier, Phil Ens, Peter Erb, Louis Groarke, Jim Horne, Matthew Keeping, Leonard Krahn, Michael Lantz, James MacCormac, Stephen Maitzen, Lyn McGinnis, Jan Narveson, Joe Novack, Don Roberts, Joe Velaidum, and, as always, my students. In the course of preparing the *Primer*, various anonymous reviewers have made wonderful suggestions and I am deeply grateful to them. At least some of those reviewers, I suspect, are theists, which goes to show how much the world of academic freedom and respect differs from other worlds. Thanks also to Greg Janzen for helping bring this (very) long-term project to a close. And without Alex Sager's vision, enthusiasm, and insight, this project would never have been expressed. But most of all I thank Pat and Emma.

PREFACE

This little book lays down reasons for atheism. To the question, "Does God exist?" the resounding answer is "No!"

Individuals may believe whatever they want, of course. There is no shortage of untenable beliefs. I am not addressing one's *right* to believe whatever one wants. That is not in question. What is in question is whether a belief we have concerning God is true or false. To answer this question, we must pay attention to the kinds of belief atheists are rejecting. The main focus of these short chapters, however, is not *what* people believe. Rather, our concern is with the epistemic warrant of the belief: we want to know whether the belief is true, or likely to be true.

Focussing on whether beliefs about God are true or false presupposes that we prefer our beliefs to be more likely true rather than more likely false. Those who reject this underlying assumption will not need to read this (or any non-fiction) book. To decide whether a particular belief is more likely true rather than false, we have to examine it somehow. We have to do more than note that we believe it. "Well, I believe it," is no answer to the question, "Is your belief true?"

Although this book lays down reasons for atheism, the intended audience is not restricted to atheists. It is important that the arguments for theism be as strongly presented as possible. My intention is to avoid *ad hominem* and straw man attacks against theism. My hope is that theists can read the arguments supporting theism and have no reason to say, "But you've got it wrong!" Only then will the rejoinders resonate with them. For that matter, nor does it do theists any good to reject straw man versions of atheist arguments. So, I see *The Atheist's Primer* as being of interest to dedicated theists as well. Whatever side of the fence we sit on, the beliefs we preserve ought to be well-founded. To see if our beliefs are well-founded, we must look into the face of the best arguments of the opposite camp. Although I side with atheism, my intention for this primer is to offer the best reasons going for both sides. Atheists can use them at their discretion. Theists should be well-informed of them (if not assent to them).

13

My intent is not to insult anyone. My intent is to raise the challenge. If you think these arguments fail to rid you of your belief in God, your challenge is to explain where my arguments have gone wrong. Rather than call me a fool, help me out of the snares I set before you.

SUMMARY OF PARTS

Part I: Preliminaries

The four chapters included in Part I are to help situate our discussion. Chapter 1 explains why being an atheist is better than being merely an agnostic. Chapter 2 considers the objection that atheists dismiss the existence of something no theist ever claimed existed. Atheists invent an impossible being and call it "God" and then proceed to explain why "God" — so defined — doesn't exist. Related to that objection is the worry of religious diversity. How can an argument showing the non-existence of a *particular* god be sufficient to show the non-existence of *any* god? The answer is easy if we are allowed to abstract, so a defence of abstraction is given as well. Chapter 3 distinguishes the atheism that I am advocating from a recent trend in theology called religious atheism. A religious atheist rejects notions of a godhead, while retaining notions of spirituality. Chapter 4 raises the fairly well-known objections against taking sacred texts, such as the Bible or the Koran, literally. It takes a further step, however, by claiming that the usual theistic response — treat sacred texts metaphorically, not literally — has a serious problem in its own right.

Part II: "Proofs"

The chapters included in Part II review the arguments given for why one should believe in God. These include the ontological argument (Chapter 5), the cosmological argument (Chapter 6), the argument from design (Chapters 7 and 8), and the moral argument (Chapter 9). For the most part, these are well known. Most people — even many theists — concede that they fail, but the reasons for their failure seem to escape them, since many continue to appeal to such proofs as soon as one's back is turned. Part of the reason for the continued appeal of these "proofs," I suspect, is that the explanation for their failure often tends to be a bit obscure. For example, "Existence is not a predicate," says Kant, as if that is all the explanation one needs to discount the ontological argument. And the appeal to evolution succeeds in destroying the argument from design only so long as one is clear on evolutionary theory — something not everyone gets quite right. My goal in Part II, therefore, is to clearly articulate first, why the arguments do sound plausible, and secondly, why they nevertheless fail, and to do so without — or with minimum — jargon. The argument from design receives two chapters, since there are two ways of showing why it goes astray: by appeal to evolution as an alternative to the appearance of design (Chapter 7) and by explaining its structural weakness when contrasted with good analogical arguments (Chapter 8).

Part III: Attributes

An attribute of a being is a trait ascribed to that being. If I am lame, one of my attributes is lameness. There is much discussion, usually theological as opposed to philosophical, about the attributes properly ascribed to God. It may seem that atheists need not be bothered to discuss God's attributes. Whether a unicorn has a beard like a goat or not is a matter that presupposes the existence of unicorns. For those who do not believe in unicorns, the discussion about whether it would have a beard is idle. Similarly, some may think that since atheists reject the supposition that God exists, further discussions about God's attributes — whatever those discussions may be — are irrelevant.

But the normal attributes claimed of God are so peculiar that they provide atheists added ammunition. Particularly, if God is defined as a being with specific attributes, and those specific attributes are impossible, or self-contradictory, then God, so defined, cannot exist. Atheists point out that many of the particular attributes normally ascribed to God are, indeed, impossibilities. Examining some of the attributes claimed of God, then, provides another route to atheism. In Chapters 10–14, I shall examine the standard attributes of the Judeo-Christian God: goodness (Chapter 10), omnipotence (Chapter 11), omniscience (Chapter 12), atemporality (Chapter 13), and love (Chapter 14).

It is true that one may believe in a god that does not require these problematic attributes. If so, this part may be skipped. What I wish to rehearse for you in Part III is to: (a) detail the problems with the specific attributes; (b) examine the major defences within the standard Judeo-Christian tradition, and; (c) explain why these defences either fail to solve the problem or create other problems. The problem of suffering (Chapter 10) is better known as *the problem of evil*. How can a good God allow bad things to happen? I think that this worry is fairly decisive in showing the inadequacy of belief in any sort of god. The concept of a deity of some sort that cares about your affairs is more universal than the concept of a deity that knows how many hairs are on your head, or that can lift a large rock, or is outside of time.[1]

Part IV: Faith

Atheists' attempts at discrediting proofs for God's existence are often of no concern to theists. Belief in God is largely a matter of faith. Many theists feel the existence of God in their very souls, and that is proof enough. Or is it? The chapters in Part IV suggest otherwise. Chapter 15 expresses why faith is an inadequate justification for one's belief in God. In normal circumstances, merely because one feels conviction about something doesn't make that belief true. Just because you hope that you have the winning lottery ticket, for example, does not mean that you do have the winning lottery ticket. Not all theists maintain that faith is *intended* as a justification, however. Variations on what faith is intended to do are discussed in Chapters 16–18, and these include existential and fideist arguments (Chapter 16), mystical arguments (Chapter 17), and postmodern arguments (Chapter 18). In all cases, however, the conclusion is not much different. The appeal to faith reduces to the claim that the speaker believes in God. But since *that* was never in doubt, the diversion was idle. Chapter 19 looks at Pascal's famous approach to faith. Most recognize it to be unconvincing, but my role here is to explain clearly why it is unconvincing. Chapter 20 uses a logical positivist notion, the principle of non-falsifiability, to help explain why many faith claims are vapid. In doing so, however, I am careful to divorce the view from any other logical positivist notions. The extrapolated view is simply this: if you refuse to allow anything to count against your belief, even in principle, then your belief doesn't really count for much. And this is the main problem with (at least many) appeals to faith.

Part V: Implications
The last five chapters examine that existential fear that often accompanies persons who consider giving up their belief in a god. What happens to morality? Does one have a reason to keep on living? What happens after death, then? The answer to the first question is, "Nothing" (Chapter 22). The answer to the second question is, "Yes, of course" (Chapter 23). The answer to the last question is, "Nothing, sorry" (Chapter 24). Meanwhile, Chapter 21 addresses mystical experiences. Often religious thinkers conceive mystical experiences as evidence for God's existence. Others highlight it in terms of at least being present with something supernatural, something metaphysical. In either case, it would seem that atheism must thereby reject the existence of mystical experiences. Such a move jars with testimony, however. My response, instead, is to distinguish the experience from the interpretation. Mystical experiences are real phenomenal events; real replicable brain states. Atheists need only deny that mystics commune with anything supernatural.

The final chapter, "Error Theory," tackles the vexing question: "If belief in God is so wrong, why do so many people across so many cultures and times believe in some sort of a god?" This is an interesting question so long as it is not intended to be used as evidence for God's existence. As to why religion persists despite lack of epistemic warrant, some kind of error theory — an account of why the error persists — will be needed. But whatever the correct error theory is won't make any difference to the question this little book addresses: Is belief in God epistemically warranted? My answer to *that* question is NO!

NOT DISCUSSED

The Atheist's Primer is not intended to exhaust the literature. Arguments and variations of arguments abound, but what I offer in *The Atheist's Primer* is intended to be the main corpus.[2] Further discussion and debate are always possible, but I hope without ignoring the points raised here. That said, at least four things that might be expected in an atheist's primer will not be found here: the argument from bad consequences, the argument from pluralism, a history of atheism, and a concerted effort to discuss world religions.

The Argument from Bad Consequences

Consider the claim that most of the evils humans cause other humans is done in the name of religion.[3] I may agree with this claim, but I do not discuss the wholesale slaughter humans have committed in the name of religion, because it is irrelevant to the debate at hand. It shows only that religion has a great potential to incite great passion, and sometimes that passion may move people to do evil things. If the claim is taken as a reason to abandon religion, then it is purely a prudential, or utilitarian, calculation. What it would not show is that a god does not exist, or that it is epistemically wrong to believe in God (even if it is prudentially wrong to so believe). As noted already, my concern in this book is merely with the epistemic warrant of a belief in God. For that matter, the fact that people, or zealots perhaps, mistake what religious doctrine in fact recommends, can hardly convince more sane religious believers to abandon their beliefs. The lessons of Jesus, or Mohammed, or Gautama are clearly counter to the conclusions reached by religious warmongers.

Moreover, religion has brought about good consequences, too: music, architecture, art, charitable organizations. Such benefits can't establish God's existence, of course, any more than bad consequences of belief in God shows God's non-existence. Nor can we forget that people have caused wholesale misery to other people for non-religious reasons. To blame religion for all our evil deeds — to people, to animals, to the environment — is not to look at humans closely enough.

The Argument from Pluralism

The second topic not discussed concerns the argument for atheism from religious pluralism. As David Hume noted in 1757, accepting multiple religions is inconsistent.[4] If each religion says that it — and only it — is the right one, and embracing any other is idolatrous, then to embrace them all is to guarantee error. Meanwhile, to choose only one among a throng of religions, each professing itself to be the only route to salvation, the chances of your having chosen correctly is slight. Take any religion that you want, the chances are that it's the wrong one and not worth believing in. As an argument based on probability, this isn't bad, so long as there really is no overlap of core ideas across competing religions, and the number of realistically contending religions is really as large as Hume pretends. Both points are dismissed by the respected philosopher of religion, John Hick.[5] But even if Hick were wrong, and Hume correct, the argument from religious pluralism would still not be sufficient for atheism. Although any individual may be hard pressed to know which religion is uniquely right, it would leave the possibility that one is indeed right. This means that it would leave unscathed the basic premise that God (of some description) exists. But "God (of any sort) exists" is precisely the proposition that *The Atheist's Primer* intends to reject, and so the argument from pluralism is not to the point.

History of Atheism

The Atheist's Primer is not an historical analysis. Its focus is purely epistemic. That is, it examines whether belief in a god is warranted. Whether a belief is warranted is largely independent of the lineage of the belief. The term "atheism" is obviously coined after the term "theism," and so in that sense atheism is an upstart rebel teenager compared to theism. But so what? The belief that the world is flat was held before the belief that the world is round. Besides, if we take atheism to be part of the commitment to seek naturalistic explanations for events in the world, atheism has a much longer lineage than it is typically credited.[6]

World Religions

In the main, I am addressing the belief in a deity within the Judeo-Christian tradition. Variations make brief appearances in Chapters 2, 3, 4, 21, and 25. Many will see this as a shortcoming, and perhaps it is, but my arguments are addressed primarily to the inability to back the underpinning metaphysical claims that are needed to keep deity beliefs afloat. In that sense, the epistemic worries that arise for belief in the Judeo-Christian God will apply to any god concept. Variations within the different religions typically concern the nature of the deities, and the things that one has to do to reach salvation. But none of these things worry the atheist, for they are all predicated on the preliminary presumption that some kind of deity exists. It's *that* belief that *The Atheist's Primer* rejects. Given that, a catalogue of world religions won't be found here.[7]

READING TIPS

For the most part, I have tried to make these arguments as accessible as possible. Some chapters are less so than others, however. As far as the accessible chapters go, they are 1, 2, 6, 7, 9, 10, 11, 14, 15, 19, and 23. Chapters that are more technical, or more specialized, are 3, 5, 8, 12, 13, 16, 17, 18, 20, and 21. The remaining chapters are divided between having accessible and less accessible parts. These hybrid chapters are 4, 22, 24, and 25.

For those pressed for time, a few key chapters express the main points for atheism. These are Chapters 1, 7, 10, 15, 22, and maybe 23. For those already well versed in the philosophy of religion, and who want to get into a bit more depth, I suggest that you also include Chapters 3, 16, 17, 18, and 20.

I have tried to keep referencing to a minimum. The benefit of referencing is to give credit where due and to provide a source for further reading for those so inclined. Thus, each chapter has accompanying notes that may be found at the end of the book. Sometimes these notes offer more technical details and/or raise controversies not discussed in the main text.

PART I. PRELIMINARIES

———∞———

WHY NOT AGNOSTICISM?

There are three broad views concerning the belief in God: *Theism*, a belief in some form of a god or gods; *Atheism*, a belief that there is no such thing as a god; and *Agnosticism*, a fence-sitting position between the first two.[1] Atheists claim that there is no God. They hold such a belief largely on the grounds that no proof exists as yet to convince them of such an entity. Atheists cannot prove that God does not exist, however. Agnostics and theists alike think that this fact is enough to forever discredit atheism. Consider, for example, the famous debate between Copleston and Russell.

> Copleston: Well, my position is the affirmative position that [God] actually exists, and that His existence can be proved philosophically. Perhaps you would tell me if your position is that of agnosticism or of atheism. I mean, would you say that the non-existence of God can be proved?

> Russell: No, I should not say that: my position is agnostic.[2]

But Russell already stumbled. Let us see why.

PROVING NON-EXISTENCE

Atheists should not be reluctant to accept the following proposition:

(1) Nothing can prove the non-existence of God.

Not all atheists are willing to accept this bold claim, mind you.[3] Accepting (1) however, is not to say that we cannot disprove specific arguments for God's existence. There are plenty of reasons to reject every argument yet given for God's existence. Offering such a catalogue is precisely the point of this *Primer*. Showing why a particular argument fails to prove X, however, does not constitute a proof for not-X.

Many will think that if we accept (1), we should be either a theist or an agnostic, but certainly not an atheist. Atheists, after all, are those who believe that there is no God. But if nothing can prove the non-existence of God, shouldn't this count against atheism? The correct answer is "No."

There are two ways of being unable to disprove the existence of something. 1. We cannot definitively prove the non-existence of things for which we already have definitive proof of their existence. 2. We cannot definitively prove the non-existence of things which do not exist. When I say we cannot definitively prove the non-existence of God, I do not mean to invoke the first reason. The second reason is not well understood, however.

Consider the proposition that there is a goblin under the bed. Perhaps your daughter has woken you up in the middle of the night to make such an assertion. How should you appease her? Perhaps you will get down on your hands and knees and look. You report your findings: a stray sock, a book, some dust, but no goblin. Does this test prove the non-existence of goblins? Not if one of the magical properties of this goblin is the ability to become invisible. Your not seeing an invisible goblin is perfectly compatible with the existence of an invisible goblin. Even your daughter understands this logic. So, you take out a broom and sweep under the bed. Your broom has not struck anything that you cannot see. Does this prove the non-existence of an invisible goblin? Again, such a test is to no avail if another of the magical features of this goblin is to disappear when faced by non-believers. Your not striking a goblin that can magically avoid being struck can hardly count as proof against the existence of such a goblin. You now realize that all such tests will similarly fail. The magic nature of the thing being investigated is such that no definitive test can prove its non-existence.[4]

That we cannot definitively prove the non-existence of the magic goblin under the bed does not stymie us, however. We do not say, "Ah, then I guess it's reasonable for us to assume the existence of magic goblins." Nor would we think it reasonable to simply withhold judgement until some definitive proof comes along. Rather, we think it eminently reasonable to believe in the non-existence of goblins, magic or otherwise. Why? Are we wrong to come to this decision absent proof? Let us examine this more closely.

Notice that we cannot simply say, "It is reasonable to not believe in goblins because it is a fact that there are no goblins," since we have just shown that we cannot definitively know any fact concerning the non-existence of goblins. Likewise, we cannot be atheists *because* it is a fact that God does not exist, for that would beg the question. To beg the question is to sneak the conclusion in as one of the premises. If we ask, "Why do you believe God exists?" it begs the question to say, "Because God exists." If we ask, "Why do you believe there was a shooting star?" you would not say, "Because there was a shooting star." You would say, "Because I saw it, and I know shooting stars are possible events, because scientists have well documented them, and for that matter, I have seen them before," etc. Similarly, we all believe in the non-existence of magical goblins, and rightly so, but that doesn't make it a fact that there are no magic goblins. Rather, we reasonably hold that no magic goblins exist because no evidence can be offered to support their existence. We don't see goblins, we don't feel goblins, we don't hear goblins, we don't smell goblins, we don't taste goblins, and any effects that happen in the world can be explained without recourse to goblins. Those reasons are good enough.

THE BURDEN OF PROOF

In courts of law, we presume that a person is innocent until proven guilty. That is, absent proof of guilt, we treat the person as innocent. The *burden of proof* resides with the prosecution. If the prosecution fails to provide reasonable evidence of guilt, the verdict lies with the *default* position: innocence. One might suggest that we should say "not guilty" rather than "innocent" when proof of guilt is not confirmed, and this is fine so long as we don't think a "not guilty" verdict is a "not innocent" verdict. The best way to avoid such a conflation is to say that anyone deemed "not guilty" is *ipso facto* "innocent." That is all we mean by "innocent." We reverse the burden of proof if we think that the defence must conclusively prove its case. Everyone would be presumed guilty unless proven innocent. To deny that anyone has the burden of proof is to admit that agnosticism concerning guilt or innocence is the reasonable position to take when neither side can conclusively prove her case. Making either guilt or agnosticism the default position would severely undermine the justice system.

The analogy, so far, should be clear. Those claiming the existence of something have the burden of proof. Absent a good case being made for said existence, the default position is disbelief in the existence of that thing. Theists make the claim that God exists. Therefore, it is up to the theists to prove their case. And should all their arguments come to naught, the reasonable position is atheism.[5] Theists who maintain that the atheist needs to prove her case have reversed the burden of proof. Agnostics, meanwhile, believe that no one has the burden of proof in the God debate.

FALLIBILISM

Of course it is possible that guilty men go free and right beliefs are rejected. This is inevitable. We are merely human, after all. Error alone is not sufficient to reverse the burden of proof. Instead, we are *fallibilists*. That is, we admit the possibility that we are wrong. Taking a stance while admitting that one may be wrong is different from not taking a stance precisely because one may be wrong whichever stance one takes. Agnostics assume this latter position. It is unwarranted. The sincere atheist need not pretend to have proof of the non-existence of God. All she needs is to point out that the side with the burden of proof has not sufficiently demonstrated his case.[6]

Similarly, because we can't prove conclusively that aliens have never landed on earth, or that magic goblins do not exist under your bed, does not mean that the status quo is to believe that aliens have landed on earth, or that magic goblins exist. The task is to prove that aliens have landed on earth and magic goblins exist, and failing that proof is sufficient reason to stick with the status quo belief that aliens have not landed and that magic goblins do not exist.

THE COMMON SENSE VIEW

Some may contend that arguing for the existence of something is not the criterion for having the burden of proof. Instead, they claim, the burden of proof should lie with those who oppose the commonly accepted view. Consider, for example, furniture. Because it is common to accept that furniture exists, the statement, "Furniture exists," is not doubted. If someone said, "Furniture doesn't exist," that person would be the one who would have the burden of proof. If so, existence is not the criterion for the burden of proof; common belief is. Because it is common to accept that God exists, atheists should have the burden of proof, not theists.

While initially plausible, the common sense view of the burden of proof fails for two reasons. First off, notice that a commonly held belief is not accepted *because* it is commonly held. As our mothers may have reminded us, we would not jump off a cliff (without water below, or being strapped to bungee cords, parachutes, or hang-gliders) merely because others were to do so. If a belief is commonly held, then there must be independent grounds to believe it as true other than the mere fact that others believe it. It can't be the case that each member of the common group believes it on the basis of the group's believing it — for how could the first or subsequent members ever come to believe it by such means? This suggests that there must be independent grounds for common beliefs to be true other than the fact that others commonly believe it. Let's take an example. It is common to believe that it snows in Saskatchewan in winter. Do we believe this *because* it's common to believe it? Or can we appeal to our experience with snow in Canadian climates? Presumably it's the latter. That is, while it may well be common (in Canada) to believe that it snows in Saskatchewan in winter, the reason Canadians believe it is *not* because other Canadians believe it. Rather, each Canadian believes it snows in Saskatchewan in winter because each Canadian independently relies on evidence common to all Canadians. In order for us to take belief in God as the default position, *because it is common to believe in some kind of god*, we need to be able to point to common evidence for that belief, not merely to point to the fact that the belief is common.[7]

Secondly, the common view argument needs us to sincerely believe that no proof for furniture's existence is compelling. We need to deny that our seeing the chair, our touching the chair, our sitting in the chair, count as compelling proofs. Indeed, there is a philosophical argument to make such a case, but it is hardly a commonly held notion. Philosophers are concerned about how we know anything at all. To know whether the chair exists as it appears to us, we need to see what the chair is like independently of how the chair appears to us. To do this, we can no longer rely on our senses. If we use our senses, that contaminates the experiment. But without the use of our senses we can no longer tell anything about the chair. Thus we are stymied. My seeing the chair cannot definitively prove that the chair is really as it visually appears to me. All we have — and all we can ever have — is the appearance of reality, not a proof of reality. So here is a case where our belief in furniture is the default position despite sufficient evidence. Such an argument, then, denies that the burden of proof lies on those maintaining existence. Some theists use this to their advantage. While there may not be sufficient evidence to believe in God, nor is there sufficient evidence to believe in furniture. But since we do rightly believe in furniture, we can thereby rightly believe in God.[8]

Such a reversal of the burden of proof is unconvincing, however. We don't believe in the existence of furniture because it is common to believe in furniture. If it is a common belief, the belief must be linked to something commonly accessible. It is: our senses. In fact, thinking of why we believe in furniture reveals how we are forced at a fundamental level to trust our senses. This may fall short of an indubitable proof, but the demand for indubitable proof on such matters is where the problem lies. On the reasonable assumption that we can generally trust our senses, the proof of the chair's existence is sufficient, if anything is.[9] Theists, therefore, need to give reasons why we should completely distrust our senses if they want to reverse the burden of proof. Good luck to them.

IS ATHEISM ITSELF A METAPHYSICAL BELIEF?

Once we see that atheism is the default position, we see that it is misleading to conceive of atheism as a metaphysical doctrine. In courts of law, the absence of proof of guilt entails the (fallibilistic) belief of innocence. In the absence of any evidence of an invisible monster under the bed, we do not suspend judgement; we accept (fallibilistically) the default of non-existence. Similarly, absent convincing evidence in favour of a god, atheism is the reasonable (fallibilist) position. In this sense, one needn't presume that atheism requires a belief structure to back it up. Nor does one need to know the history of atheism. Thinking so makes the mistake of putting atheism on a par with theism as far as holding a web of metaphysical beliefs. Atheism is simply the default position.

SUMMARY

Those who maintain the existence of something always have the burden of proof. Theists maintain the existence of God. Therefore, theists have the burden of proof. Should those proofs fail, the reasonable position is atheism, not agnosticism.

Of course, this does not show that the theists' arguments fail. We would need to look at each individual argument for that. And that is what I plan to do in the following chapters.

2

———∞———

WHICH GOD ARE
YOU DENYING?

We seem to need to know what God is before we can decisively say no such being exists. But there is no consensus on what God is. There are many religions. Within these religions are further factions. Within a given faction there are many believers with varied interpretations. Is it possible to define "God" in terms general enough to accommodate all these varied beliefs? As one anthropologist puts it, "Whatever commonality of religion is found, anthropologists can come up with a countercase."[1] Given the lack of consensus on stipulating what God is, atheists face the following problem: the God that we claim does not exist may not be a god anyone ever claimed to exist. And whatever we say, then, we are not saying anything about the true God. My intent in this chapter is to explain how I may proceed, notwithstanding this obstacle.

For a preview, I claim that whatever picture of God you have, so long as that entails metaphysical agency, atheist arguments apply. Agency entails an intentional stance.[2] If something thinks, or loves, or intentionally does stuff, that's an agent. A metaphysical agent is one who can do those things without physical presence. Atheists admit that there are things without physical presence. Atheists also admit that there are agents. Simply, they deny the two can go together.

KIDNEYS AND HEARTS

To answer whether or not God exists, we seem to need to know what God is. Is God an X, a Y, a Z? We may agree that God defined as an X doesn't exist, but that wouldn't end the discussion unless we agree that God is properly defined as an X. Perhaps God is best understood as a Y. But expecting agreement on our defining God as a Y is imprudent. As it turns out, fortunately, we need no wholesale agreement on the full nature of God. All we need are a few key characteristics. To encompass as wide a range of concepts of God as possible, these few key characteristics will be abstractions. I fully acknowledge that most theists never come to think of their God in these abstract terms. To them, God is more personal, more concrete, more real, than abstract. To them, God is not definable in philosophers' terms.[3] This does not mean, however, that God cannot be properly defined in abstract terms.

The complaint about rejecting an abstract God is irrelevant. Consider the fact that you are a human being. Your identity is rich and full and unique. Your experiences, successes, failures, relations, careers, hobbies, keepsakes, cultural values, parental values, peer values, social status ... all these and more intertwine to form who you are. For me to define you as simply something with kidneys and a heart would seem woefully inadequate. As unique individuals, we resist being treated as mere things. Any generalization of human types will invariably sound cheap.

Nevertheless, having kidneys and a heart is a true characteristic of you. That you cannot deny. I can use this information. Let's say that I have a device that beeps when it detects kidneys and hearts; I hold it up to a box, and it doesn't beep. Given this information, I am free to infer that you are not in the box. That you are more than just kidneys and a heart detracts nothing from the accuracy of my conclusion. That having kidneys and a heart is not what you would consider essential to your identity is irrelevant to my making use of that definition. Similarly so with God.

WHAT IS GOD?

So we need to come to some agreement on what the kidneys and heart of a god is in such a way that all, or most, conceptions of God share these bits. Such shared characteristics tend to include: God is an agent; God is unique; God exists externally, not merely in the imagination of believers; God has a spiritual presence, not a physical presence; and God is the creator of all existence.[4] Other characteristics may be thrown in, but these will do.[5] Minimally, God is a supernatural agent. God's being an agent means God can do things, like love you, or perhaps curse you, and God can create stuff, like the universe. God's being unique highlights the supremacy of God (or gods, so long as the set of gods is unique). The supernatural or spiritual presence of God highlights the resistance to any natural reduction of God. God's being the creator of the universe highlights that God has something to do with existence. That God is responsible for creating the universe out of nothing (*ex nihilo*) is a central doctrine of Christianity, Judaism, and Islam.[6] That God (or a god) created the world out of stuff already existing is common to a variety of other religions and myths.[7] Variations exist about the nature of the creator, of course. For gnostics, the true God is not the creator. Rather, according to gnostics, matter was created by a demiurge. Doing so was a deviation from the true God's will, since the creation of matter divorced humans from God. Be that as it may, even gnostics accept that the universe was created by a deity of sorts. Deism is the belief that God created the world, but does not maintain or care about the world after He created it. Process theologians believe that God is still in the act of creating the world. Judeo-Christian theists maintain that not only did God create the world, He is still very much presently concerned with the world. But all of these variants agree on the kernel that the world was created by something god-like.

True, these essential characteristics of God do not exhaust the nature of God. There are others. Certainly, some of these others may well be thought far more crucial to many theists' understanding of their God than the bits cited here. For example, God is thought to have a great interest in our behaviour. But so long as the abstract parts cited here are components of what they would agree as being attributable to their God, then they will do — just like your being defined as something with kidneys and a heart will do if our only concern is to tell if you exist.

Consider the uniqueness of God. If someone holds that gods and skunks are of the same genus, we would suggest that they misrepresent gods or skunks. If God is unique, defining God in terms of something we already know exists (things not unique to God) will not do justice to God. Given God's uniqueness, when we tell someone, "God is like a Y," we will always have to admit somewhere along the line, "... but of course, God is *more* than just a Y." This addendum removes the connection needed for us to accept God's existence. Our acceptance of God's existence is predicated on our acceptance of Y. If God is *more* than a Y, however, the predication is no longer apt. What is *more* than a Y? Not Ys, anyway. Conversely, if God is defined as simply a Y, and Ys exist, then we ought to conclude that God exists. In this sense, it is easy to prove God's existence, so long as we agree to define God in terms of things that we accept exist. The question of whether we ought to so define God in such terms remains, however. Is it helpful to describe God as a Y? After all, we can say, "Of course God exists if you define God *that* way, but is *that* really what you mean by God?"

The problem lies in the uniqueness of God. God is always one step removed, one step beyond our limited conception. As the existential theologian Paul Tillich believed, God is beyond even the concept of existence.[8] Some will marvel at this. How brilliant! What but God could be so enormous, so puzzling? Fine, but having a concept — like the biggest thing ever imaginable, or the smallest thing ever imaginable, or the thing that is both the smallest thing ever imaginable and the biggest thing ever imaginable at the same time — by itself is idle. Saying the concept of God is beyond all concepts is simple to say, impossible to fathom. Concepts are easy. Whether they actually refer to anything is the hard part. On what basis is that inference made? That I have a concept of a magic spoon doesn't entail the existence of a magic spoon. If such abstraction is as good as we can get, this won't stand in its favour. (For more on this worry, see Chapters 5 and 17.)

An implication of God's uniqueness is inexpressibility. God, being so unique, refers to the unknown, that which exceeds our understanding. Thereby to denounce the existence of such a thing presupposes that one can understand such a thing: proof that the atheist simply fails to get it. But why name an unknown? Wittgenstein imagines a situation where everyone has a box that no one else can see into and whatever is in each person's box is called a "beetle." In such a case, the word "beetle" wouldn't be the name of a thing. The thing in the box would have "no place in the language-game at all; not even as a *something*: for the box might even be empty."[9] And if we were to name all that we don't know, we would possess an awkward language. We would have more terms for things that we don't know than for the things that we do know. I don't know how many species of horseflies there are in Alberta; shall I invent a name for that specific lack? Besides the impracticality of the practice, how can one *believe* in something that one admits one doesn't know? Do you believe that you don't know it? Is that all you're saying?

To claim that something exists, we have to know what it is. But according to the Anselmian view, *The Cloud of Unknowing* view,[10] the view that God's nature is infinitely removed from our ken, then any pretensions of our knowing what God is, is proof that we've got the wrong concept. If it is impossible for us to know what X is, it is impossible for us to say that X exists. The impossibility of saying that X exists hardly justifies believing in X. The default is non-existence. Recall (from Chapter 1) that it is up to the child to make a case for the existence of the monster under the bed, and failing that, it is reasonable to hold that no monster exists. That is how reason works. Why should we subvert that when we speak of God?

MAGENTA AND PINK

Or is it possible that some things are inexpressible without our doubting their existence? Describing colour to a blind person will be difficult for the blind person to understand. She might give up. My attempts mean nothing to her, but it wouldn't stop *me* from believing in colour.

Unfortunately, the colour analogy is notoriously poor. It would have us believe that some people "see" God. Those who don't are defective. There is a problem in explaining the defect. Is God a worthless manufacturer to have shipped off faulty merchandise? Generally, theists explain sin as the fault of the sinner due to free will, rather than ascribe the fault to the manufacturer. But here we are speaking about defects in perception and/or cognitive ability. Such defects can't be blamed on sin. For the colour analogy to work, it would have to make sense to speak of someone abandoning belief in colour in the first place. Similarly, why would one have sinned in the first place if God's glory is evident to one prior to the sin? Aquinas's attempt to avoid such worries was to claim that it wasn't the knowledge of right and wrong embossed in our souls, but the *capacity* to know right from wrong that is embossed in our souls. Our having a capacity to know right from wrong doesn't preclude our needing good instruction concerning what is right and what is wrong.[11] Saying it this way, however, doesn't help theists too much. We also have the capacity to murder people. For that matter, we also have the capacity to disbelieve in God. So telling me that certain aptitudes or capacities are naturally ingrained in us is not to tell me much at all.

We can avoid this worry, though, by altering the analogy slightly. I say, "That's pink," and you tell me, "No, it's magenta." I first wonder whether you speak my language, but soon I discover that you do understand the concept of pink. We agree on other things that are pink. You point out the distinction between the thing you call magenta and the things that we both call pink, and I come to see the difference. I say to myself, "Aha, so that is magenta." I now know how to apply my new knowledge. I understand how the term "magenta" is used.

In explaining magenta without a magenta artifact, the case will be slightly different. You will say, "Magenta is like pink, but different," or "Magenta is pinkish, but not pink." I will be hard pressed to correctly use this new bit of information, but I will at least understand a rough approximation of what magenta is. I will know it's nothing like yellow, or blue, that it is more similar to pink. Similarly, you may tell me that God is like a Y, but different. I will have some idea. The fact that Ys exist will lend some support to God's existence. But at the same time, we are not reducing God to a Y. If we did that, I would say, "Well what's the point of introducing this new term?" If magenta were completely reducible to pink, I would ask, "Why should I worry about the existence of magenta when my concept of pink is perfectly adequate?" Magenta wouldn't have any use to me. Similarly, if God is reducible to Y, I wouldn't be moved to say that now I have proof God exists. I would be moved to dismiss God as an unnecessary appendage. I would stick with my Y.

Alternatively, God is reduced to a Y, but I reject the existence of any Ys (God is a "grand spirit," for example). Ys, to me, are as much a metaphysical flight of fancy as was God. If so, the attempt at making God credible would have failed. It is precisely because of this realization that neo-theists try to make a case for God's nature in terms even the atheist would accept, like love (see Chapter 14) or an ultimate concern (see Chapter 17) or aesthetic appreciation (see Chapter 3) or even nature (see below). In doing so, they apply the magenta analogy. Their telling me that God is like Y when I already accept Y's existence is not to trick me into believing in God's existence (*so defined*) but to guide me in the right direction. God is like love, in important respects, but different, unique, greater still.

But the magenta analogy fails. In the end, there's something at which one really can point in cases of magenta. What can we point at in the case of God? If we had such a thing, the discussion wouldn't ensue. We all admit that we can never point at God.[12] Both theists and atheists agree on that. We tend to look with suspicion at those who believe that they're really pointing at God.

One thing's being like, but different, than another works well for things that belong in the same category. Magenta and pink are both colours, at least. However different bats are from us, there is some useful similarity between us and bats since we're both mammals. Molluscs and humans, however, are not just different species, but different clades. To liken molluscs to humans would be to stretch things too far, but even molluscs and humans have more in common than humans and God. At least molluscs and humans are both physical creatures discernible by perception and governed by laws of biology. God is not any of these things. When God is defined as being beyond all categories, being utterly unique, comparison talk is meaningless. God cannot be *like* anything at all — except maybe other gods. Whereas I do see other colours, I do not see other gods.[13]

TOLERABLE MISDESCRIPTIONS

Part of the problem in discussing notions of God is the miserable state of language itself. The words used carry with them mundane denotations, yet are meant more figuratively, symbolically, and any attempt to pin them down to mundane denotations is uncharitable. We speak of sunsets although the phrase contains a false referent. The error is harmless, though. We still *use* the phrase. It is poetic, or at least simpler, to speak of sunsets and not earth revolutions, which in any event wouldn't capture the image we wish to speak about. The subject isn't the earth, but the sunlight. So, we tolerate the error and don't believe that anyone today misunderstands physics when he says, "Look at the beautiful sunset." The same speaker does not say, "Look at the pole passing the car." Saying, "Look at the sunset," does not preclude an understanding of motion. Perhaps speaking of God is similar. When people use the term "God," they really mean Y. In this sense, then, we can say, "God, so understood, exists."

For example, theists may point at God so long as the pointing is inward, not outward. For philosophers Whitehead and Hartshorne, we do not expect to perceive God, but we can *prehend* God.[14] Prehension is a non-sensory mode of perception. Memory, for example, is an act of prehension. We don't perceive our childhood traumas, though we remember them. Nor do we perceive pain as we perceive the object that caused the pain. We prehend pain. Similarly, though we don't perceive God, we prehend God. And just as we cannot point at God, nor can we really point at our prehensions. When I point at the pain in my toe, all you see is me pointing at my toe. My pointing at my toe does not convince you that my toe is in pain. But perhaps I do not care to convince you that my toe is in pain (unless you are my mother, or my physician, or my coach). Likewise, my belief in God is not something that I care (necessarily) to convince you about. I *prehend* it, and that is surely enough. And supposedly, I prehend it every time I love, or when I feel grateful, or when I recognize a morally good action, etc. But an atheist can love, have gratitude, and know what's good without adding this extra belief, this nomological dangler. So *what* is it we prehend? Is it just the prehension, or something more? The existence of false memories, false pains, hallucinations, delusions, and moral error should be sufficient to undermine the authority of prehension.

When we tell people who speak of sunsets that the sun isn't really setting, that it's the earth that's spinning, that when the pole appears to pass the car, it isn't that the pole is passing the car, but the car that is passing the pole, we are not likely to meet resistance. "Of course, what do you take me for, a fool?" they will say indignantly. But this reaction is not what one expects from a speaker about God. "When you use the term God, do you realize that that's merely a shorthand term for the secular concept *Y*?" They will respond, "Don't be absurd. I mean to refer to God, not merely to *Y*. I mean to refer to an existing being." Theists use the term "God" as if it refers to an existing being, a metaphysical agent — not as a short form for love or whatever we've selected as our *Y*.

Of course, if "God" is used in this way, and meaning is defined according to how it is used, as Wittgenstein maintains,[15] the concept of "God" would have meaning. Therefore, meaning is not limited to that which has a referent. Very well, but this does not show that "God" has a referent. It only shows that people *believe* "God" has a referent. These are different things.

LIFE FORCE

Take the now typical reply, "I don't believe in God in the traditional sense: I believe in God as a life force." Is one to deny that a life force exists? Certainly not. Life exists. It's a force. But where does this get us? Atheists need not deny life forces, at least not if a life force is something biology studies, as opposed to *élan vital*, for example. Atheists know that at death, the body rots, the nutrients leak out and are absorbed by the forces of life. Recognition of the food chain does not compel us to accept a metaphysical agent. Some maintain, however, that this is evidence of a soul, a sign of everlasting life, not of mere physics.

There is nothing in the world that can support the further claim of continued identity. That part of my life force that gets sucked up into a willow tree and some other part that gets absorbed temporarily by slime mould is unlikely to capture what people typically mean by life after death. There is no evidence that it is *me* that continues. Parts of me may move on after my death, but not the parts with which I can identify. That *something* continues after my death is nothing to me. The notion of a continued existence of a soul is not demonstrated by pointing out nature's rejuvenating forces. (For more on the death state, see Chapter 24.)

Talk of immortality is not necessarily connected to talk of God, of course, although the two are often related. Presumably, persons who speak about God as a life force do not mean to equate God merely with the subject of biology. If pressed, they probably mean that God is the *ground* of the life force, the ground of biology.[16] Usually, however, there isn't a ground to a force — only the force itself. When one speaks about biology, one isn't looking for the ground of biology. To the extent that one is looking for the ground of biology, one isn't looking at biology anymore. A force like gravity isn't explained by an appeal to *another* force. To think so means that you don't understand the explanatory force that gravity offers, or the explanatory force that biology offers. It's as if, after explaining to someone that thunder is not due to God's being angry but electrical discharges momentarily cleaving air masses, the person replies, "Yes, but God must be angry to do that." The replier is looking for the *ground* of the scientific explanation; and thereby isn't doing science anymore.

If the above is not clear, consider the following. The assumption, "Everything has a natural cause," is what scientific inquiry presumes. Science cannot empirically test that presumption. What it can test is whether any particular effect has a natural cause. If it fails to find a natural cause for a particular effect, it doesn't say, "Gee, I guess there's a non-natural cause, then." It keeps looking. But that all tests reveal natural causes will only tell us that observed effects have natural causes, not that *every* effect has a natural cause. That's an inference beyond the observational data.[17] To ask, "Why does everything have a natural cause?" then, is not open to scientific inquiry other than by continuing with particular observations of natural science.

Similarly, we can say that a being exists (who can deny that?), but to conclude that therefore *being itself* exists, is to confuse categories. The "existence" of being is a different sort of thing than the existence of any being. Consider a dog and the concept of a dog, which we'll call *doghood*. A dog will bark, but doghood will not bark. A dog will wag its tail, but doghood will not wag its tail. A dog will have fleas, but doghood won't have fleas. Does this mean that doghood is greater than dogs? Does this mean that doghood is responsible for dogs' existence? Such reification is confused. Doghood did not create dogs. We created doghood to account for dogs. Similarly, say the atheists, to reify being itself is insane. God is simply our own creation to account (poorly) for being.

What this shows is that people cannot simply equate God with biological life forces. People cannot support their use of "God" with an appeal to the natural sciences. To do so is to either be misinformed about the meaning of "God," or to be misinformed about natural sciences. When theists speak of God as being the ground of being, they are speaking of something beyond the realm of scientific inquiry. And so long as they do so, they cannot appeal to science for support. Such news shouldn't be shocking to most theists, but it kills the loose talk attempt of equating God with nature or life forces.

THE ARGUMENT FROM EXPERIENCE

Some people claim to have had direct contact with God. This is not a see-a-face-in-the-clouds type experience. It is not a God talking to them. It is a personal experience. Whatever the experience is, it is an event that leaves the experiencer little recourse but to admit that God exists. Such people may not be theologically savvy. Their experience tells them nothing about God's nature; it tells them only the brute fact that He is. Such personal experiences vary, of course, and to a large extent, they seem to be ineffable. The description hardly does justice to the phenomenon. One student of mine could only cry as she tried to explain her personal experience with God during the horrendous aftermath of an earthquake in Mexico City. So I will tell you mine. I was trapped on the face of a cliff near Port Eliza on Vancouver Island. After exhausting my options, I, perhaps rashly, lunged to try to reach a ledge some distance above me. In the process, I felt what I can only describe as the hand of God lifting my foot to safety. Being an atheist, I also knew that my immediate description of the experience was implausible. Knowing that, however, did not diminish the feeling that I had experienced some metaphysical intervention.

I take it that my Port Eliza event captures the kinds of personal God experiences that some people have. The best alternative explanation I can come up with has something to do with adrenaline, and I concede that it sounds lame. What is important, however, is to recognize that it is false to say that I directly experienced God. Rather, I experienced a sensation that my foot was lifted. That was the immediate sensation. Even that "sensation," presumably, was the output of faulty interpretation. The fact that I immediately felt the hand of God, or felt my foot lifted, does not mean that no interpretation occurred between the bare event and my phenomenal experience. Rather, I had an experience that I immediately interpreted as my foot being lifted by the hand of God. Putting it this way highlights that the experience itself cannot count as confirmatory of the interpretation. (For more on the distinction between interpretation and sensation, see Chapter 21.)

OUR NATURAL BEING

A disciple went to a Zen master and asked what he needed to do to become enlightened. The master struck him across the head.[18] The moral is that you are already the Buddha. It is merely our rationalizations that have seemingly cut our conscious selves off from who we really are. And discovering this inner nature is to discover the Buddha inherent in us all. Perhaps what is often meant by a god is not the white bearded sort of thing, but something like what Zen Buddhists mean: a personal contact with nature. If so, denying the existence of a god *so defined* seems senseless.

But what is meant by this Buddha in us? For Zen Buddhists, it appears to be the realization of how much a part of nature we are.[19] And voilà, we return to the mundane. The message is that we should learn to become more in tune with our natural being. There is nothing counter to atheism in this. Does being in tune with our natural being give evidence of a god? Why? What does this addition do? A skunk and a fish are more in tune with their true natures than most humans. Does this mean that they are more in tune with God?[20] If so, the term "God" has been so watered down as to mean nothing but what atheists mean by "nature." And saying that some people are more in tune with nature than others is not something atheists need deny.

THE POINT

The intention of *The Atheist's Primer* is to offer reasons for why belief in a god is unwarranted. As we have seen, a problem immediately arises: what sort of God? There are a number of traditional religions, countless variations on those traditions, even more non-traditional beliefs, and yet more personal god beliefs. To reject one religious belief will hardly mean one should thereby reject all religious beliefs. So this preliminary chapter was offered to narrow our scope.

In the main, I am addressing the belief in the Judeo-Christian deity. My arguments are addressed primarily to the inability to back the underpinning metaphysical claims that are needed to keep such a belief afloat. In that sense, the epistemic worries that arise for belief in the Judeo-Christian God will apply to most other brands of religions. If I can show that there can be no such unique, metaphysical agent who is the creator of existence — or at least no warrant so far given throughout the course of history that a being with these characteristics exists — I will have shown that there can be no justification for belief in God. This is so, *whether or not I have fully captured what you understand by God*. All that I would need is that you concede that whatever you mean by God, this God is a unique, supernatural agent that created the universe.[21]

Admittedly, some non-traditional beliefs in personal gods may escape being defined by these abstract qualities. God is simply the state of being alive, say, or God is simply my inner conscience, or God is simply the character I invoke when I am fearful or thankful or hopeful. To the extent that such views do escape the charge, so I have avowed, they become too secular to be of any concern to atheists. Where they resist being secular, they fall back under the more traditional conceptions — those that may be rendered in limited abstract terms.

Do not be fooled into thinking that such an abstract definition of God does not capture the essential characteristics of God merely because it does not capture the full picture. That would be a mistake. The danger that atheists dismiss the wrong thing when they dismiss merely some necessary, abstract bits is wildly overstated. Theists understand God to be a supernatural agent. Atheists deny the existence of supernatural agency. What else theists understand God to be is irrelevant.

3

――――∞――――

RELIGION WITHOUT GOD?

RELIGIOUS ATHEISM

Ricœur says, "Atheism clears the ground for a new faith."[1] This should strike atheists as a weird thing to say. Atheists aren't in the job of creating new faiths, you'd think, but a recent move in Western theology says otherwise. They want to get rid of God, yet for religious reasons.[2] We shall call this trend, "religious atheism." If it seems odd to get rid of God but not religion, recall that a number of Eastern religions have no God, so a precedent has long been set. According to Altizer, "Christian scholasticism followed Aristotle by defining God as pure activity, *actus purus*, [and by doing so] wholly isolated God from the world [and made him] inactive and impassive."[3] This was a mistake. *That* God is dead. By removing scholastic notions of God — the atheist part — religious atheists wish to remain truer to the ground of being — the religious part. They reject the notion of God, but accept spirituality.[4]

Religious atheism is a way of absorbing atheism into religion. As such, we should be suspicious. If religion is so great a sponge that even atheism is absorbed by it, atheism proper is non-existent. As Altizer claims, "The death of God is an event that can only be perceived by faith."[5] Accordingly, as soon as you proclaim yourself an atheist, it means that you have faith. Usurping the concept of atheism for religious purposes is something to be avoided. In fact, defining concepts in such a way that removes any distinguishing feature of that concept is generally to be avoided. So let me be clear: the atheism that I am arguing for in this primer is not religious atheism.

True, an atheist is one who believes that God does not exist, and true, God is merely one sort of metaphysical agent, so technically, an atheist could believe in a host of other metaphysical agents, like bogeys and ghosts. Generally, however, the arguments upon which atheism rests (at least those outlined in this book) will also commit atheists to abandoning the metaphysical baggage upon which any religion is established. When I speak of atheism, I mean this broader picture. Atheism, as I mean it, is the rejection of metaphysical agency.

As noted in Chapter 2, metaphysics concerns what lies beyond the physical, or phenomenal, realm. It concerns itself with the ultimate nature of reality. Saying, "Nothing exists beyond the physical realm" is itself a metaphysical statement. My complaint, therefore, is not with metaphysics *per se*, but the very specific belief that there is at least one metaphysical agent. Agency entails the ability to take an intentional stance. To believe in God is to believe that something beyond the physical/phenomenal realm can take an intentional stance. Atheism, as I mean it, rejects that.

Given the existence of religious atheism, some suggest that what I would call "atheist" is better described as "areligious." (The irreligious, presumably, are those who simply never entertain the question at all.) But being areligious allows for the belief in a personal god without the accoutrements of formalized religion. So, I would need to say something like "areligious atheism" to distinguish my brand of atheism from "religious atheism" (let alone "religious theism" or "areligious theism"). Such terms are clumsy. Instead, I shall argue that religious atheism doesn't deserve the name "atheism." Atheism, as I mean it, is the rejection of all the metaphysical baggage that is essential to religions of any sort.

Clarifying that, *for me*, atheism does not include religious atheism is sufficient in terms of understanding the arguments presented in this primer. But we can do more than provisionally stipulate: we can show why religious atheism is one of the tenets that atheism rejects. Religion is vast and amorphous and is associated with many good things that atheists need not reject. Religious architecture, religious music, and religious painting can be beautiful and intrinsically valuable, even to atheists.[6] And religion has been a useful glue for communities, perhaps even a passable opium against existential angst. But what makes religion uniquely religious is not these things. Rather, what makes something religious has to do with the affirmation of spirit. When (areligious) atheists reject God, they do so because they have no good grounds to believe in the spirit world at all. So, for us, the concept of religious atheism is nonsensical.[7]

SPIRIT

Whether we are religious atheists or areligious atheists depends on what we mean by "religious." For example, some define religiosity in terms of archaic and rigid institutions.[8] Rejecting such things is not the same as accepting atheism. Ray Billington, a former Methodist minister who now considers himself a religious atheist, describes a religious experience as the encounter of "a metaphysical, spiritual essence of the world that is beyond the merely material."[9] For proof, he claims, "[H]uman experience over the millennia suggests ... that the world of metaphysics is a reality, not a fantasy, much less an aberration."[10] And, "If the religious experience is unreal, it follows that billions of people, from widely differing levels of existence in a variety of contexts have been deluding themselves that the euphoria or sense of absorption that they feel on certain occasions were something more than brain cells stimulated by one catalyst or another."[11]

If we allow such subjective phenomenological introspection to count as evidence, we can "prove" the existence of witches. People really did see witches. They weren't hallucinating. Our telling seers of witches that they are deluded is not a comment on their perceptual abilities: it is a comment on their conceptual interpretation. Likewise, with the religious: telling us that the phenomenal state of witch-seers or religious-seers can't go any way to support the validity of what they think they see.

Apart from jumping on the bandwagon, Billington also cites the appreciation of art and of nature as counting as a religious experience. As he says, art is "holy" — even if unacknowledged by the artist. Through music, we can experience the divine. To be moved by Wordsworth's "Lines Composed a Few Miles Above Tintern Abbey," is to have a religious experience. And appreciating nature is to appreciate the spiritual: to be able to see, as Blake does, "a world in a grain of sand ... Eternity in an hour."[12] In other words, a "religious experience is to have a profound sense of awe."[13]

Difficulties abound. The basic worry is definitional. The implication is that to be a *true* atheist, one must be indifferent to poetry, to nature, to art, to music, to love, to being awed ... otherwise, one endorses religion. Lubac is explicit: "Atheists reject everything attributed to God, including love and personal relations and wisdom and justice." Since (areligious) atheism results in "the annihilation of the human person," atheism is built upon "resentment."[14] Such superciliousness is suspect. Atheism annihilates the human person only if we define the human person as divine. Absent such definitional fiat, the suggestion is ludicrous. Shrugging off my belief in God is not like shirking my parental responsibilities to become a deadbeat dad. The epistemic rejection of a belief in any god is not based on "resentment," or "wanting to be free." It is based purely on the lack of epistemic warrant. When one abandons one's belief in a tooth fairy, it isn't because one wants freedom, or that one is resentful, or that one imbues humans with tooth fairy attributes. If someone does abandon her belief in tooth fairies for those reasons, we would call her insane.[15]

Merely because I like poetry, or nature, or painting, or love, or justice, or wisdom, or music, or architecture, hardly justifies metaphysical claims about the divine. And it does no good to say that people over the course of history have experienced awe at seeing nature. No one need ever maintain that such an experience is unreal. We need merely doubt that such awe is a recognition of a metaphysical reality, of a spiritual domain (an issue we'll return to in Chapter 21).

Billington anticipates my reduction of aesthetic appreciation to the non-spiritual: "Some may reduce the experience to no more than the effects of matter in motion, but this still leaves open the possibility that the effects have been caused by a force in the universe which is other than physical."[16] Here Billington equivocates on the uses of physical. In one sense, physical means matter. In this sense, we can reply, "True, but not all non-matter is spiritual." For example, gravity is a force, not matter, or a relation between matter (directly proportional to the product of two masses and inversely proportional to the square of the distance between them), but noting this does not commit us to calling gravity a spirit. The other sense of "physical" that is used in the sciences includes gravity as a physical force. Gravity is one of the things that the discipline of "physics" studies. Other non-spiritual non-matter include "holes, jokes, metaphors, propositions, numbers, legal systems, laws, rules, interest rates, theorems, conversations."[17]

The simple point is this: our rejecting the existence of spirit does *not* mean that we are abandoning art, or love, or a deep appreciation of nature. No metaphysical hocus-pocus is required to appreciate any of these things. So, to think that materialist reduction still leaves room for spiritual explanation is to misunderstand the materialist reduction. After being told that thunder is not caused by God, but by air masses colliding, someone may insist that such a materialist reduction still leaves room for God's decreeing that the air masses collide, and (this is the catch) therefore the materialist reduction is wrong. But the use of the "therefore" is invalid. The scientific explanation of thunder does not require anything else to account for the phenomenon. Or, let's say that you love someone, perhaps a child. Would you feel any need to eradicate that love if you came to learn that there were no such thing as the spiritual? If you have even the slightest inclination to answer yes, we presume that you did not actually love at all, not that the spirit world has been confirmed.

From the religious atheist's stance, to reject spirit is to be a materialist in the non-philosophical sense, as if atheists of my ilk were interested in only conspicuous shopping, as if no atheist were interested in poetry, or sunsets, or music, or can experience profound awe. Religion wishes to conceive itself as offering something unique and sensible. But what's sensible about religion is not unique, and what's unique about religion is not sensible.

THE BACKDOOR GOD

Another worry about religious atheism is the feeling that some sort of god gets snuck in through the backdoor. Although Billington doesn't want to speak of God, he is happy to speak about the "ground of being," and the "godhead."[18] Robinson, after dismissing God, speaks of "the ultimate depth of all our being, the creative grounding and meaning of all our existence."[19] Ricœur sees atheist faith recovering "the true meaning of the God of consolation, the God of Resurrection."[20] Altizer's atheism has it that God willed his own death to enter more completely the world of his creation: "God has actually died in Christ."[21] The word "actually" is rather startling. Atheists of my ilk would never admit such a thing. The God-is-dead theology presupposes that God *did* exist, that God *really did* create the world, and that *in time* God entered the world. For Altizer, one must reject "the God who alone is God and give himself to a quest for the God who *is* Jesus."[22] And "the death of God ... makes possible [our] transition into what Blake hailed as 'The Great Humanity Divine,' or the final coming together of God and man."[23] Such talk, combined with the premise that one is an atheist, is incoherent. In any event, none of this is the atheism that I am advocating.

Atheism (properly understood) would never say, "God is dead," for that presupposes that God once was alive. Hamilton and Altizer clearly believed that there was once a god, but is now no more. Normally, such a view can be subsumed under deism, the view that God created the universe then abandoned it (so long as dying counts as abandonment). Altizer and Hamilton wish to distance themselves from deism, however. They claim that deism is the inevitable result of the orthodox or "scholastic" representation of God. They want a god (or godhead) who is immanent in the world.

In this sense, the term "atheism" is inapt. The religious atheist movement is more closely aligned with agnosticism in the technical sense (see Chapter 1, note 1). Agnosticism, in the technical sense, is the belief in a personal, immanent god that is utterly and absolutely beyond human conception. To conceive of God is to necessarily limit God, and that limitation necessarily distorts. Take any conception of God; agnostics would not believe in that. So superficially, the agnostics may appear to be atheists, for they deny the existence of God, *so defined*. To call them atheists, however, merely for rejecting your particular picture of God, is too fast. As Buber noted, the problem with a belief in God is when it's a belief in an *it*, not a *thou*.[24] Recognizing the thou in human relations is to recognize the thou in "God." In this sense, divinity is manifested through humanity. So when religious atheists express their fears about having a distorted conception of God, they are emphasizing agnostic arguments of old. Agnosticism in the technical sense is well captured by Wittgenstein: "Whereof you cannot speak, thereof you must remain silent."[25] But for theistic agnostics and religious atheists, religious silence has to be understood as worship,[26] and herein lies the problem: speech and thought are integrally connected. The problem is not that I cannot formulate in words my picture of God, but that I cannot formulate any concept in thought either. Worship, however, entails forming some concept of the worshipped. Worship entails that *something* is deemed worthy of worship and it is difficult to formulate what that could be while maintaining that the thing worshipped is beyond conception. A rock is not typically deemed worthy of worship, while an Olympic athlete or a virtuoso violinist may be worthy of worship. This illustrates that things deemed worthy of worship must be distinguished from things that are not. But how is this to be done if one refuses to hold any conception of God at all? The agnostics' party line commits them to holding that God cannot be so distinguished. So, even worship is a form of going astray.

But if any worship is going on — and to that extent if any religiosity is going on — the concept of a godhead is formed, even if only through a *via negativa*.[27] That's what makes agnosticism a *kind* of theism, and likewise, that's what makes so-called religious atheists *kinds* of theists as well.

CONCLUSION

A standard critique of atheism is to suggest that atheists are denying the existence of a god no one ever believed in. Such a worry is not wrongheaded. It is an instance of the general philosophical rule to avoid straw man arguments. On the other hand, if one automatically assumes that any atheist critique *must* be such a straw man, one is falling prey to another sort of philosophical error: begging the question. I hold that atheism is not dependent on having a precise image of God. All that is needed is to understand God as a metaphysical agent. It is the existence of metaphysical agents that atheism finds problematic. Revamp your picture of metaphysical agency all you want, but so long as you believe in a metaphysical agent, atheist arguments apply.

The point of religious atheism is to emphasize the importance of human relations, of communion with nature, of love, of spiritual immanence, without getting caught up in the scholastic picture of an it-God. Theists can affirm God's objective, independent reality without treating Him as a thing, however.[28] And atheists proper can still reject any of the spiritual baggage clinging to religious atheism. This problem with religious atheism was noted by Alasdair MacIntyre (a theist): "[A]ny presentation of theism which is able to secure a hearing from a secular audience has undergone a transformation that has evacuated it entirely of its theistic content.... [T]hat which is credible ceased to be theistic, and that which remains theistic ceases to be credible."[29] I concur.

4

METAPHOR AND
SACRED TEXTS

Man Lives 930 Years (Gen. 5:5)
Woman Turns into a Pillar of Salt (Gen. 19:26)
Man Lives Inside Whale (Jonah 1:17)
Sea Defies Gravity (Ex. 14:21)
Water Turns to Blood (Ex. 7:20)
Water Turns to Wine (John 2:9)
Man Walks on Water (Matt. 14:25)
Giants Roam the Earth (Gen. 6:4)
Man Rises from the Grave (Mark 16:3–6)
Sun Sets in a Muddy Spring (Koran 18:86)
Clot of Blood Turns into a Foetus (Koran 23:14)
Talking Ants Found in Desert (Koran 27:15)
Jews Turn into Apes (Koran 2:65–66)
Christians Turn into Swine (Koran 5:60)

We should expect such headlines in *The National Enquirer*, not in some
sacred text.[1] Or, if a text is sacred, we shouldn't expect obvious absurdities.
A text may well be *memorable* for such surprising tales,[2] but not all memorable stories are sacred. This leads many to ask, ought sacred texts be taken
literally or metaphorically? Either way causes problems for theists. If it is
literal, there is a need to explain not merely its countless improbabilities
and inconsistencies, but also why we generally and safely ignore many of
its dictums (for example, don't wear wool and linen together (Deut. 22:11)
and support capital punishment for Sabbath-breakers (Ex. 31:14, 35:2,
Num. 15:32–36)). On the other hand, if we take the Bible and the Koran
metaphorically, this severely weakens their authority. So I shall argue.

INCONSISTENCIES

Everyone has their favourite examples of inconsistencies found in the Bible. In Genesis, Adam and Eve are claimed to be the first people (2:7, 21). They give birth to Cain and Abel (4:1–2). Cain kills Abel (4:8) then is sent off to Nod where he marries and has children (4:16–17). Later, Seth is born to Adam and Eve (4:25) and he too marries and has children (4:26). Who do Cain and Seth marry? Where did these wives come from? There is no inconsistency if Adam and Eve also had daughters. That the Bible fails to mention anything about Adam and Eve having daughters doesn't mean that they didn't, since women are not generally deemed worth mentioning. But even if they did have daughters, we wouldn't expect these women to have fled before or with Cain to the land of Nod, since this was Cain's punishment for killing Abel. Also, Cain is marked to let "every" person know not to kill him (4:14), but what other people are there? There are only his parents and maybe a sister or two. It is far more plausible to assume that Adam and Eve were not really the first people.

Perhaps you prefer other inconsistencies. Was man created before or after other animals? After (Gen. 1:25–27). No, before (Gen. 2:18–19). The ark is said to have contained the two tablets given to Moses and "nothing else" (1 Kings 8:9), yet it also contained manna and Aaron's rod that had "budded" (Heb. 9:4). Those that seek God shall find Him (Prov. 8:17, Matt. 7:8, Luke 11:9–10), yet elsewhere it is admitted that many will not find God even if they seek Him (Ps. 18:41, Prov. 1:28, Lev. 3:8, 3:44, Amos 8:12, Luke 13:24). Apart from one ram, what is the proper sacrifice to God during the new moon? Two young bullocks and seven lambs (Num. 28:11). One young bullock and six lambs (Ezek. 46:6). Should we rejoice when our enemies suffer? Yes (Ps. 18:10). No (Prov. 24:17). Can a divorced woman remarry? Yes (Deut. 24:1–2). No (Luke 16:18). Is it okay for a theist to marry an atheist? Yes (1 Cor. 7:12–14). No (Cor. 6:14–17). Is long hair on men good? Yes (Num. 6:5, Judges 13:5, 1 Sam. 1:11). No (1 Cor. 11:44).

Other incongruities include: God loves man (Gen. 1:31; Rom. 12:10; Gal. 6:2), yet He later recants (Gen. 6.6,7) and drowns them (Gen. 6:17). Or God is both a loving God (Ps. 107:43, John 3:16) and a jealous God (Deut. 5:9, Ex. 20:5). Sadly, some people might not see an inconsistency here. At best, jealousy is no virtue. At worst, it is a warning sign of an abusive relationship. True love cannot be abusive — not even in a god.

Notice that none of these inconsistencies can be discounted by speaking of the differences between the Old and the New Testaments. The discrepancies concerning the contents of the ark, for example, can't be based on philosophical differences. Inconsistencies concerning love can be found in the Old Testament as well as the New Testament, and not merely between the Old and the New. For that matter, philosophical differences across the two testaments couldn't be attributed to a change in God, since God is supposed to be immutable (unchanging) (Mal. 3:6, Heb. 6:17, James 1:17); nor can we blame some of the writers for getting it wrong without abandoning the notion that the text isn't divinely inspired, and nor can we suppose that the two books simply speak of different gods, since writers of the New Testament endorse tales of the Old Testament. For example, Matthew (Matt. 1:23) quotes Isaiah's prophecy about the virgin birth (Isa. 7:14) and John (John 1:23) refers to the prophecy in Deuteronomy (Deut. 18:15).

The Koran has its own inconsistencies, some of them identical to those found in the Bible. Man (as a species) is said to be created from water (24:45, 25:54), from clay (6:2, 32:7, 55:14), and from dust (3:59, 30:20, 35:11). The Koran is said to be written by Allah Himself (4:82) yet the author of the Koran often breaks into prayer *to* Allah (1:1–7, e.g.). A single day to us is said to be comparable to both 1000 years to Allah (22:47, 32:5), and 50,000 years to Allah (20:4).

Such inconsistencies are, in themselves, trivial. If we find a typo in Chekov, we wouldn't cross Chekov off our list of great writers. Things are different, however, with sacred texts: texts claimed to be written or inspired by a divine, omniscient, perfect being. We can expect errors in non-sacred texts, but not in sacred texts. To find such patent mistakes, then, indicates that the error-filled text is not sacred; it is merely the work of mistake-prone people who happen to believe themselves inspired — if even that.[3]

IMPROBABILITIES

The "headlines" above may well be exaggerations, or perhaps misconceptions in some respect. If so, it is natural to assume that other parts of the book are also exaggerations or misconceptions.

Consider the story of Jonah. He was swallowed by a "great fish" (for trying to avoid a task assigned to him by God) and he remained in the belly of the fish for three days (Jonah 1:17). A man who knows nothing about great fish (perhaps whales) except that they're as big as a house might make the biological error in thinking that the inside of a fish or whale would also be like the inside of a house, though darker. But a god, who is claimed to have made fish and whales (Gen. 1:21) could not make such a mistake.

Another illustration that the authors of the Bible were not in tune with the authors of the universe occurs in Genesis. God created light on the first day (Gen. 1:3–5), yet the source of light (the sun and the stars) on the fourth day (Gen. 1:14–19). In the Koran, the sun sets in a muddy spring (18:86), foetuses come from blood clots (23:14) and the purpose of mountains is to hold down the fields like giant paperweights (Koran 16:15, 21:31, 31:10). Such inaccurate descriptions of nature are understandable in humans, but not a being claimed to have made nature and to know everything. Where mistakes about nature are made, whether about anatomy or physics, we must assume that the mistakes are made by man, and not by God. But because there are mistakes of this sort in the Bible and the Koran, it is surely not unreasonable to assume that this is because such texts are written by man, and not merely the mistaken parts.

Perhaps the Bible was written by man, but under divine light? The light must be heavily filtered to permit such blatant errors about the world that God made. In short, these improbabilities lead one to believe that the Bible is not the authoritative voice of God. If a biography of me is filled with errors and false facts about my actions, we must assume that I didn't approve it. We must assume that it is not authoritative.

IGNORED DICTUMS

There are many pieces of advice given in the Bible and the Koran, most of which, fortunately, we ignore. For example, don't wear wool and linen together (Deut. 22:11), let the state put to death anyone who breaks Sabbath (Ex. 31:14–15, 35:2, Num. 15:32–36), make women subservient to men (Gen. 4:6; I Tim. 2:11–15), weight women one half the worth of men (Koran 2:282). Apart from not making graven images of God, "Thou shalt not make ... any likeness of any thing that is in the earth beneath, or that is in the water under the earth" (Ex. 20:4). Such a decree makes a bronze fish and a ceramic worm as problematic to God as idolatry, which is as heinous as murder and theft. Does anyone today feel sinful for disobeying such rules? Can we give credence to such dictums, let alone worship the source of such dictums?

Moreover, advice is provided for sacrificing animals (Ex. 20:24, e.g.), keeping slaves (Ex. 21:3, Koran 8:51, 70–71), having sex with slaves (Deut. 21:11–14, Koran 4:24, 24:58, 30:28, 33:25–26) and killing homosexuals (Lev. 20:13). In fact, recommending death is common fare. God killed Nadab and Abihu for offering incense as a peace offering (Lev. 10:1–2) even though incense as a sin offering is encouraged (Lev. 16: 11–13). Other biblical reasons for execution include breaking the Sabbath (Ex. 31:14) and, of course, anyone (and his or her progeny) who fails to believe in the right God (Ex. 22:20, Jer. 5:12–13, 2, Peter 3:7, 2, Chron. 15:15, Ps. 78:21–22, 31–34). The Koran's preferred method of killing non-believers is beheading (Koran 8:12, 47:4).

Among some good advice (don't lie, don't cheat, don't steal, be charitable) and how to butcher which animal for which sin, the Bible also forbids shaving (Lev. 21:5), cutting one's hair or trimming one's beard (Lev. 19:27), touching a woman during her period ("her sickness") or anything she touches (Lev. 15:19–27, 20:18), getting tattoos (Lev. 19:28), eating rabbit or pork (Lev. 11: 6–8), eating lobster, scallops, or mussels (Lev.

11:10–12), and it also forbids the blind, the lame, the deaf, the blemished, the flat nosed, the club-footed, the broken-handed, the crooked-backed, the dwarfed, and the scabbed, to approach the altar, for they, like homosexuals, are deemed "profane" (Lev. 21:18–21).

You cannot force your favourite sacred textual bits on others if: (i) you omit other bits from that text; and (ii) your justification is no more than that the normative advice occurs in your favourite sacred book. You can foist on others normative advice that can be found in so-called sacred texts, but not *because* it is found in the so-called sacred text. Independent (and good) reasons must be offered. Otherwise, one is cheating.

PARTIAL LITERALISM

Inconsistencies, improbabilities, and tendentious advice found in the Bible and the Koran make it difficult to treat either the Bible or the Koran literally. (And that's ignoring the problem translation raises for literalists.) The sensible position is not to take everything in sacred texts literally.[4] From here, one can be a literalist for parts of the texts and a non-literalist for the remainder, or one can take no component of any sacred text literally. The problem for partial-literalists, is how to decide which piece of the sacred text to keep and which to dismiss. Non-literalists cannot defend whichever piece they choose by its mere presence in the Bible or Koran. Being non-literalists, they agree that such arguments are void. Some other argument is required. Theologians appeal to theological tradition, but that's just kicking up dust when the issue is precisely whether the tradition itself is worth continued acceptance. The answer can never be, "Because it says so in the Bible," or, "Because it says so in the Koran." They must provide reasons for abiding by what it says in the Bible or Koran independently of its being said in the Bible or Koran. Similarly, someone may give you good advice, but if it is good advice, it isn't good advice *merely because the person said so.*

For example, charity is praised in both the Bible and the Koran, but so too is the belief that homosexuals should be killed. To decide that the former should be kept and the latter discarded, some argument other than "the Bible (or the Koran) says so" needs to be employed. Presumably we can defend the merits of charity independently of its appearance in sacred texts. It helps someone else. It builds community. Those are good reasons for atheists and theists alike. And the mere fact that such good advice can be found in a particular source doesn't make that source authoritative unless we feel convinced that: (i) all things that source tells us are equally good advice (they aren't); and that (ii) no other source provides the same pieces of good advice (but many other sources do so, too).

METAPHORICAL READING

The difficulty with taking sacred texts literally, or even partially literally, leads many to treat such texts metaphorically, or analogously, or symbolically.[5] Being held captive in the belly of a "fish" for three days, for example, may be intended as a metaphor of Jonah's struggle to do the right thing. Even so, I am doubtful that all the above problems dissolve. What is the intended metaphor for the message that we should kill homosexuals? Nevertheless, a new problem arises.

Sacred texts lose their authority if we are to view them metaphorically. The dictums may be very wise. The morals and parables may be excellent lessons. But if we are merely to view them metaphorically, we lose all claims to the literal existence of God.[6] If the big fish is a metaphor for Jonah's doubts, why can't God, who speaks to Jonah, be a metaphor for Jonah's conscience? Once we abandon any pretension of literalism, then talk of God or Allah must itself be interpreted metaphorically, likewise, talk of heaven and hell, and talk of Jesus as a son of God, yet another metaphor.

A metaphor of what, one might ask? Well, we know "God" can't be a metaphor for God. It would have to be a metaphor of something we *can* take literally, i.e., something secular. Whatever the metaphor is — a parent figure, evolutionary forces, or something else — "God" would stand for something non-God like.

We needn't deny that the Bible and Koran give some good advice. The overall message might go something like: "You ought to be nice to your neighbours. We're all related in the sense that we're stuck on spaceship earth and we would do well to work together rather than in competition." Surely we can say and mean this without inferring the existence of a literal God. On the metaphorical reading, if it is good advice, it is good advice for reasons independent of taking the existence of God to be a literal truth. It would be good advice given the literal circumstances in which we find ourselves. It is advice that atheists could endorse.

On a metaphorical reading of the Bible, the authority of the advice does not come from above and beyond; but from us.

RICŒUR AND COMPANY

Paul Ricœur, among others, suggests otherwise. Ricœur claims that metaphors can point to a real referent that normal denotation cannot get at. Metaphors can help us see through the veil of limited language to a transcendent truth. As he says, "Metaphor discloses a relationship of meaning hitherto unnoticed.... [Metaphors] say something new about reality."[7] In this sense, metaphors are not translatable into literal language, nor do they simply give a colourful way of describing something literal, something non-metaphysical. Thus, all that I have suggested above is false.

Ricœur gives an example: "Time is a beggar." This metaphor, he says, is not just another way of telling us what we already know about time; it gives us new insight, it provides a new referent. Likewise, when we speak of the Bible's being metaphorical, we mean it in this transcendental way; not as a simple substitute for secular referencing. Meaning, for Ricœur, is overlaid on, not reduced to, the text the way that dualists think mind is overlaid on, not reduced to, brain functions. This is why metaphor cannot act as the link between signifier and signified, or word and object.[8]

In contrast, Donald Davidson, a philosopher of language, rejects the notion that metaphors convey meaning beyond the literal referents. Metaphors cannot be ineffable, mysterious, or beyond the information given, even if the speaker herself is unable to articulate precisely what she means. Understanding metaphor is the same kind of activity as understanding any other linguistic utterance.[9] H.P. Grice, another philosopher of language, offers a slightly different account from Davidson, but he too agrees that metaphors are reducible to non-metaphorical utterances once the context of flouting linguistic convention is understood.[10] That philosophers of language disagree with Ricœur on the magical properties of metaphor doesn't by itself mean that Ricœur is wrong. But nor does it do any good to use a Ricœur-like defence of metaphor to support theism without first being prepared to explain why most other philosophers of language have got it wrong.

Perhaps what Ricœur is getting at is akin to noting the different sensibilities between persons who can find beauty in poetry, and those who cannot. Those who tend only to see the literal in Shelley's *Ozymandias*, say, find an account of a statue in the sand. Those who understand poetry see so much more in it. There is nothing about hubris stated in the poem, but that, presumably, is what the poem is *about*. In a similar way, treating religious metaphor as simply pointing at some secular referent, as opposed to lifting the veil of language to reveal the mysterium, is missing a key element. But Davidson and Grice's view of metaphor can accommodate poetry without supposing some mysterious tendon linking the literal to the metaphysical.

Besides, it is well known that metaphors vary in quality. It is easy to come up with metaphors. God is a taxi driver. Science is a bright balloon. Juxtapose any two subjects and a metaphor is born. If all metaphors reveal a truth, provide insight, then the concept of truth and insight itself is cheapened. But if we judge metaphors as good or bad, as better or worse, presumably we judge them according to our notions of "pre-metaphor" reality. Thus, metaphors point at something we already know; something we *can* put in a variety of other terms, something which already has a referent. Or, at least, they point at something that the metaphor user already knows. That is to say, even in the case where I learn something new about the world through metaphor, the metaphor composer obviously didn't come to that special insight through the metaphor (unless she creates metaphors haphazardly and every now and then some resonate). Rather, someone wishes to describe the way that the world appears to her and she searches for a fitting metaphor. That is, the conception comes before the metaphor, not afterward. For example, we can speak of hubris without reference to Shelley's *Ozymandias*. Our talk of hubris may be less poetic than Shelley's, but unless poeticism is the point of metaphor, this shows that metaphor is simply a language tool for referencing — not to be confused with the referent itself. (If poeticism *is* the sole point, then we can have empty metaphors, something Ricœur, at any rate, rejects.) Given this, metaphor is a referencing tool. But now we return to our original problem: what is the referent of God?

Ricœur's reply is that metaphors don't say *literally* what things are, only what they are like. But now we return to the problem of God's uniqueness raised in Chapter 2. My saying that X is like Y can't be right if I at the same time maintain that X is wholly unique. God can only refer to something that can have no reference other than to Himself. But saying this does not in any way show that God exists. Instead, it reveals how dubious appeals to metaphor have been in the hope of rescuing sacred texts.

PART II. "PROOFS"

5

ONTOLOGIC ILLOGIC

A PRIORI AND A POSTERIORI ARGUMENTS

Generally speaking, there are two kinds of arguments: *a priori* and *a posteriori*. Conclusions of *a priori* arguments are made independently of experience, whereas conclusions of *a posteriori* arguments are made on the basis of experience. An example of an *a priori* argument is the following: if Sally is taller than Beth, and Beth is taller than Peter, we are entitled to infer that Sally is taller than Peter. Our inference is not based on observing how tall Sally, Beth, or Peter are. The inference is based simply on our understanding logical relations. We don't even have to understand the concept "taller than." The argument would work just as well if we replaced "taller than" with "phlibbier than." We would still be entitled to conclude that Sally is phlibbier than Peter, whatever "phlibbier" might mean. Similarly, we know that if you had ten apples and I took four from you, you'd have six apples. We know this because we can count. It doesn't matter what it is that we're counting — apples or phlibbles. Nor does it matter whether the episode actually takes place, for our counting does not rely on observational data: only our conceptual understanding of numbers and math. You form your conclusion based on your understanding arithmetic not on your conception of apples. You don't need to conduct a survey of apple owners, or run an experiment where, after one hundred occasions of taking four apples from ten, you conduct statistical analysis to derive the average remainder. Instead, the conclusion "six apples" is forced upon you by *a priori* means.

On the other hand, let's say you want to know how tall Beth is, or you want to know how many apples you have left after you've seen me lurking around your bushel, but you don't know whether I've taken any, or if I did, you don't know how many I've taken, or even if you do know how many I've taken, you don't remember how many apples that you originally had. To get these kinds of knowledge claims, you have to go and observe the world. You have to measure Beth. You have to go and look at your bushel of apples. The conclusions that you reach, thereby, will be *a posteriori*. Any conclusion that relies on empirical observation will entail that the argument is *a posteriori*. Or let's say you notice human-shaped footprints in the sand. You infer that a human has passed this way ahead of you. You make your conclusion based on empirical observation. Therefore, it is an *a posteriori* inference. There is nothing *a priori* in assuming that a human passed this way. A human's not having passed this way is a logical possibility.

Most arguments for God's existence are *a posteriori*. We see footprints in the world and infer that the maker of such prints is God. I shall analyze such arguments in Chapters 6 to 9. One argument for God's existence, however, is purely *a priori*. This argument is called the *Ontological Argument*, and is credited to St. Anselm, and resurrected by Descartes. This is the argument that we'll examine in this chapter. Few believe that the argument succeeds, but it is very clever nonetheless and extremely useful to review — especially since tacit appeals to the ontological argument crop up even amidst avowedly *a posteriori* arguments.

THE ONTOLOGICAL ARGUMENT

St. Anselm's famous *Ontological Argument* makes the case that God *necessarily* exists.[1] That is, we know *a priori* (or non-empirically) that God exists. In brief, the argument is as follows:

1. God, by definition, is greater than anything that can be conceived (as a concept).
2. Existence is greater than non-existence. (It is better to exist in reality than to exist merely in concept.)
3. Therefore, God must exist (in reality).

Premise One

The first premise, if understood correctly, should not be problematic. Atheists, theists, and agnostics all agree that part of the meaning of God is that God is greater than anything that can be conceived. Atheists merely believe that nothing satisfies the definition. They don't (or need not) disagree with the definition itself.

If we ever conceive of something greater than God, this would not show that the premise is wrong. It would show only that we have not actually been looking at God in the first place. We've been led astray somewhere or other. That you can come up with a better toaster means that the first toaster wasn't the perfect toaster. The perfect toaster, then, cannot be bettered by a rival toaster. This is the same with God. Jones's saying, "Here is something greater than God," reveals merely that Jones has got the wrong image of God. God, *by definition*, is absolutely perfect — and this implies that *nothing* could be greater — not even in one's conception. God is, by definition, above all that.

So far so good. Anselm wants to show that once we accept this definition of God, which most — perhaps all — monotheists do, then we are
actually committed to recognizing that God in fact exists. "Only the fool
will fail to see this," says Anselm, resorting to a time-favoured *ad hominem*. Is Anselm right about this? Let's move to the next premise.

Premise Two
Existence is greater than non-existence. That is, we would think more
highly of something that really exists compared to something that exists
in concept only, all else being equal. It turns out that as soon as we accept
the definition of God (from premise one), we also accept the notion that
God "exists," at least in concept. For example, if I say, as I may be wont to
do, that "God doesn't exist," then I must have some concept of the thing
that I'm denying exists. So, it turns out, I must have in my mind's eye, so
to speak, a concept of God. Once this is recognized, then it seems possible
to speak of the existence of that *concept*.

Barring the peculiarity of saying that a concept "*exists*," we must first
recognize that this really doesn't get us far. Simply by saying, "Witches
don't exist," doesn't mean that witches must exist, seeing as how we know
in our mind's eye what it is we want to deny: things that fly on broom-
sticks and cook up lizard innards with toad drool, etc. So, having a thing
that exists only as a concept isn't all that special. Just as we can have a
concept of God, we can have a concept of a unicorn even while knowing
that no such thing exists in fact. We can even have a concept of a squared
circle (since we have a concept of each component) while recognizing that
the realization of that concept is an impossibility.

But existence in *reality* is greater than existence in mere concept (or
understanding) only. That is, it's not very great if it doesn't really exist.
This is the point of Anselm's second premise. Consider two great plans,
plan *A* and plan *B*, both designed to make you a million dollars. All things
being equal, if only plan *A* would *actually* make you a million dollars,
while plan *B* would make you a million make-believe dollars, which plan
would you choose, *A* or *B*? Obviously *A*, since *A* turns out to make the
million dollars exist *not just in concept*, but in *reality*. On the same principle as this, a god existing in reality would surely be *greater* than a god
that exists in one's imagination alone.

A slight modification to this second premise is needed. It is not the case
that *anything* that exists in reality is better than that same thing existing in
concept alone. When the child fears that there's a monster under her bed,
it is not normally considered better that the monster be real than imaginary. When the student has nightmares that he will fail all his exams, it is
not normally better that his dream be realized than not. So, let us politely
modify Anselm's premise to apply to *good* things only. It is better that *good*
things exist in reality than in mere concept. With bad things, it is "greater"

that they remain in concept only. Since God is good, presumably (though see Chapter 10), this emendation will not affect Anselm's argument.

The Conclusion

So, what's the point? Well, from the second premise, we learn that an existing god is greater than a god merely imagined, and from the first premise, we learn that God *must* be the greater of the two. Since an existing god is greater than a non-existing god, then, by the very definition that even atheists accept, God must exist, rather than not exist.

Notice that Anselm is speaking of God's *existence*. According to Paul Tillich, for example, God is greater than even existence.[2] Existence is too confining for God. According to Tillich, existence is normally applied to *things*, whereas God is a "no-thing." To treat something as a *thing* is bad. We feel used if we discover that someone treats us as a thing, an object, an instrument. Such a person fails to recognize that we are autonomous beings deserving respect. We are not things. We are not objects to be used. If it is wrong to treat *us* as a thing, imagine how wrong it would be to treat God that way! Such idolatry is what Tillich is trying to avoid when he speaks of God as a "no-thing." When Tillich says that God is not a thing, or that God is beyond even existence, he is not saying what atheists say: that no such being as God exists, that no concept of God has any referent. Rather, Tillich's notion is an extension of Anselm's first premise, and Anselm would not be (or at least should not be) averse to the suggestion. But this doesn't alter anything. Anselm still needs to move from something that exists in the imagination alone to something that is non-imaginary, real. He needs to show that a belief in God is not a false belief. He needs to move us from the definition of God as being really great to a god that is really real. After all, believing in a particular "no-thing" does not exempt one from having a false belief.

So goes St. Anselm's proof for the reality of God. Now let's see why it fails.

NULL SETS AND HYPOTHETICALS

Gaunilo, one of Anselm's contemporaries, showed that the ontological argument will work for almost anything.[3] Let's go back to witches. Imagine if someone says the following: There exists a witch so great in witch power that no other witch is greater. Well, a witch that actually exists is surely greater than one that doesn't. Therefore, this witch must actually exist.

We need to know why this example is not convincing. In the witch case, we may want to say something like: That's all very true, I suppose, *once we accept the possibility of witches existing*. But if we do not accept the possibility of witches existing, telling us about a really great witch won't move us. Accepting the concept of a great witch doesn't prove the existence of witches. And a very similar thing can be said for the ontological argument.

To show this, let's go back to the definition on which atheists, theists, and agnostics agree. It is not anything like "God exists. And he is greater than anything else." Rather, if we flesh it out a little, it looks far more like this:

1*. If God exists, then God is greater than anything that
     can be conceived.

To defend this translation, first off, the two propositions ("God is greater than anything that can be conceived" and "If God exists, then God is greater than anything that can be conceived") are logically equivalent (in three steps using the logical rules of addition, implication, then transposition).[4] Secondly, let us note that propositions have a subject and a predicate. In the proposition, "Emma broke the vase," the subject is Emma, and the predicate concerns the breaking of the vase. If I say, "Emma broke the vase," and you say, "No," we can assume that you mean Emma didn't break the vase, not that you mean Emma doesn't exist. If I say, "A ghost broke the vase," and you say, "No," we can assume that you mean to (also) deny the existence of the ghost. In other words, sometimes we wish to deny the predicate, and sometimes we wish to deny the existence of the subject.[5] In the case of "God is greater than can be conceived," it is the subject that atheists wish to deny, not the predicate. To make that clear, the re-translation into the hypothetical form is helpful.

Notice that hypothetical (or if ... then) statements have two parts: the part that occurs after the "if" (the antecedent) and the part that occurs after the "then" (the consequent). Logic demands that conditionals carry through the argument until an affirmation of the antecedent or a negation of the consequent occurs. That is, if the premises are all if ... then ... statements, the conclusion must also be an if ... then ... statement. Therefore, we need to translate the remaining parts of the argument accordingly. So:

2*. (Since existence is greater than non-existence) then if
     God is greater than anything that can be conceived,
     God must exist.
3*. Therefore, if God exists, God must exist.

You can now see why there is nothing very illuminating in this argument. This is the sort of conclusion for which we don't need any complicated argument. Anselm could have said that right off the bat. We can all accept the claim, "If God exists, God exists," without ever being committed to the *quite different claim* that God exists.

To put the point another way, notice that a definition defines a particular set. A definition of "dog" defines a set of all dogs. If the definition is well made, we will find only dogs in the definitional set, and no dogs excluded from the definitional set. When we come across any object in the world, and we wonder whether it is a dog, we look to the definitional set of "dog" and decide whether the item in question belongs in the set or not. We look to see what actually fits in that set. In this case, any dog we happen to come across. Bras and automobiles, among other things, do not belong.

But there is nothing in set theory that dictates that a set needs to be filled in any particular case. The set of all witches, for example, will be an empty (or null) set, as will the set of all unicorns, and the set of all squared circles. The sets of witches, unicorns, and squared circles will be sets without any members. To decide whether a set has any members can never be determined by examining what defines the set alone. The criteria for deciding the set of witches will differ from the criteria for determining whether anything actually satisfies that set. We have to go out into the world, beyond merely forming the conception of the set, to see if anything actually belongs in that conceptual set. The definitional set of a unicorn is one thing; whether anything satisfies that definitional set another. Similarly, the definitional set of a god is one thing; whether anything actually satisfies that set another. Atheists are those who say that's just what we don't find: any members to fit the set of all entities greater than anything that can be conceived.

This is Kant's point when he says, "Existence is not a predicate."[6] Kant is wrong if he's making a grammatical point, of course. In the proposition, "God exists," God is the subject, and existence is the predicate. But Kant is not making a grammatical point. Let us say, instead, that existence is not a *property*. Existence is not something which *adds* to the description of a thing. If I ask Santa for a dollhouse for Christmas, I might indicate certain attributes of the dollhouse: that it have a two-car garage or that it have a widow's walk. Those additions mean something. But if I also tell Santa to make my dollhouse exist is not to tell Santa anything more than I've already said. Likewise, if a couple plans on buying their first house, they may say things like, "It should have ample closets," "It should have a good view." But to say, "It should exist" is weird, since this is already presupposed by speaking of the house in the first place. Saying, "It should exist," adds nothing, because existence is not a property. Otherwise, my dreaming of a mansion that belongs to me for free, has ample closet space, has a good view, and exists in fact, would be all I would need to own a new home.[7]

BARRETTELESS AND IMAGINARY DOLLS

One might object that there is a difference between an imaginary doll and a real doll.[8] Imagine asking for a doll for Christmas and receiving, instead, an imaginary doll. Your parents explain, "Don't worry, since existence is not a property, there's no difference between this (imaginary) doll and a real doll." You wouldn't be convinced. Similarly, perhaps you like dolls but not ones with barrettes. So you ask for a doll without a barrette. That the doll is barretteless is one of its attributes. But this attribute concerns non-existence. So, if non-existence can be an attribute, surely existence can be. In both cases (imaginary and barretteless dolls), existence seems very much to be a property. Kant appears to be wrong.

But Kant is not saying that there is no difference between existing and non-existing things. When he denies that existence can be a property, he isn't denying that existence may be properly applied to subjects. "A doll that doesn't exist" is not grammatically the same as "A doll that has a barrette." We can admit that being barretteless is a property of "a doll without a barrette," without abandoning the notion that existence is not a property. Rather, when we examine whether the Christmas request is satisfied, we ask, "Does the doll have a barrette or not?" The question of existence concerns the barrette, not the doll. That is, the barrette is the subject, not the predicate. A barretteless doll is different than a non-existing barretted doll, even a non-existing barretteless doll. This is why Kant spoke of predicates, not properties. The subject either is or isn't. What the subject is *like*, its nature, is the domain of the predicate. The predicate only speaks of nature, not existence. To put the matter another way, God's existence cannot be vouchsafed by an *a priori* argument alone. It requires an *a posteriori* argument. (We will examine *a posteriori* arguments for God's existence in Chapters 6 to 9.)

NECESSARY EXISTENCE

Adding new information to a subject is the job of predicates. Existence doesn't do that. Thus, one may admit that existence is not a property. Even conceding this point doesn't end the discussion. The ontological argument doesn't ascribe to God mere existence, but *necessary existence*.[9] It is one thing to say that I get no new information from your telling me that your doll exists after you've told me that your doll has no barrette, but if you tell me that your doll necessarily exists, that's something new, something surprising, in fact. Necessary existence is very different from regular existence. So, if God necessarily exists, that tells me that God is not like other things that exist. That's new information. So, if what counts as a predicate is the addition of new information to the subject, then necessary existence is a predicate.

To accommodate Anselm's argument with necessary existence (so that the terms in each premise match), we have to change the second premise to:

2†. Necessary existence is greater than non-necessary existence.
  (It is better to necessarily exist than to contingently exist.)

The original premise 2 (that existence was greater than non-existence) was easy enough to grant. Our accepting premise 2† is more difficult, for it requires that we are able to compare necessary existence to contingent existence. But the only things that have hope of counting as necessary existence will be *a priori* truths, like "2 + 3 = 5," or "A pickle is a pickle," neither of which are things that have any agency. We don't say that "2 + 3 = 5 loves you," or "A pickle is a pickle created the universe." If we do not believe that existence without agency is better than existence with agency, and since the only plausible candidates for necessary existence have no agency, we would reject the claim that necessary existence is better than contingent existence. But if we reject premise 2†, we cannot arrive at the conclusion that God necessarily exists.

The above criticism assumes that we have some sense of what necessary existence could mean. A more general worry is to say that we cannot possibly know what necessary existence could mean, because combining "existence" with "necessary" is already to misunderstand what we mean by "existence." To say that something exists is to conceive of the possibility that it doesn't exist. The very concept of existence is integrally connected to contingency, but now we're asked to throw this conception out to make the ontological argument work.

To put the matter differently, inserting the concept of necessary existence into the ontological argument amounts to the following syllogism:

1**. If God is a necessary being, then God exists.
2**. God is a necessary being.
3**. Therefore, God exists.

Such an argument is valid. That is, if the premises are true, the conclusion follows. The first premise, moreover, is perfectly fine. Atheists would complain about the second premise, however, since it presumes the very thing the argument was trying to establish.

SUMMARY

That my ball has the property of being round and red presupposes that I have a ball. Similarly, saying, "God has the property of being omnipotent, omniscient, and good," presupposes that God exists. But presupposing God's existence is not the same as verifying that God exists. When I say, "A unicorn has the property of being a cross between a horse, a rhinoceros, and a swan," I am not committed to inferring that such a beast exists in fact. The ontological argument is mistaken precisely for making such inferences. Simply put, definitions cannot prove existence. And that's the problem when one plays fast and loose with concepts. That we have a concept of something — even a wouldn't-that-be-awesome kind of a concept — does not mean much in itself. Concepts are easy; whether they refer to anything is the hard part.

6

WHY IS THERE SOMETHING
RATHER THAN NOTHING?

THE COSMOLOGICAL ARGUMENT

The Cosmological Argument is proposed by those who believe the mere fact that there is something (the universe, for example) pushes us toward belief in a supernatural creator.[1] Mere stuff can't come from nothing, can it? So, it must come from something. But whatever it comes from can't be the same *kind* of thing as the stuff itself. The creator of the universe, whatever or whoever that is, must be different in kind from the stuff of the universe. It seems, only a god could fit the bill. I mean, what else? Stuff just always existed? Surely such a proposition seems more absurd than a belief in a god. Aquinas's version of the cosmological argument may be put in the following form:

1. For every effect, there's a cause, and every cause is itself an effect of a previous cause.
2. But such a string of causes and effects can't be stretched back to infinity. (If there were no first cause of anything, there wouldn't be an effect, and if there were no effects, there wouldn't be anything at all, but obviously there is something (the universe).)
3. Therefore, we posit a first cause (a self-causing being) and that's what we mean by God.

The cosmological argument asserts that something must have started the universe. The posited starter is God. It is common to suggest the Big Bang as an alternative starter. But such an objection misses the force of the cosmological argument. A vague reference to the Big Bang doesn't forbid us from asking what got the Big Bang going. The Big Bang is an explosion of something, presumably, not an explosion of nothing. Where did those gaseous bits that exploded come from?[2] One cannot say "From the Big Bang itself." To dismiss the cosmological argument, we have to dig deeper.

INCONSISTENCY

Many have charged the cosmological argument with being internally inconsistent. We don't know where the world came from. We also recognize that something cannot come from nothing. So, we postulate God. But neither do we know where this God came from. So now what? If God can just be, why can't the universe itself just be? If the thought that the universe simply popped into existence is too weird for us, why is a god who popped into existence (or always existed) less strange? Theists, however, believe that this critique plays more into their hands than into the hands of atheists. After all, the only thing that can start the whole process must be significantly different from any constituent member of the process itself. Minimally, if members of the chain are caused, then the creator must be uncaused — otherwise we're pulled back into an infinite series of creators, and the question concerning the origin of *that* series would still be left unanswered. An infinite series of creators is as problematic as an infinite series of mere stuff. Since the creator of stuff is so different than the stuff created, however, it is not inconsistent to say *stuff* can't create itself while a creator can. For this reason, proponents of the cosmological argument maintain that there is no inconsistency.

Is the response adequate? Is there no inconsistency, then? There is certainly no inconsistency once we admit the existence of a magical self-creating creator, but why would we do that? Why is such a solution deemed credible? We weren't supposed to *start* with that belief; we were supposed to *arrive* at that belief. The inconsistency is avoided by relying on the possibility of a god. The cosmological argument was supposed to lead us to the possibility of a god, however, not presuppose one. The "God" solution to the origins of the universe avoids the question of how a god could come about. Even if we think that God is self-creating, there must be a time before such a self-creating being existed.[3] That is, we seem forced to admit that the self-creating being must have itself come from nothing. But the cosmological argument starts from our recognition that something can't come from nothing. It is not fair to say, "Well, magical beings can come from nothing, given that they're magical." And even if so, why wouldn't there be a whole proliferation of magical beings? The solution is more arcane than the problem with which we began.

Most theists readily admit that God couldn't have come from nothing. Instead, they assume that God has always existed. If God has always existed, this would avoid the problem that God arose from nothing. It does not avoid the inconsistency charge, however. Not only did we begin by saying it is impossible for something to come from nothing, we also began with the premise that a thing's simply existing forever is implausible. If something can exist forever, why not mere stuff? The charge of inconsistency stands. (At least for now: the section on Necessary Beings will review another tactic aimed at avoiding the charge of inconsistency.)

INFINITY

The cosmological argument makes the case that stuff either has existed forever or was created by an uncaused cause. To arrive at the uncaused cause, therefore, it is necessary to dismiss the possibility of stuff's being around for infinity. Both Aquinas and Samuel Clarke thought that was easily managed by noting that an infinite series obviously precludes there being a first cause.[4] But if the first cause doesn't exist, the effects of that cause wouldn't exist either. If your father didn't exist, nor would you. Since there is something rather than nothing, the supposition that a series of contingent beings existed for an infinite amount of time must be false.

But this argument confuses matters. If I deny that I'm the father of your child, I am not denying my existence: I am merely denying the purported status of being the father of your child. Likewise, if I deny that any particular contingent being is itself uncaused, I am not denying its existence. I am merely asserting that for any contingent being in the infinite series, you will always find some other contingent being which is its cause.

So far, all that has been shown is that neither Aquinas's nor Clarke's reasons for rejecting an infinite series of contingent beings succeed. This does not mean that an infinite series of contingent beings should be accepted. For that matter, even accepting the existence of an infinite series of contingent beings doesn't end the discussion. We can still ask, can we not, why the infinite series itself exists. For example, if we ask, "Why do Canadians eat pigs, but not horses?" the answer, "They've always done so," does not really suffice. Similarly, saying, "There is an infinite series of contingent beings," does not answer the question of how the infinite series of contingent beings got going in the first place.[5]

Paul Edwards disagrees.[6] He raised, what we may call, the Five Inuit Problem.[7] If we see a group of five Inuit waiting to cross a downtown street, we might wonder how the group got there. To answer the question, we go and ask each member of the group. We discover that one is there for a conference, one is there for a job interview, one is there for a vacation, one is there as the spouse of another, and one is there because her car broke down. After gathering this information, we do not need to ask the further question, "Yes, but why is the *group* there?" We don't ask this further question because the explanation for the group's being there is fully explained by the reasons provided by each individual member being there. Similarly, we *have* given an account of why there's something rather than nothing by giving an account such that for any given member of the group of existing things, it was caused by some other previously existing thing, and this account holds for that existing thing itself, *ad infinitum*.

The Inuit analogy may not work, however. Once we learn the individual reasons for the Inuits' presence downtown, we at the same time realize that *this isn't really a group at all*. If a group is understood as a collection of objects *belonging* together, then a mere cluster of objects needn't be understood as a group. In this case, groups are supposed to have some feature that unites the individual members beyond inessential contiguities. If so, we mistook the collection of Inuit individuals for a group. To believe otherwise is to commit the fallacy of composition: assuming what is true of the parts is true of the whole. There is a difference, for example, between: (a) a collection of bricks and globs of mortar; and (b) a wall comprised of bricks and mortar. The wall is not simply a collection of parts, but an arranged order of parts. As such, we can speak of the formation of a group independently of the reasons for a particular set of individuals joining that group. For example, I have heard of a golf club members' association still holding meetings long after their golf course was consumed by postwar development. Why current members join the club cannot possibly explain the reason for the club's initial institution. If so, explaining the reasons for current members joining may explain the continued existence of the group, but not the original existence of the group.[8] So although there may be cases where giving an account of the individual members *ipso facto* gives an account of the set, it does not follow that every such set is fully explained by an account of the individual members. Likewise, the lore of the Montréal Canadiens is not fully explained by explaining the skills of each of the current members of the team. And so whether the set of past, present, and future contingent beings is explainable within the set or without is still an open question.[9]

One way to suggest that the set must be explained from without is to note a general assumption: everything has an explanation. In that sense, we may legitimately ask for the explanation of the existing set as well as the explanation for each member of the set. Of course, deciding that the question is itself legitimate does not mean that the answer to the question is "God." For although we may accept that everything has an explanation, it doesn't follow that anything has a supernatural explanation. To the extent that we understand God as a supernatural agent (see Chapter 2), the cosmological argument grinds to a halt. Perhaps we mean (as do scientists) that everything has a *natural* or *non-metaphysical* explanation, and if so, the answer "God," won't be tolerated. Furthermore, the assumption that everything has a cause needn't rule out chance or coincidence as the explanation. Finding out that you and a stranger have a mutual friend does have an explanation: one involving chance.[10] Moreover, noting that everything has an explanation does not commit us to assuming that the explanation is not already had by the account of the individual members. Perhaps the set of all existing things should not be mistaken for a group at all. If so, the Five Inuit analogy works after all. But even if we feel that we require a further explanation for the group of existing things than that supplied by the explanation of the individual existing things themselves, this does not mean that we *know* what the explanation is. That we admit a causal explanation probably exists does not mean that we're forced to accept "God" as that causal explanation.

Questions about the nature of explanation aside, however, asking for the cause of the infinite series of contingent beings is not legitimate. It is not legitimate for reasons other than the Five Inuit problem. An infinite series cannot itself have a creator, for that would entail that the series is finite. To seek a causal explanation for the series is to already assume that the series must have started at some point, the point at which it was created.[11] But this is simply to deny that it was infinite. If it begins at the point of its being created, it has a beginning, and anything with a beginning has not existed forever. So, one cannot accept both that the series is infinite and that it was created by an external agent. The question, "What created the infinite series?" makes no sense given the meaning of an infinite series.[12]

None of what I say above means that an infinite series of contingent beings makes sense. In my case, anyway, it plainly doesn't. Understanding infinity is the point beyond which my brain hurts. I cannot fathom it. But merely because I cannot fathom the concept of infinity, or have no adequate answer for why there is something rather than nothing, it does not mean that I should accept a metaphysical answer. To do that would be a form of appealing to ignorance, a move we dismissed as fallacious in Chapter 1. So, atheists don't know everything. Fine. Who said we had to?

THE KALĀM ARGUMENT

I think the above definitive, but one objection, referred to as the *Kalām Argument*, suggests that my difficulty to grasp the infinity of contingent things plays into the hands of theists, not atheists. The argument makes the case that an actual infinite series of contingent things is impossible. From there it suggests that the world had a beginning, and that beginning was due to a personal creator. I shall ignore the latter components of the argument, and very briefly highlight William Lane Craig's account of the impossibility of an infinite series of contingent things.[13] An infinite series of things has the following peculiarity: Remove half of the series, say every second object in the infinite series, and you will not diminish the length of the series by one iota. An infinite series of only even numbers is still as infinite as the infinite series of even and odd numbers. While we may tolerate such absurdity with formal concepts like numbers, Craig believes we cannot tolerate such a result with actual physical objects. Take the revolutions around the sun of Saturn and Jupiter. Jupiter revolves once every twelve earth years, and Saturn once every thirty earth years. If the universe were eternal, both would rotate around the sun an infinite amount of times, yet Saturn still more times than Jupiter. But how can one infinity be larger than another infinity? Or if the number of souls were infinite, so would half that number of souls be infinite, or for that matter, twice as many souls. Likewise, take an infinite series of books, and remove every second book, you would now have two infinite series of books, each with as many books as the first set of infinite books. Such absurdities are unfathomable. Because we cannot tolerate the absurdity of infinity with physical objects, we cannot conceive of an infinite series of physical objects. Since the series of contingent events the cosmological argument is trying to explain is a series of physical objects, we cannot seriously entertain the thought that the universe just always existed.

For the Kalām argument to work, however, Craig would need to show how a given property becomes contradictory when it belongs to an infinite series of such properties. Only then could we say the property's contradictory nature makes impossible the circumstances that caused such a contradictory nature. But the Kalām argument shows no such thing. That an infinite series of books, say, contains as many books as half that infinite series does not reveal any contradictory nature of books. It reveals only what Craig already accepts, that the concept of mathematical infinity is peculiar, and this is so whether it's applied to points on a line, souls, books, planetary revolutions, or cookies in a jar. What would be contradictory is to take every second book of a *finite* series of books and discover that the remaining collection contains the same number of books as the original collection. This shows that Craig can't get his head around the concept of an infinite series of objects; not that an infinite series of objects is incoherent. So it isn't clear that an infinite series of objects has been shown to be unthinkable. Jupiter still circumnavigates the sun once every twelve years, and whether it's always done that (something the infinity argument needn't even accept) wouldn't affect a thing.

NECESSARY BEINGS

So far, the objection against the cosmological argument rests on: (i) pointing out an internal inconsistency; and (ii) showing that the reason for rejecting an infinite series of effects fails. Both criticisms are thought to be avoided if we distinguish between contingent and necessary beings. A contingent being depends on something else for its existence. A necessary being does not. Therefore, there is no inconsistency to say a contingent being cannot cause itself while a necessary being can. Similarly, so the objection goes, even admitting the possibility of an infinite series of contingent beings leaves open the possibility of a necessary being standing outside that infinite series and being the cause of that infinite series. That is to say, there must be a necessary being to get the series of contingent beings going. By the logic noted above, if the thing which got the contingent series going was itself contingent, this would not be a way out of the infinite impasse, so it must be something wholly other. If the cause is not contingent, it must be necessary. Note, this is not saying that it necessarily follows that God exists. Rather, it is saying that God is a necessary being (and — supposedly — from this it necessarily follows that God exists).

There are two problems with the necessary existence manoeuvre. First, the objection is supposed to proceed even if we allow the possibility of an infinite series of contingent things. But this is false. Even if the cause of the series of contingent effects is a necessary cause, that the infinite series has a cause entails that it has a beginning (the point at which it was caused). If it has a beginning, it is not an infinite series.

Secondly, the concept of a necessary being is a contradiction in terms, much like the concept of a square circle.[14] A being is the kind of thing that may not be. A necessary thing is the kind of thing that cannot not be. That two plus one equals three is necessary, but not a being. That a necessary being is a contradiction in terms follows from what I've already discussed in Chapter 5. Basically, existence cannot properly be inferred from definitional fiat.[15] That a doll has certain characteristics may be part of what we mean by a doll, but that a doll exists cannot be ascertained by an understanding of the characteristics of a doll. We have to go out into the world to see if any such objects in existence satisfy the definition of a doll. This is the same with God.

One might object that the cosmological version of the necessary being argument is different than the ontological version of the necessary being argument. For example, William Rowe makes the case that, in the cosmological argument, we infer from the *principle of sufficient reason* that there must be a necessary being above and beyond the contingent existences that we generally find in the universe: otherwise, the series of contingent beings couldn't get going at all.[16] But if the concept of a necessary being is incoherent, it doesn't matter *how* we arrive at that conclusion — whether by *a priori* or *a posteriori* means — we know something's gone amiss.[17]

Since the concept of a necessary being is incoherent, it cannot be the case that the mere existence of matter entails a necessary being. If, instead, one means only that the cosmological argument shows that it is necessary to infer a God (as opposed to our inferring a necessary being), then we return to the inconsistency charge as well as to the worries against rejecting the possibility of an infinite series of contingent effects. Either way, the distinction between necessary and contingent is a dead end.

BEST EXPLANATION

So far, the cosmological argument forces upon us only two options — the stuff of the cosmos has always existed, or it came from something outside the cosmos — and neither appears plausible. As such, one can admit that the cosmological argument fails to move us in any direction, save facing our own ignorance concerning the origin of the cosmos. This is the atheist's answer. Alternatively, one can say, but look: between the two options: complete mystery or a theistic answer, it would seem preferable to opt for theism. The theistic answer at least explains the thing we set out to explain: the existence of the universe. The alternative doesn't even do that. Even when we admit that the God answer contains some unknown mysteries itself ("Where did God come from?" and "Why did He do it?"), it doesn't diminish the fact that we have an answer. If we find our living room window broken and we find a baseball on our living room floor, we have an answer to the question: "How did the window get broken?" The answer "The baseball did it," is not to be retracted merely because we don't know where the baseball itself came from, or why it came to be here, on our living room floor. Similarly, if the question is "How did the world come about?" theists have an answer, and atheists don't. Thus between the two alternatives, it would appear that theists win. That is to say, a theistic answer to the origin of the universe is the best explanation going. Theists can even be fallibilists about the explanation. That is, they can maintain their God belief until something proves them wrong. But until then, among the viable options, the theistic answer is the only answer going. The atheists claim mere ignorance, but that's no explanation. That is, although theists can agree that their answer is not proven, all they need is the recognition that it's still the best answer going. Such thinking about the matter is referred to as *the argument from best explanation*, or *the argument from sufficient reason*, and its proponents include Leibniz and more recently (though he rejects it in the end) William Rowe.[18]

The argument is more than that an answer is better than no answer, since one might imagine some events have no causal explanation at all. The argument from sufficient reason, then, adds to the mix that every event has an explanation. Given that, finding that the atheists provide no explanation, while the theists provide an explanation, everything being equal, the principle of sufficient reason suggests you opt for the going explanation over the non-explanation.

To diffuse the argument from best explanation, we needn't dwell on cases where the principle of sufficient reason seems to be false. (For example, in quantum theory, the breakdown of atomic particles randomly creates other particles, or the sum total of all contingent facts can't itself be given a contingent explanation since there is no contingent fact outside of the set of contingent facts to be explained.) All we need remind our audience is that the atheists aren't saying that *no* explanation exists for the existence of the universe: only that the God answer isn't anywhere near adequate. And its non-adequacy isn't simply because some *further* mysteries about God exist; the God answer is itself a mystery. To return to the baseball, we don't doubt that the baseball exists. So saying the baseball broke the window counts as an adequate explanation even if we don't know anything else about the baseball, *but its brute existence*. But in the case of God, we have to *infer* His existence from the fact of the universe. To match the baseball analogy, we would have to infer the existence of a baseball from the fact of the broken window, and once we make that leap, it is easy to suppose the baseball broke the window. When someone points out that we find no baseball to corroborate the story, how inadequate a response must it seem to say, "But there must be *some* explanation rather than no explanation, therefore I'm sticking with my baseball theory."

The best explanation argument fails. There is no added explanatory value given by the appeal to God, so the God answer cannot satisfy the principle of sufficient reason, even if we think such a principle generally correct.

CONCLUSION

The cosmological argument forces upon us only two options — the stuff of the cosmos has always existed, or it came from something outside the cosmos — and neither appears plausible. As such, one must admit that the cosmological argument fails to move us in any direction, save facing our own ignorance concerning the origin of the cosmos.

7

DESIGN OR EVOLUTION?

THE DESIGN ARGUMENT

The design argument for God's existence comes from noting how well everything fits together. For example, trees take in carbon dioxide and spew out oxygen while we breathe in oxygen and exhale carbon dioxide. That's a perfect fit! And such examples of perfect fit are abundant in the universe. From how well diverse parts of the universe fit together, an inference to a designer is natural, since usually diverse and complicated parts that have such an intricate fit are designed that way. Once we infer design, it is natural to suppose a designer. What else could count as a designer of the whole universe, but a god?[1]

Is this a good argument? I am devoting two chapters to explain why not, not merely because it is quite likely the best argument going for God's existence, but because there are two distinct ways of defeating it. The first is by an appeal to evolution (the present chapter). The second is by getting a better understanding of analogical argument structure, and then applying that skill to the design argument (the next chapter). A version of the design argument that claims to bypass the evolution alternative (the fine tuning or biogenesis argument) is also raised and dismissed in the following chapter.

I remember seeing on a linoleum floor the perfect outline of Atlas holding the globe on his shoulders. And once I had seen the pattern, I could not help but believe it was really there. But what could "it was really there" mean? Was Atlas really holding up the earth? Was this one of a series of Greek myth flooring lines? Or was the only thing really there merely a pattern that had the look to me of being something akin to Atlas holding up the earth? Was my linoleum Atlas "really there" in the same way that dots on the wall are really there when motes on my cornea cause me to see dots while I am looking at a wall?

It seems that we have a psychological need to impose structure on random data. Likewise, if we are not careful, we are quick to see in random events confirmatory evidence of a pet theory. Seeing design in the universe is the same sort of thing as seeing patterns in ink blots and linoleum floors. So I shall argue.

But first, let's rehearse what makes the design argument so appealing.

THE APPEAL

Aquinas's version of the design argument goes as follows:

> We see that things which lack knowledge, such as natural bodies, act for an end, and this is evident from their acting always, or nearly always, in the same way, so as to obtain the best result. Hence it is plain that they achieve their end, not fortuitously, but designedly. Now whatever lacks knowledge cannot move towards an end, unless it be directed by some being endowed with knowledge and intelligence; as the arrow is directed by the archer. Therefore some intelligent being exists by whom all natural things are directed to their end; and this being we call God.[2]

Paley adds a bit more colour to the argument. If you stumble upon a watch in the woods, you would infer that the watch was designed. You would make this inference even if the watch doesn't work, even if you don't understand what all parts of the watch are for, and even if you've never seen a watch before. The reason that you would infer design is because whenever you find intricate parts working together, you naturally infer design. The cogs and wheels of the watch are so well fitted together that simply by seeing that fit, you would infer that someone designed it, and this is so even if you have no idea what the design is for. The universe, meanwhile, has an intricate fit of separate pieces, just as the watch does. So, if it is natural to infer a designer of the watch, it is natural to infer a designer of the universe.[3]

As you can see, both Aquinas and Paley dismiss chance as the explanation of the intricate fit of the universe. Of course, for many people, we marry someone who we met by chance. That we met them by chance doesn't mean that we value them less than had it been an arranged marriage, a marriage by design. But still, design *seems* to be a better explanation than evolution for the immaculate fit of life on earth. The impetus behind the theory of evolution is often thought to be chance. People commonly wonder, though, how *chance* can explain all this. It seems especially unlikely, and we ought not to bet on the unlikely, so we are moved to the theory that the world was designed. And who but a deity is capable of such a task?

Consider: the earth is perfectly distanced from the sun. Farther away, and we'd freeze; closer, and we'd burn up. What is more, the moon is itself the right size and the right number. The earth's rotation axis is not perpendicular to the plane in which it orbits the sun. It is offset by 23.5 degrees, and it is this tilt that explains why we have the seasons we do. If our moon was bigger or smaller, or if we had more moons or less, the axial tilt and/or spin rate of the earth would alter, which would greatly impact the earth's temperature. For example, moonless Venus rotates slower than it orbits the sun, so that its day (sunrise to sunset) is actually longer than its year (one loop around the sun). Its year is about 225 earth days, while its day is about 243 earth days. A day on moonless Mercury, meanwhile takes about 176 earth days. If you could stand on Mercury (at certain latitudes), you could witness the sun rise, move directly overhead, then stop, then retrograde back, then proceed back on its westward track. Uranus, with twenty seven moons, rotates on its side so that its rotational axis is in the same direction of its orbit around the sun, thus leaving its equatorial edges always facing away from the sun. With such alterations to day lengths, and seasons, the earth's average temperature (vacillating between extreme heat and extreme cold) would likely be uninhabitable — at least to humans.[4] Consider, too, our neighbouring planets. They have a role in our survival. There is evidence of a horrific meteor shower that would have devastated our little planet had it not been for the larger inert masses surrounding us to have taken much of the brunt. Moreover, life (our life anyway) requires the correct mixture of carbon and oxygen: a slight adjustment to any number of physical constants would have made it impossible for these two elements to be formed. A faster production rate of carbon (produced in the interior of stars) would mean that there would be less helium, which would mean that there would be less oxygen. A slower rate of carbon production would mean that most of the carbon would burn into oxygen given the larger amounts of helium. The complexities of the ecosystem, as environmentalists and biologists like to remind us, are awe-inspiring. And the complex fit between planets, chemicals, and ecosystems is nothing compared to the complexity found within living organisms. Our heart pumps blood, our eyes sees, our skin heals, our lungs breathe, our muscles contract. To imagine that such a complex and wonderfully functioning organism that happens to have found itself on a perfectly suitable planet came about by *chance* is too far-fetched to contemplate seriously. What are the odds of our planet being both so perfectly situated and so perfectly constituted? Pretty low.[5] Hence, a better bet than that everything came about by chance is that everything was placed with intent.

THE EVOLUTIONARY ACCOUNT

The above argument interprets the evolution argument as an appeal to mere chance. It deems the odds of such a chance so astronomically low that the supposition of a god is a better bet. But this is a wildly inaccurate way of describing the evolutionary account. Evolution provides a much better account of the seeming "design" than the theory of design itself. Natural selection means that the things that can survive in an environment do so, while those that can't, don't. What can we expect from this? Since those that will survive are those that fit in best, we are left with only those things that fit, and not any of those things that don't fit. Consequently, looking at how everything fits together so nicely cannot count in favour of the design argument. The fit is exactly what the evolutionary theory predicts as well. Given the existence of oxygen in our atmosphere, things which find oxygen poisonous have not survived. Things which find oxygen non-poisonous, or beneficial, have survived.

Something that manages to have survived has offspring. These offspring carry most of the traits of the parents, and since the parents survived long enough to reproduce in their environment with whatever traits they had, the offspring itself has a good chance of reproducing, and so long as the environment remains relatively stable, these successful traits take over the population. Sexual reproduction doesn't produce exact replicas of one's parents, however. Some variation exists. If these variants confer advantage, the variants get passed on to future generations. If the variants are disadvantageous, the strand dies out. Since altering something that works is more likely to make it not work, most variants are disadvantageous. In fact, the greater the variation, the greater likelihood of disadvantage.[6] This is why evolutionary changes will be by very small increments. But some variants provide an advantage, and that anomaly, over time, becomes the norm in the population.[7] Sometimes those variants provide an advantage in the existing environment compared to the parents and siblings. More commonly, however, the advantage from variation is due to changes in environment. What trait used to work well in one environment won't necessarily do so well in a different environment. Since the environment is itself in flux, variation in offspring is an essential ingredient in evolution.

The concept of "advantage" and "disadvantage" concerns natural selection. What is advantageous is a purely relative concept: relative to the existing environment. The environment includes the physical geography as well as other species. That is to say, a particular organism might do well so long as it has ample resources, no competitors for such resources, and no predation. But should any organism be so lucky, there is an obvious niche for invaders. In other words, when evolutionists speak of environment, they mean to include competitors, prey, and predators, let alone parasites and germs. Environmental disasters can also wipe out an otherwise successful species, as seems to have happened with dinosaurs. That the lowly shrew survived but not the dinosaur reveals that the phrase "survival of the fittest" is a purely relative concept, not to be equated with a "might is right" interpretation. Natural selection, then, simply concerns whether or not an organism has grandchildren. If yes, it has been selected. If not, it's been selected out. The conditions in which it will have grandchildren depend on the variable conditions of the environment in which it and its offspring happen to live. Understanding this basic pattern of replication, variation, and natural selection is all one needs to fully account for the appearance of design in the world. The dynamics of natural selection are not themselves a matter of chance. Existing traits fit with other existing traits, generally because those that didn't fit this particular group of existing traits have died off.[8]

So far, we have two accounts that explain the appearance of design, the design argument and the evolution argument. An important and often overlooked fact makes evolution not merely an alternative to design, but a far better account of the way the world is. If the design theory were right, we wouldn't expect many things to have been designed that wouldn't fit. This is doubly so if the designer is deemed to be perfect in every sense. If the design theory were true, what we have should be pretty much what was designed. The evolutionary theory makes no such suggestion. Rather, the evolutionary account predicts that the currently existing things should be a tiny fraction of what there has been and will be. Alas, fossil evidence supports the latter theory and counts against the first theory. The number of species existing today is less than one per cent of the species *known* to have existed. It seems a poor design if only one per cent of it survives. To put it another way, the design argument is based on finding an intricate fit, and from that mere intricacy of fit, a designer is invoked. Now we see that design argument proponents are not looking at the whole picture. They are only looking at a current time slice and see an intricate fit incorporating most of the existing organisms. But if we look at a larger time slice, we see that only one per cent actually has fit. The inference to a designer from immaculate fit is no longer feasible. So much for the design argument. (A modern resurrection of the design argument, called the *fine tuning* argument, will be examined in the next chapter.)

CHANCE AND FRUIT FLIES

Above, I highlighted the dynamics of natural selection in a way that does not appeal to chance. This is not to say, however, that chance makes no appearance in evolution. Consider a typical Canadian fruit fly. Canada is a cold place. In cold climates, things that can survive the cold generally do better than things that cannot survive the cold. In the case of the fruit fly, it turns out that a genetic mutation in a previous strand of fruit fly caused a particular fruit fly to have an (at the time) abnormally thicker thorax. This thicker thorax had the benefit of keeping the fruit fly warmer without impairing its flight. This added warmth helped the fruit fly to last a bit longer than the other fruit flies. Since the mutation was at the genetic level, the gene causing the thicker thorax passed on to future generations. Since the thicker thoraxed fruit flies did better than their thinner thoraxed compatriots in terms of reproduction (due to their longevity in the cold climate compared to other fruit flies) the population of thicker thoraxed fruit flies increased. In this story, chance is a factor in two places: (i) the genetic mutation causing the thicker thorax in the first place (due to a chromosome inversion); and (ii) the circumstances in which the mutated trait finds itself. A thicker thorax in a warm climate may not have done so well. A thicker thoraxed fruit fly would not have evolved if the early prototypes happened to be swatted or eaten prior to their reproducing. In neither case, however, is the role of chance understood as improbable. A mutation of a thicker thorax requires an existing thorax. We can't get a thorax out of nothing. Similarly, the environment in which the trait finds itself (among swatters and predators, say) is itself due to the fitness of those bundles of traits, each governed by Darwinian natural selection; not chance.

But, even if chance played as large a role in the evolutionary account as design advocates allege, the role of chance is itself not well grasped. If we ask, "What are the odds of your winning the lottery?" we know that the odds are going to be slim. But if we ask, "What are the odds of *someone's* winning the lottery?" the ratio (if the lottery isn't fixed) is 1:1 — a guarantee. Similarly, if we ask, "What are the odds of this little planet having all the right conditions to support life?" the odds are slim. But if we ask, "What are the odds of *some* planet having all these conditions?" the odds have vastly increased in direct proportion to the number of suns and planets and moons in the universe: a bunch.

Peter Van Inwagen, a modern proponent of the design argument, calls the sort of "let's switch things around" response that I've just given "the most annoyingly obtuse argument in the history of philosophy."[9] He compares it to noting that while the odds of five coins all coming up heads on a single toss (HHHHH) are low (0.5 x 0.5 x 0.5 x 0.5 x 0.5 = 0.03125), the odds are actually the same odds as *any* specific configuration of a five coin toss. The odds of THHTT, for example, are also 0.03125, as are the odds of HTHHT. And although such reasoning is fine, it merely shows that the odds of *any* configuration are low. But when we couple the argument with noting that not any configuration will produce life, the "let's switch things around" rebuttal I used above is off the mark. Imagine, instead, that I give you five coins to toss and if they come up all heads, I'll spare your life, but otherwise I'll kill you. If you toss the coins and they *do* all come up five heads, you would naturally assume that it was *more* likely that the coins were trick coins — designed to come up heads — as opposed to thinking that you were just lucky today.[10] In other words, not only are the odds incredibly low, but the significance — life itself — is incredibly high.

It is that combination that makes the "it's all just chance" response totally lame. At least, this is Van Inwagen's argument.

If someone offers you an extremely unlikely bet, and you win, it may be reasonable to suspect that the bet was fixed, that the person intended for you to win, that the outcome was designed. In such cases, note, there is no doubt that the person offering you the bet is an intentional agent. We are only wondering whether this particular outcome is intended, not whether the agent herself can have intentions. In the case of God, things are different. We don't start with an intender and wonder if this unlikely outcome, the world, happens to be intended. We are asked to start with the supposition that this world is intended and from that infer an intender. Van Inwagen's comparison is inapt.

Moreover, Van Inwagen admits that if you happened to know that millions of people were also being given exactly the same choice, you would calculate that roughly three per cent of participants would be lucky, and that, therefore, it is conceivable that you might be one of those three per cent. In other words, if you think of the lottery as being indefinitely run, you would more likely think "chance" a suitable explanation for your good fortune of being alive.[11] He wants to suggest that this latter supposition is itself unlikely, but his distinguishing between single-shot and indefinite run lotteries reveals a misunderstanding of expected utility theory. Suppose that the proposed lottery is the following: if you throw five heads, you win $1000; anything else, you pay $100. The expected utility of such a lottery is determined by the amount to be won multiplied by the odds of winning, subtracted by the amount to be lost multiplied by the odds of losing. In other words, $1,000(.03) - $100(.97) = $-67.00. That's to say that you stand to lose $67.00, on average, by playing this game. If you happen to win $1,000, the expected utility hasn't changed, or been in any way abrogated, any more than occasional winners at casinos refute the claim that the odds favour the house.[12] The expected utility of any lottery remains true, whether or not the game is offered a million times or once. Of course, on no given game of the lottery described above can you lose exactly $67.00. You will either gain $1000 or lose $100. To think this alters anything is to misunderstand the expected utility. Even if the specific lottery is only offered once, the correct interpretation of its expected utility is determined as if it were played a sufficient number of times. To treat the calculation of the odds of a single game differently than the calculation of the odds of a large number of games is to misunderstand the calculation of chance.

Rare events do happen purely by chance. No other explanation is necessary. Still, when people utter things like: "Hey, there was one in a million chance of that happening, and it *did*," such an utterance belies the belief in an unexplained force. Likewise, we can't accept that we met our wonderful spouse by chance. Instead, we assume that "everything happens for a reason." But saying that something has a one in a million chance of happening is not saying that there is *no* chance of it happening. Rather, given a million occurrences, it will probably happen once. This is exactly what did occur. So what's the big mystery? The same goes with the first meeting of your spouse. The odds of your marrying this person instead of any other socially eligible person are slim. But given people's penchant to marry, the chances of your marrying *someone* are considerably high. This argument is hardly "obtuse" and certainly far from being the most obtuse "in the history of philosophy." There are better candidates for that award.

In fact, the law of probability guarantees that, as the number of events increases, the number of coincidences will increase. The probability of flipping a coin and its coming up heads five times in a row is .03. So that is an unlikely event. But, if you flipped five coins at once, 100 times, the probability of at least one of those trials coming up all five heads is .96.[13] That is, in one hundred trials it is *very likely* that this rare event, this coincidence, will happen. What people tend to forget is the base rate information: that the number of occurrences in which coincidences might occur is itself very large.

Coincidences in one's own life are memorable. This helps to distort their importance. An uninteresting day is not very memorable. We more easily recount many of the remarkable coincidences that happened to us, and tend to forget the mundane events. Thinking of so-and-so and her phoning, or being late for the bus and thereby meeting the person who you ended up marrying, etc. These cases stick in our minds. More mundane events get forgotten. How many times did you miss a bus and nothing happened? How many people did you meet whom you didn't marry? When we compare the remarkable coincidences in our lives that we remember with the unremarkable events that we tend to forget, it is not surprising that the former seem much more salient. This is due to distortion in memory. We tend to forget or ignore the base rate information.

Although the evolutionary account appeals far less to chance than design proponents seem to assert, even the element of chance that is involved is misunderstood.

INTELLIGENT DESIGN?

Evolution and God's creating the universe are not logically incompatible. One can (try to) evoke the cosmological argument and make the case that God created all the elements necessary for evolutionary processes to get going. But given the failure of the cosmological argument, such a move isn't going to go anywhere. Another tactic is to point out that evolution is just a "theory" and that not all the empirical data supports the wide claims of evolutionary theory. Darwinian evolution, recall, makes the case that small random changes at the genetic level may infer advantage at the level of the organism (or the gene). In this sense, we do not say a change was designed to help the organism. We do not say that the chromosome inversion took place *in order* to produce a thicker thorax in the fruit fly, *in order* for the fruit fly population to better withstand the Canadian winter. Saying this puts intention ahead of the act, and then we need to posit some candidate to be the appropriate intender–presumably, God. This intentional model was the version of evolution that Darwin's predecessor Jean-Baptiste de Lamarck came up with. According to Lamarck, an organism saw what was needed to confer advantage to itself, like having a longer neck to reach foliage higher than its competitors, and so altered its physical shape to better adapt itself to its environment. The organism then, somehow, passed on this physical alteration to its offspring. In other words, if you deem it worthwhile to lop off your pinky, your children will be born pinkyless too.[14] Needless to say, Lamarck didn't know anything about genetics.[15] Darwin's model, on the other hand, was fully naturalistic. No intending was required. If a trait conferred advantage, given the environment, and was reproducible, the trait would thrive in future generations so long as the environment remained relatively stable. If a new trait didn't confer advantage, there would be no guarantees that it would continue. If a new trait were disadvantageous, it would die out.

As Richard Dawkins likes to remind us, Darwin's model predicts incremental increases.[16] New trait variations must be possible mutations from existing morphological features. One can't suddenly wake up with fully functioning wings when one hadn't even the beginning of wings. One can't wake up with a fully functioning mammalian eye if no light sensitive organ existed. It is precisely this incremental restriction on Darwinian evolution that proponents of intelligent design take umbrage with. We can track the evolution of long legs through various extensions of existing shorter legs, but such a process doesn't work for everything. Take a wing: a part of a wing won't allow the organism to fly, but a whole wing can only come about by variations to organisms with partial wings. Since partial wings can't be expected to confer any flight advantage, no organism with partial wings can be expected to have passed on its genes. Hence, no organisms with full wings could be expected to have ever come about. Yet, organisms with full wings certainly exist. Hence, the Darwinian incremental picture must be wrong. Similar stories are told by the much publicized intelligent design advocate Michael Behe concerning blood-clotting systems and flagella.[17] In order for such irreducible complexity to have evolved incrementally, a better explanation, so the argument goes, is some sort of intelligent design.[18]

The intelligent design argument, however, misses the role of what Gould and Vrba call "exaptation."[19] An exaptation is a trait that has adaptive use, but originated for some other reason. For example, bird feathers are now widely believed to have originated, not for flight, but for heat insulation.[20] Only later did this temperature regulating device get co-opted for flight. Similar tales are told about flagella and blood-clotting systems. Flagella, the oft-cited example of irreducible complexity, turns out to be reducible, after all. In brief, some parasitic bacteria have a type-three secretory system (TTSS). The TTSS uses some of the same proteins as are in flagella to inject chemicals into their hosts. Given the protein base, the TTSS is a partial, or "incomplete" flagellum, yet useful to the bacteria (not the host organism!), even though the use of the TTSS to the bacteria is different than the use of the whole flagellum. This demonstrates that the flagellum is not as irreducibly complex as intelligent design proponents avow; simpler forms also serve useful — albeit different — functions.[21] Given the prospect that initial states in development confer some benefit to the organism (or gene) that is different than the benefit that later stage mutations confer, there is no need to invoke "intelligence" to the natural process. The basic Darwinian model remains intact.

FINE TUNING
AND ANALOGY

THE DESIGN ARGUMENT (AGAIN)

As noted in the previous chapter, the myriad things of the universe have an intricate fit and work together with amazing harmony. Usually things that have such fit and harmony are designed by someone with a special purpose in mind. So, it is natural to infer that the universe probably was designed by a being with a purpose in mind: presumably, God. This is the structure of the design argument.[1]

In the previous chapter, I highlighted the argument for the evolutionary alternative. In brief, since organisms with fit survive and organisms without fit don't survive, organisms that survive are likely to fit with their environment, including other organisms. This fully accounts for the appearance of design in living things. Further, fossil records show that about ninety-nine per cent of known species are extinct and that the evolutionary model better explains this empirical fact than does the design argument. Moreover, the odds of this planet sustaining life are low, but the odds of *some* planet sustaining life increase as the number of stars and planets increase, etc.

In this chapter, I wish to explore two further arguments related to design: the fine tuning argument, and the appeal to proper analogical structure. The first is an argument for God's existence that claims to bypass the evolution alternative. The second is David Hume's pre-Darwinian argument against the design hypothesis.

FINE TUNING AND BIOGENESIS

Evolution explains how the bits and pieces of life fit together with such precision that it could appear to be the result of design, but evolution does not explain how the bits and pieces came together for there to be life at all.[2] If the rate of the universe's expansion after the Big Bang varied by more than one part in 10^{55}, then the universe would either expand too quickly or collapse back unto itself.[3] Either way, the formation of galaxies, hence our solar system, would not happen. The probability of such an event happening by chance seems less likely than that it was designed. Likewise the chance assembly of the first reproducing molecule. As put, this captures the *argument from biogenesis* (the origin of life), and the *fine tuning argument*.

If we wish to bake a certain size cake, we set the temperature at 350 degrees Fahrenheit, and set the timer for 30 minutes. Alter the temperature (sufficiently) while keeping the time constant, or alter the time (sufficiently) while keeping the temperature constant, and the cake won't work out. In this sense, the two dials, temperature and time, are fine tuned and complement each other. If we set the two dials randomly, the odds of getting an edible cake at the end are pretty low. Assume the temperature dial increases by 25 degrees up to 600 degrees. Then we can say there are, including the 0 setting, twenty five possible temperature settings. Assume the time setting is by ten minute intervals and goes up to four hours. Including 0, there are twenty five possible time settings. The possible permutations between temperature and time, then, are 25^2. The odds that the dials are each properly set by chance are 1/625, or .0016. That's better than the odds of winning a typical lottery, but still pretty low.[4] If the cake comes out fine, we suspect it is due to a baker fine tuning the dials on purpose, not randomly. For the origin of life itself, there are more dials than temperature and time, although those are probably two of the dials. Perhaps another dial regulates the production of carbon, or hydrogen atoms, or helium atoms, etc. How many settings such dials would have, I confess not to know, but suffice it to say we are asked to picture a lot of dials, each with a lot of settings. Alter any one setting on any one dial, and the precursors for life to evolve couldn't exist. A commonly cited permutation is that the odds that the stuff necessary for life is 1 in 10^{55}.[5] And even once those precursors exist, the odds of the required molecules randomly coming together to produce the first life are still very low. When the odds of the cake coming out by chance are so low, it is natural to infer an intentional baker. Similarly, so the fine tuning argument goes, when the odds of the stuff of the universe existing at all are so low, it is natural to infer an intentional designer of the universe. When the odds of all the ingredients in the cake coming together in the right proportions by accident are also low, we might infer design again. So, as the argument from biogenesis goes, since the odds of the first living molecule coming together are low, it is again natural to infer a designer.

As put, the biogenesis and fine tuning arguments make a probabilistic claim. One can't say that the extremely low odds of the cosmological constants being just right or of the right molecules coming together are impossible. Rather, given that there's life at all, and given that the odds of such life are incredibly low, it seems more likely life came about by intent than by chance. A bit more technically, the probability of life given that life came about by chance is lower than the probability of life given that God intended life to come about, or

Pr(Life | Design) > Pr(Life | Chance).

What might seem surprising about such a claim is that atheists can accept it as true. The probability that the cosmic dials will be set in the right way for our life if the universe is designed by a God intent on giving us just this kind of life is greater than it would be if the dials had been set by chance. The comparison presupposes the prior existence of a supernatural designer. That's why our accepting it doesn't commit us to anything. For after all, saying Pr(A | B) speaks of the probability of A given B. It does not speak of the probability of B itself. The probability of buying a lottery ticket given that you've won the lottery [Pr(bought | won)] is very high while the probability that you've won a lottery given that you've bought a ticket [Pr(won | bought)] is very low. I can even say, "Given the existence of gremlins (and the non-existence of squirrels), the noise in my attic is more likely caused by gremlins than by squirrels." I can say this even if I reject the prior probability of gremlins. Ditto with the probability of the circumstances of life being fine tuned given a fine tuner.[6]

Perhaps I am being unfair in my formula. Perhaps the fine tuning argument should be written so:

Pr(Design | Life) > Pr(Chance | Life).

If so, then what we are saying is that design is a more probable explanation given the fact of life than chance is given the fact of life. But this formulation is not at all obvious. Apart from the difficulties in determining what the value is for Pr(Chance | Life),[7] consider the difficulty in determining the value for Pr(Design | Life). Here, we are appealing to a supernatural agent. As Hume noted, we have no prior experience with gods or universes.[8] Wherever we look, we find natural explanations of events, not non-natural explanations of events. Relying strictly on experience, we should expect that Pr(Chance | Life) > Pr(Design | Life), *no matter how low the odds are* of Pr(Chance | Life).

Probabilistic comparisons rely on background information. In the cake example, we have plenty of experience with intentional bakers, so the prior probability of the cake being intentionally baked is higher than the prior probability of the cake being perfectly baked by chance. Whereas in the case of the universe, we have no prior probability of any supernatural agent intentionally designing a universe. So, however low the odds of a habitable universe or the first life coming about by chance, it would seem to be still higher than the "0" probability we would assign the alternative.

The above argument holds however low the odds are that chance is the cause of the universe being so fine tuned. An independent argument can be offered to show that the chance explanation isn't quite so improbable, anyway. While the evolution of organisms cannot account for the origin of the cosmos, the mechanics of evolution may still suffice: namely replication, variation, and fit. For this to hold, we need to conceive of a whole slew of cosmoi, each with random settings of their innumerable dials. The cosmoi that happen to have the right settings on each dial get to exist. The ones whose settings are off (or sufficiently off given the other dial settings) on any of their innumerable dials, die off. Under such a picture, the fact that our cosmos happened to have all the right settings isn't surprising given that it hasn't died off. Asking "What are the odds that *our* cosmos had the right settings?" is the wrong question. Instead, we ask, "What are the odds that *some* cosmos has the right settings?", and the higher the baserate of cosmoi, the higher the odds. Similarly, while the odds of you winning the lottery are low, the odds of someone winning the lottery are high. True, when we win, it seems natural to demand some other kind of explanation. It seems miraculous given the odds against us. We say to ourselves, "I understand that probability theory can explain why somebody won, but it doesn't explain why *I* won." But such a feeling is a kind of observation bias, and should be discounted. Similarly, the fact that our cosmos happened to be one of the lucky ones doesn't need any further explanation than the evolutionary mechanisms on cosmoi production has already provided. So, basically the same kind of answer for the appearance of organismic design can be given for the appearance of cosmic design.

A difficulty with this answer, however, is it requires our accepting the prospect that there are perhaps millions, or billions or perhaps an infinite number of cosmoi, whereas even accepting one other cosmos is not something that we can base on our limited experience. We've witnessed one. That's it. So how can we generalize to others? This isn't quite the same mistake as witnessing only natural events and inferring a supernatural event, mind you, since our inference to cosmoi is a mere increase in number, not in kind. In fact, in the case of biogenesis we *do* observe trillions upon trillions of solar systems besides our own, so the odds of the first reproducing molecule coming together by chance in at least one of them may well be rather high — and finding one lottery winner among trillions of players doesn't suggest design. So if there are trillions of solar systems, why not trillions of cosmoi? Still, the cosmoi theory may itself seem implausible to many.[9] The need to understand the cosmoi argument does not actually impel us to accept the existence of other universes, however. Even hypothetical cosmoi will do as far as determining probabilities of events. That is, even if there is only one big bang, one shot at getting all the dials correctly set by pure chance, we are not in a position to say that that event couldn't happen, given that we are here. To say chance is less probable than design is too strong, if the only evidence we have to go on is the bare fact of our existing in a universe with its precondition dials all properly fine tuned. What's more, the alternative explanation (design) requires some prior non-contentious experience with supernatural agency, whereas the prior probability of evolutionary mechanics as an explanation is considerably high.

Summary

Owing to the fact that we exist, and our existence is contingent on the constants of the universe being just right for existence, we are bound to observe that the constants are just right. But this is so whether or not the universe was designed or came about by chance. While the probability of the dials being set exactly this way is ridiculously small, the sheer number of such universes would virtually guarantee that *some* of them would possess the dials set in such a way that life could arise. And even if the prospect of other universes is itself a problematic assumption, relying on probability theory is all that is needed to remove the sampling bias. Once done, the sheer implausibility of the dials being set exactly this way lessens. Moreover, the fine tuning argument proponents cannot merely rest on getting us to admit that the probability of the preconditions to life is low. They also have to argue that the probability of a supernatural designer is higher. While evolution counts in favour of the prior probability of natural explanations to things, there is no equally probable account of supernatural agency to back the designer hypothesis. In terms of straight prior probabilities, then, chance beats out design.

ANALOGICAL ARGUMENT STRUCTURE

In this section, I wish to provide a summary of the argument that David Hume gave in the *Dialogues Concerning Natural Religion* against the design argument. He noted that the design argument was a kind of *analogical argument*. Analogical arguments can be good or bad. By exploring the structure of what good analogical arguments are supposed to look like, we can better see what a poor analogical structure the design argument actually has.

An analogical argument takes the following form:

1.   Entities a, b, c, and d have attributes P and Q.
2.   Entities a, b, and c have attribute R.
3.   Therefore, entity d probably has attribute R.

Let us call the *analogues* those entities represented by a, b, and c. We'll call the *primary subject* entity d, the subject of the conclusion. We'll call *shared attributes* those attributes represented by P and Q. Lastly, we'll call the *target attribute* the attribute identified by R, or the predicate of the conclusion. Given these terms, the structure of an analogical argument can be represented as:

> A number of analogues share in common with the primary
> subject a number of shared attributes. Because these analogues
> also have the target attribute, we conclude that the primary
> subject also has the target attribute.

A good example of an analogical argument is the following:

> John, his brother Sam, and their parents smoked two packs of
> cigarettes a day since they were teenagers, and ate a diet rich
> in fatty foods. Sam and John's parents all died prematurely
> of heart attacks. Therefore, probably John will die of a heart
> attack also.[10]

A poor example of an analogical argument is the following:

> Both Jack and Jill have cars. Jack crashed his car. Therefore, Jill
> will crash her car, too.

What distinguishes a good analogical argument from a bad analogical
argument concerns at least the following three conditions. (1) The number
of analogues. Generally speaking, the more analogues the better; the fewer
analogues the worse. (2) The number of shared attributes. In general, the
more shared attributes there are, the better the argument. The fewer shared
attributes there are, the worse the argument. (3) The number of disanalogies. The fewer number of relevant disanalogies between the primary subject and analogues, the better. More relevant disanalogies than analogies,
the worse.[11]

The heart attack argument makes a plausible prediction because there
are relevant analogues (brother and two parents) and at least three relevant
shared attributes (genetics, smoking, and diet). Plus, it is difficult to imagine a relevant disanalogy, although there may be some (perhaps John exer-
cises, while his parents and brother didn't). Meanwhile, the prediction that
Jill will crash her car is unconvincing. There is only one analogue (Jack)
and only one vaguely relevant shared attribute (having a car). Moreover,
there are countless relevant disanalogies to consider. Does Jack drink while
driving, speed excessively, and tailgate while Jill does none of these things?
Is Jack a teenager while Jill is in her thirties? Since there are so many plausible differences between Jack and Jill, pointing out one similarity (their
each having a car) is wildly insufficient.

Given that quick lesson in what distinguishes good from bad analogical
arguments, we are now set to see why the design argument is more like the
car crash argument than the heart attack argument.

WATCHES AND ASTROLABES

Recall from the previous chapter, Paley's comparison of a watch to the universe. His idea was that should you stumble upon a watch in the woods, say, you would infer that someone had designed that watch. You would make such an inference even if you had never before seen a watch and had no idea what its purpose was. Perhaps you are too familiar with watches to grant Paley's point. Think, instead, then, of stumbling across an astrolabe. If you are like me, you wouldn't know what an astrolabe is, nor what it is intended to do, but you would still infer that it was designed. Paley's claim is that you would make the inference of design (and hence, a designer) from the mere intricate fit of disparate parts. Likewise, we can infer an intelligent designer of the universe merely from the intricate fit of all the disparate pieces of the universe. In analogical terms, Paley's design argument goes as follows:

> A watch could not assemble itself. The complex arrangements
> of parts into a working watch is possible only because there
> is a craftsman who designs and constructs the watch. In just
> the same way, the complicated parts of the world could not
> arrange themselves into the natural order. So there must be a
> designer of the world, and that is God.[12]

In this case, the conclusion is that the world must have been designed. Therefore, the primary subject is the "world," and the target attribute is "being designed." The analogue is that which the world is being compared to. In this case, that is a watch. So, the analogue is a "watch." What do the world and watches have in common? That is, what is the shared attribute? In this case, it's the intricate fit, or in Paley's terms, the "complex arrangements of parts."

There is only one analogue here, a watch. Basically, a watch is being compared to the world. We (now) know that the fewer the number of analogues, the worse the argument. Of course, a watch is simply *an example*. We could cite many such examples. Notice, though, that we cannot cite *natural* examples, like eyes and ecosystems, since whether they are designed is what the conclusion is trying to establish. They are examples of the primary subject. The analogue must consist of only *human-made* stuff, like toasters and nuclear reactors and computer chips, etc. The whole array of such examples, however, can only count as a single analogue: human-made stuff. The analogue is human-made stuff and the primary subject is natural-made stuff. Thus, the argument still counts as having only one analogue.

The shared attributes between a watch and a world is that both are comprised of complicated parts that intricately fit together. Whether this counts as one or two attributes, it is not a lot to work with — especially when there are alternative explanations for such fit (see Chapter 7). After all, we might note that things made by humans require many prototypes before the bugs are worked out, often break down, are by and large poorly designed, are made by teams, or are outsourced, and are made for the profit of the producer, not for the things themselves. All designers *we* know are mortal, work in teams, build on the designs of previous designers, have made previous and botched designs, are in no way perfect, do it for the money, cut corners, have limited intelligence, and interrupt their work to defecate and fornicate and eat. In other words, all designers *we* know are mortal. Thus, perhaps we should conclude that many botched worlds have occurred prior to this one, this world is destined to break down, is poorly designed, is made by a team of mortal designers, not a single god, and that we, as part of the creation, must be mere tools of the designer deities. Picking out only one shared attribute over others leaves one open for such *reductiones ad absurdum.*

This leads us to imagine countless relevant disanalogies. Watches are crafted on an assembly line or in a jeweller's shop, but much of what we see in nature is birthed, or hatched, or grows from seeds. This seems to be a relevant disanalogy. Finding disanalogies is easy when the number of shared attributes is small; especially when we link one aspect of the world to account for the whole. If we pick another part of the world, say the birthing of a calf, we might conclude that the world was not designed, but birthed. Or, to use Hume's analogy: "Since a spider web and the universe have an intricate fit, and the spider web comes from the belly of a spider, the universe must come from the belly of a spider."[13]

So far, the argument by design isn't doing well. Things get worse. Even if we accepted that the universe was designed, we couldn't possibly infer a supernatural God. As Hume noted, we can never infer an infinite being from finite beings, nor an infinite cause from finite effects, nor a supernatural cause from natural effects. To do so would be as unfounded as inferring that since something on the other end of a scale weighs more than ten ounces, it must be infinitely heavy.[14] That is to say, every effect we see in the universe has a natural cause. Therefore, we are not entitled to infer a supernatural cause from empirical, or *a posteriori*, grounds alone. But, the design argument was supposed to be an *a posteriori* argument.

SUMMARY

The structure of the analogical argument is weak. It has only one shared attribute (fit) and one analogue (human artefacts) and relevant disanalogies between the analogue and primary subject are easy to point out. Pointing out eyeballs, organs, ecosystems, ozone layers, etc., does not help the case, since these cannot count as analogues: whether they are designed or not, is precisely what the argument was trying to show.

Basically, the design argument collapses into asserting that because human-made objects have design, natural stuff also has design. Such an argument has exactly the same structure as the following bad argument:

> Because both mammals and fish are alive, and since mammals
> have lungs, fish must have lungs.

Such an argument isn't made better by listing all the various mammals that have lungs, or listing all the various kinds of fish that are similar to mammals in being alive.

And all this ignores recognizing that evolution perfectly — in fact, *better* — explains the appearance of organismic design in the universe. For that argument, return to Chapter 7.

9

THE MORAL ARGUMENT

The bare fact of morality gives us a reason to believe in God's existence. This line of thought is referred to as *the moral argument for God's existence*. There are several variations on the moral argument for God's existence. The more common one stems from the response to Nietzsche. Nietzsche believed that if God were truly dead, everything would be permissible.[1] If everything is permissible, nothing is impermissible. If nothing is impermissible, there is no such thing as a moral wrong. And if there is no such thing as a moral wrong, there is no such thing as morality. The theist accepts Nietzsche's logic, but points out that we do have morality: therefore, God must not be dead.

The problem with this version of the moral argument is that it begs the question. Where is the argument that morality is a decree of God? Where is the argument that morality cannot be a good thing to have even if there were no God? Until we rule out as impossible a godless morality, the conclusion does not follow. So, a good step for atheists is to provide conceptions of morality that reasonable agents would endorse even if they knew that there is no God. Such conceptions exist aplenty.[2] But to really make this case, the argument needs to shift to conceptions of morality. I shall hold that off until Chapter 22.

In this chapter, I wish to examine the moral argument originated by Aquinas and made famous by Kant.

AQUINAS'S VERSION

Aquinas's version goes something like this: we distinguish degrees of goodness. For example, we may say that Sue is nicer than Fred. But this entails a maximally good thing (or maximally nice thing) of which others partake to various degrees. We call that maximally good thing "God."[3] In other words, the fact that we can distinguish good from bad, better from worse, entails that we have a concept of something that is of the utmost good, the *summum bonum*, and that's God.

It is difficult to see why such an argument carried any weight at all. Do I really need to infer an absolutely good being in order to make the judgement that Sue is nicer than Fred? Do I need to similarly conceive an absolutely tall being in order to make the judgement that Fred is taller than Sue? And would it then follow that that same absolutely tall being is absolutely short since I also make the judgement that Sue is shorter than Fred? And — you guessed it — since I likewise infer that Fred is more evil than Sue, there must be an absolutely evil being. So, either there are count-less such gods, one really tall, one really small, etc., or all these absolute traits belong in one infinite being. The former is denied by monotheists, and even polytheists wouldn't admit to so many gods. If the latter, then God is both absolutely good and absolutely evil, both absolutely tall and absolutely small. Such an absurdity follows from Aquinas's poorly con-ceived argument.

Perhaps Aquinas is not entirely to blame. The source of the problem lies with Plato's Theory of Forms.[4] The Theory of Forms is Plato's answer to the question, "What's really real?" We see stuff, a daffodil, say, and we wonder: is the daffodil really as it appears to us, or is the real daf-fodil somehow different than its appearance? But, if the real daffodil is different than the apparent daffodil, what is the real daffodil really like? Obviously, not as it appears to us. So therefore, it must be wholly other. For Plato, what is real is beyond appearance. Since it is difficult to speak of something beyond appearance, he speaks of "Forms." The Form of the daffodil is real, the appearance of the daffodil is not, or at any rate is of a lesser reality, something that exists merely because it partakes in the *real* daffodil, the daffodil Form. Forms are eternal and changeless, appearances are neither. Things we call beautiful participate in varying degrees with the Form of Beauty. Things we call good, participate in varying degrees with the Form of the Good. It's the Form of Beauty that explains why the daf-fodil is beautiful. It's the Form of Good that explains why charity is good, theft bad.

I should note that something in the concept of Forms is perfectly sane. We do have to match what we see in the phenomenal world with our men-tal categories. I see something sticking out of the ground and my mental categories tell me to call that, first, a plant; second, a flower; and third, a daffodil. In making such distinctions, I need to appeal to something going on in my mind. The daffodil criteria in my mind is different in kind from the daffodil growing in the ground. The distinction between the daffodil and the form of a daffodil, then, shouldn't be that surprising. It is even more evident when we notice the difference between the fact of the daf-fodil and the value that we attach to the daffodil. That we call the daffodil pretty, instead of ugly, highlights that the daffodil is one thing, what we think of it another. This gap between the fact and our assessment of the fact is more noticeable when we cross cultural boundaries. What's pretty in one culture needn't be so deemed in another. Across species, this is even more noticeable. Flies like manure; we don't, generally. That there is a difference between the phenomenal stuff we find in the world and the concepts that we apply to such stuff lends some support to Plato's discussion of forms.

It is the same when we see a moral act. We see an action (a fact), and apply some concept in our minds (a value) to that action. The fact of handing someone some change, for example, could be a simple business transaction, or charity. We say that the second is moral, not so much the first (though it is not immoral, to be sure). The bare action is the same; the moral appraisal is different. Similarly, lighting wood on fire is not (normally) immoral, whereas lighting a cat on fire is.[5] These examples highlight that we assess phenomenal facts in the world by appealing to something going on in our minds.

Does the fact-value distinction give the Theory of Forms more credence? Not quite. Something more is going on with the Theory of Forms than pointing out a gap between facts and values, or objects and concepts. We can accept the fact-value distinction without accepting the Theory of Forms. We can "recognize" that burning cats is immoral without presupposing that such recognition is a fact of the matter. I can "recognize" my distaste of mushrooms without supposing that mushrooms are intrinsically, objectively distasteful. Plato and Aquinas, however, thought recognition of value in objects presupposed an objective domain. They thought that the Form of Beauty and the Form of Good were real things in themselves. To them, we call daffodils "beautiful" and charity "good" because they partake — in varying degrees — in the forms of Beauty and Good, respectively. Neither Beauty nor Good exist in the phenomenal world, of course, so they suppose that their existence must be in some other domain — a supernatural domain. That is, from the mere difference between fact and value, Plato infers two things: (i) concepts exist as real — though non-phenomenal — things, and; (ii) there must be a spiritual domain to house those real, but non-phenomenal, things. Neither inference is warranted from merely recognizing a gap between fact and value, object and concept.

No one needs doubt that we appeal to standards of good and beauty in our assessment of beauty and good. Pointing this out, however, is not enough to get us to call such standards objective, or God-given. Aquinas's rendition of the moral argument starts from our distinguishing good from bad, and leaps to belief in the existence of something maximally good: the Form of Good. This Form of Good not merely exists, but is more real than the things that we describe as good. It is these last inferences that are unwarranted.

Notice, by the way, that our not knowing whether a daffodil is as it appears to us is not sufficient reason to believe that it is not as it appears to us. To think so, is to confuse metaphysics with epistemology. Metaphysics concerns what is really real; epistemology concerns what we can know. You can't assume what is really real from limitations on what you can know. Leaving this objection aside, even if we accept the "existence" of a Form of Beauty or a Form of Good, it doesn't follow that such forms have existence beyond being simply a concept. The concept of the most beautiful daffodil in existence may make sense, but not the concept of the most beautiful daffodil period, let alone the concept of Beauty existing in the same sense as a beautiful daffodil existing. You can smell the daffodil; you cannot smell the concept of a daffodil. You can smell a fragrance; you cannot smell the concept of the most beautiful fragrance. So, even if we were forced to conclude the "existence" of ultimate goodness, we needn't attach that to a being. In the same way, we can understand an existing dog, and we can understand the concept of a dog to which any existing dog ought to belong, but we wouldn't confuse the concept of a dog with existing dogs. A dog has fleas. The concept of a dog does not. It is simply a concept that we employ to categorize existing things that we call dogs from existing things that we don't call dogs. The alternative view to Plato and Aquinas is that *we* ascribe value to certain objects on the basis of our dispositions and the use that we find in such objects. We like daffodils, not dandelions. Flies like manure.

A further worry, as if the above were not enough, concerns Aquinas's notion that the maximum is the cause of the minimum. This means that the supreme good is the cause of any of the good that Sue has. This partly makes sense to the extent that we will call Sue short only in relation to the fact that Fred is tall. If Sue remained at her height, but Fred were not taller, we would no longer call Sue short relative to Fred. Shortness and good-ness are relative terms. Sue's being short and nice depends not merely on things about Sue, but on things external to Sue, whether others are nicer and taller. But to say that Fred's tallness is "the cause of" Sue's shortness is to abuse the meaning of "cause." The sense of "cause" in "Fred's height caused Sue's shortness," is certainly not the same sense of "cause" in the statement, "The heavy rains caused the mud slide," or "God is the cause of the universe." Yet, it is the latter sense of "cause" that Aquinas needs. Even if we could (or need to) conceive of an absolutely tall being in order to make a comparison in height between two existing objects, we would be hard-pressed to say that that absolutely tall thing is necessarily the cause of the tallness in the objects at hand.

Aquinas followed Aristotle in distinguishing four kinds of causal expla-nations: material, formal, efficient, and final. A material cause of X details what X is made of (wood, say). A formal cause of X details what kind of a thing X is (a chair, say). An efficient cause of X details how X came about (a carpenter built it, say). A final cause of X explains why X came about (someone wanted to sit, say). When Aquinas says that the ultimate moral standard is the *cause* of moral actions, then, he means, presumably, the formal cause, or, perhaps, the final cause. My objection above took him to mean the efficient cause. But, if Aquinas sticks with talking about a final or formal cause only, his argument can't get to a god without sheer stipulation. If the maximally good is deemed a final cause, that would mean that the existence of the maximally good is *why* charity, say, is deemed good. But, apart from our supposing charity is deemed good because it helps a person out (instead of appealing to an unknowable concept of the maximally good), it wouldn't explain the (efficient) causal connection between the maximally good and the charitable act. It is one thing to say that Aquinas wasn't talking specifically about efficient cause, but if his talk has no connection to efficient cause, the talk is idle. If, on the other hand, Aquinas means to invoke a formal cause, then Aquinas conceives the maximally good as a blueprint (of sorts) for things that we call good. Nothing in saying this commits us to imagine that the blueprint is made by God, however. Perhaps we made it. No one needs doubt that we appeal to standards of good and beauty in our assessment of beauty and good. Pointing this out is not enough to get us to call such standards person-independent, or objective, or God-given.

You can see why Aquinas's version of the moral argument (typically referred to as the argument by gradation) doesn't receive much attention. Nevertheless, Immanuel Kant thought it worth resurrecting. Does he make it any more credible? Let's see.

KANT'S VERSION

Kant's version of the moral argument in his *Critique of Practical Reason* is more sophisticated. For Kant, we postulate the existence of God as the necessary condition for the possibility of the *summum bonum* — the ultimate good. The argument for this is as follows:

1. Morality dictates that we ought to pursue the *summum bonum*: therefore, since ought implies can, the *summum bonum* exists.[6] ("For it would be practically impossible to strive after the object of a conception which at bottom was empty and had no object."[7])
2. The *summum bonum* is possible in the world only on the supposition of a supreme being (since the ultimate goodness can only be contained by [or as] God Himself).[8]

In this argument, we start from the fact that we have moral duties, and arrive at the supposition that God must exist.[9]

Kant also offers another version. Since the object of morality is to achieve ultimate happiness, and since ultimate happiness is obviously not possible on earth, there must be a place where ultimate happiness is achievable, and that is heaven, and this presupposes heaven's host, i.e., God.[10] Both versions succumb to the same basic problem that beset Aquinas's version.

Firstly, let's accept Kant's claim that the *summum bonum* is possible only on the supposition of the existence of a Supreme Being. This wouldn't necessarily help theists since we can go in two opposite directions from here. Contrary to Kant, we could just as easily infer that therefore there is no *summum bonum*. My being a millionaire is a necessary condition for my owning a yacht hardly shows that I'm a millionaire or own a yacht. The assumption that there must be a *summum bonum* on the basis that there is a lesser *bonum* returns us to Aquinas's argument. No such inference need be made at all, unless one is committed to infer a *summum* tallness, a *summum* stinkiness, a *summum* drunkenness, etc. We do not require a *summum bonum* in order to recognize good from bad any more than we need a maximally high mountain in order to distinguish the Rockies from the Laurentians.

When I dismiss the notion of a *summum bonum*, notice, I am not dismissing the brute fact that we do distinguish good from bad, or that we do distinguish fact from value. To object to the moral argument for God's existence is *not* to be a nihilist about morality. To reject the moral argument is to reject the belief that morality requires metaphysical agency. If an action by you causes me net pain, I'm against it. Meanwhile, I feel fairly confident that such a sentiment is shared by most of us. Thus, most of us have an interest in reducing actions that cause others pain — if merely to lessen the chances that others will cause us or our loved ones pain. Thus, we tend to catalogue those kinds of actions that tend to cause others net pain under the heading "immoral." Similarly, since most of us tend to like the actions of others that cause us net benefit, we call such actions "morally good." (All actions that are neither "immoral," nor "morally good," like playing the violin, are what we call "morally permissible.") No appeal to a *summum bonum* is required.

Plato, Aquinas, and Kant, on the other hand, believed that moral structure is built into the fabric of the universe. As such, recognition of morality is recognition of an objective supernatural conception, imposed on the universe by a supernatural agent. Apart from Mackie's incisive criticism that objective morality is too "queer," metaphysically, epistemologically, and motivationally,[11] we don't need such a picture to distinguish good from bad, any more than we need a supernatural agent to recognize that I'm not fond of mosquitoes biting me.

Secondly, Kant claims that "it would be practically impossible to strive after the object of a conception which at bottom was empty and had no object."[12] This seems unlikely. It is certainly impossible to *achieve* an impossible goal, but it doesn't follow that it is impossible to *strive* for an impossible goal. It may be impossible for me to lower my golfing handicap to a single digit, but this shouldn't prevent me from striving to lower my handicap. J.L. Mackie makes a similar complaint. He points out what should be obvious to everyone that moral improvement doesn't require maximal improvement. All we need is some improvement to make it worthwhile to improve.[13] An abusive spouse ought to stop abusing, and this is true even if the spouse never becomes as saintly as Mother Teresa. We can admit that spousal abuse is bad without having any conception of what a maximally good spouse ought to be, let alone believe that a maximally good spouse is conceptually possible.

Thirdly, according to Kant, morality dictates that we ought to pursue the *summum bonum*. Of course, this will be false if we reject the existence of a *summum bonum*. My point here, however, is to note that even if there were a *summum bonum*, it wouldn't necessarily follow that morality dictates that we pursue it. To think so would be to confuse morality with *supererogation*. The supererogatory is the category of actions that go beyond one's duty. To go beyond one's duty may be commendable, but failing to go beyond one's duty is not blameworthy. Let's say that you have a duty to be charitable. It's difficult to stipulate exactly what such a duty entails. Are you fulfilling your duty if you give five per cent of your income to charity, or is that too low? However fuzzy the duty may be, we would still recognize that being *really* charitable may be commendable, but isn't a requirement. So, being *really* charitable would be a supererogatory act. The supererogatory may be understood as an ideal.[14] When we imagine a maximally good standard as the formal cause of goodness, we make the supererogatory the benchmark for good actions. If you start suggesting that the supererogatory becomes the standard for what counts as moral, then this confuses what is morally required with what is morally ideal. It confuses morality with religion.

Consider four different kinds of moral claims: (i) you must do X; (ii) you must not do X; (iii) you may do X; and (iv) it would be good if you were to do X. The first concerns positive moral obligations, like, "Pay your debts!" The second concerns negative moral obligations, like, "Do not murder!" The third concerns morally permissible (or prerogative) acts, like, "You may play the violin." The fourth concerns supererogatives, like, "Be more like Jesus!" or "Help the downtrodden the way that Mother Teresa does!" Note that you are immoral if you fail to fulfill your obligations, whether positive or negative. You are morally culpable for failing to pay your debts. Likewise, you are morally culpable if you murder someone. You are not immoral, however, for failing to perform a prerogative or a supererogative. You are not immoral for not playing the violin even when playing the violin would be a morally permissible act. Likewise — and importantly — you are not immoral for failing to turn the other cheek, or not giving up your career in order to help the starving in Africa.[15]

It is this latter fact that seems difficult for some people to grasp. That is because they think that there are only two kinds of moral utterances: "That's moral!" and "That's immoral!" And so they confuse failing to do what's moral with doing what is immoral. That is, they ignore the concepts of the prerogatory and the supererogatory. The supererogatory may be understood as going beyond what is morally required. It refers to (putatively) morally exemplary actions. But, if going *beyond* one's moral duty is what is equated with being moral, then what counts as your moral duty is to go beyond that duty — which is incoherent. That's like ordering the local barber to shave all and only those residents who don't shave themselves.[16] Such absurdity is the result of confusing morality with the supererogatory.

Religion's role, on the other hand, is to point to something beyond one's earthly obligations, beyond the merely moral. In other words, the supererogatory may well be fine talk for the religious, but not for what defines moral obligation (negative or positive) or the morally permissible. If morality is *defined* as a form of religiosity (the supererogatory), then of course, being moral is tantamount to being religious. But, that's mere definitional trickery and, in any event, a conflation that we have reason to reject.

Apart from my complaint of religion's usurpation of morality, the mere identification of morality with religion still wouldn't do the job. Being religious doesn't entail the existence of a god, any more than believing in alien abductions entails alien abductions.

SUMMARY

The moral argument reifies the moral ideal into a being — which is weird enough. Moreover, it completely ignores the prospect that humans have reasons to be moral independently of a belief in God. That is, our recognition of a moral standard does not count as evidence of anything that can be called "God." If we're happy to have a morality, this is presumably because we do better under certain moral constraints than not being so bound. If this is true, it is true whether or not God exists and whether or not you believe that God exists. But, I shall leave this part of the argument for Chapter 22.

PART III. ATTRIBUTES

THE PROBLEM OF SUFFERING

There is a lot of suffering in the world. We don't have to go far to see it. A thirteen-year-old girl got her hair trapped in the intake valve of a backyard pool and drowned. A five-year-old girl was trapped in her bedroom as fires slowly consumed her. An eight-year-old boy was beaten to death by his father. What kinds of deaths are these? What kind of a life is that?[1]

So long as we care about other people, know about their suffering, and can stop their suffering, we would do so. Any good person would. In the drowning case, the parents were unaware of their daughter's plight. In the fire case, the mother knew about the suffering, but was powerless to stop it. She listened to her daughter's screams but could not get into the bedroom to save her. In the beating case, the father was not good. In these three cases, suffering occurred due to either a lack of knowledge, a lack of power, or a lack of goodness. In cases where someone is good, knows that an individual is suffering, and is able to prevent that suffering, we would expect that suffering to end.

Note that God did not stop the children's suffering. God did not stop the suffering of the people jumping from the Twin Towers on September eleventh. God did not stop the suffering of the Jews in Nazi concentration camps, the suffering of victims of tsunamis, hurricanes, famine, Chernobyl, and countless other cases too numerous to catalogue. Suffering is plentiful on our little planet. By most accounts, however, God is supposed to be all good (omnibenevolent), all knowing (omniscient), and all powerful (omnipotent). There can be no suffering that God doesn't know about, nor prevent if He wants to, and if anyone is good, God is. Yet suffering exists. Something doesn't fit.[2]

Because there is suffering in the world, and because we assume that good people who know about and can stop suffering would do so, it follows that there cannot be a god who is omnibenevolent, omnipotent, and omniscient. If any such creature existed, we would anticipate no suffering in the world. But, since suffering exists, it is proper to conclude that God, so defined, cannot exist.[3]

Let us call this the *problem of suffering*. Historically, this is called the *problem of evil*. Calling it the problem of evil, however, is misleading. Not all suffering is due to evil. To be evil is to intend to harm an innocent person (or animal, perhaps). If all suffering were due to intentional acts, the problem would be less taxing for theists. The problem of suffering is greater than that. The problem of suffering casts doubt on traditional beliefs in the Judeo-Christian God. Theists are not unaware of the problem. Clever retorts have been offered, though none satisfactory. They include the following: (1) God's ways are inscrutable; (2) we have free will; (3) there is eschatological recompense (or compensation after death); and (4) suffering is needed for moral development. Let's examine these in turn.

INSCRUTABILITY

Who are we to know God's ways? God is inscrutable to us and we are deluded and wrong to question His ways. This is certainly a common type of response. That God's ways are beyond our ken is consistent with the Bible (Rom. 11:33–34, e.g.) and Anselm's concept of God's being greater than anything that can be conceived entails that God is beyond our conception.[4] Philo, one of Hume's characters in *The Dialogues of Natural Religion*, suggests that the inscrutability defence is the only possible response to the problem of evil.[5] It "solves" the problem, however, by pretending that we have never heard of the problem. It is also a brilliant example of what philosophers call the *fallacy of ignorance*. The fallacy of ignorance occurs when, on the basis of our not knowing that not-X is true, we conclude X. Concluding that the accused is guilty because her innocence was not proven, is a case of the fallacy of ignorance. This example also highlights how committing the fallacy of ignorance is a case of getting the burden of proof backwards (as discussed in Chapter 1). The inscrutability defence asserts that since we do not know how God works, any putative problem posed for belief in God must be false. How convenient.

One could appeal to the inscrutability defence without committing the fallacy of ignorance. Stephen Wykstra, for example, does so.[6] Your not knowing who your father is, is not a reason to conclude that you have no father. But then, the inscrutability defence shifts to another fallacy: that of begging the question. One begs the question when one of the premises or background assumptions is the conclusion itself. If we are trying to convince someone of something, we do not succeed by simply reasserting what it is that we want them to believe. "God exists because God exists," is not convincing. The inscrutability defence is not much different. It requires us first to believe that God exists. Once we accept that, then we can try to explain away counter evidence to God's existence by the suggestion that we may not be bright enough to understand the workings of God's universe. The problem of suffering is used to cast doubt on the assumption that any god exists at all. To respond to the problem of suffering by assuming that God's existence is true, therefore, misses the point. One might as well cover one's ears and shout, "I can't hear you!"

Theists tend to believe that the suffering in the world is compatible with the existence of a good God. Believing this isn't itself a case of begging the question. Nor is believing that God is inscrutable a case of begging the question. The trouble comes when the two are put together. We can *arrive* at the belief that God is inscrutable *from* the following premises: (i) suffering exists; (ii) a good God exists; and (iii) there is no other explanation for the seeming disparity between the fact of suffering and the existence of a good God. But, if we now use God's inscrutability to defend God's existence (premise (ii)), we have gone into a loop.

For an analogy, imagine that we look out at the untrammeled snow on my balcony. I say, "A squirrel has passed here!" You say, "Where are the tracks?" I say, "This squirrel must obviously leave no tracks." You ask, "How can that be? Have you ever seen such a thing before?" And I reply, "I don't need to, the proof speaks for itself: there are no tracks!" Now, if there were squirrels who leave no tracks, our seeing no tracks would not itself be evidence that no such squirrel passed. Granted. But, we cannot go in reverse and say, "*Because* there are no tracks, a non-track making squirrel must have passed." Similarly, once you have independent reasons for a belief in God, you might point out some track-cloaking feature of such a god, but you can't use the absence of tracks as itself evidence for the existence of such a god. And that is what the inscrutability argument does.

FREE WILL

In creating the world, God had a choice. He could make people free, or He could create automatons. Presumably God thought that it would be best if we were free. With freedom comes responsibility. Freedom and responsibility entail the possibility of sin. Sin is a necessary by-product of human freedom. With sin, suffering is inevitable. Thus, our world, complete with suffering, is really the best of all possible worlds given the constraints of allowing us to be free. Surely, we are better off being free. If so, we must tolerate suffering in the world.[7]

Though commonly offered, the free will defence is woefully inadequate. Let us accept that freedom entails the possibility of sin. One needn't accept this premise, mind you. You do not freely make your heart pump and this doesn't bother you. So, it is possible to make people free in some respects — say, in choosing a career, a spouse, one's friends, a hobby — and yet, not be free in other matters: say, having the desire to hurt someone. In other words, it's a false dichotomy to say that either we are fully free or that we are fully automatons. There is much room in between.[8]

Even if we grant that free will entails the possibility of sin, a problem remains. The existence of sin will explain a lot of suffering, for example, the case of the father beating his son to death. But, it does not explain the enormity of suffering, say that inflicted by the Nazis on Jews and Gypsies.[9] Nor does our having the freedom to sin explain why God would not intervene to protect innocents from suffering from our sin. We don't stand by and tell a victim of abuse, "I'm sorry, we can't intervene to help you since that would violate your assaulter's free will." Besides all that, and more importantly, sin does not explain all suffering. It does not explain the drowning or the burning cases, for example. Nor does sin explain the suffering caused by natural disasters: earthquakes, volcanoes, hurricanes, tsunamis, tornados, mudslides, floods, plagues, famine. Nor does sin explain harms from natural predation: attacks by lions, bears, crocodiles, sharks, boa constrictors, scorpions, black widow spiders, parasites. Nor does sin explain disease, sickness, viruses, illnesses, allergic reactions, etc.

One might maintain that sin has something to do with all these cases. However abhorrent, such an idea is consistent with the Garden of Eden story (Gen. 3:14–19, 4:1–5).[10] In this sense, suffering is inflicted on sinners as God's punishment. All suffering is due to sin. If anyone is suffering, don't help them: they deserve it.[11] That's why the tsunami hit: the villagers must have sinned. That's why the eight-year-old burned to death: she must have sinned. Why notorious sinners don't suffer similar fates will presumably be given some *post hoc* explanation as well. A slightly better attempt is to point out the fact that we freely decide to live under the volcano and in the wake of the tsunami, that we freely decide to go swimming and to heat our homes with fires. In this way, free will can still be cited as having some causal link to suffering. This overly stretched idea of the free will-suffering link fits well with the *Genesis* myth that all human suffering can be traced back to original sin. It does so at a cost, though. It removes the distinction that normal people make between the culpability of a father beating his son to death and the horror of a mother being unable to rescue her daughter from a fire. Saying, the father, in the one case, and the mother, in the other case, are both equally sinful due to some traceable causal connection between free will and suffering is to speak an alien language. The mother of the burn victim is morally blameless; not so the father who beat his son to death. No sophisticated arguments about free will can alter that basic assessment.

And besides, there are many cases where people rescue other people, and do so because the rescuers are good and have free will, irrespective of the free will of the people needing rescue. So the fact that God does not rescue other people would seem to mean God is either not as good as some people, or has no free will Himself. Neither is palatable to theism. The free will argument is nothing but a diversionary tactic.

ESCHATOLOGICAL RECOMPENSE

Eschatology concerns what happens at the end of the world, and a large part of that entails an after-death state. If there is a heaven where the innocent go, and if it is as infinitely pleasant as promised, then the suffering endured on earth may very well be no big deal. Consider all the problems and agonies that you experienced as a five-year-old: you couldn't play with the orange ball, or your mother said no more ice cream, or the little red-haired girl stuck her tongue out at you. These may all have been very traumatic for you at the time, but you can look back at them now and chuckle at the inanity of it. In retrospect, such suffering was nothing. Similarly, from the vantage of heaven, one may look back at the suffering endured in the flames, or under water, or while being bludgeoned to death by the one person you should have been able to trust the most, and laugh at the inanity of it all.

Hume's character Demea in *The Dialogues Concerning Natural Religion* appeals to eschatology in his solution to the problem of suffering: "This world is but a point in comparison of the universe: that life but a moment in comparison of eternity. The present evil phenomena, therefore, are rectified in other regions, and in some future period of existence."[12]

In Dostoyevsky's *The Brothers Karamazov*, Ivan replies to the eschatological recompense retort by saying that heaven is not worth the price.[13] Would you torture one innocent child if that guaranteed the happiness of a community of people? No, presumably, so why should God? But this misses the point of the eschatological recompense rebuttal. The argument isn't claiming that *in order to* get to heaven, one must go through this ritual of suffering. (A variant on that claim occurs next.) It is rather an argument that denies suffering altogether. What appears to be suffering, really isn't.[14]

Unfortunately, the logic of the argument moves one to the opposite conclusion. The travails of the five-year-old's not getting ice cream is nothing compared to the much more serious travails she will experience later in life: like unrequited love, the death of someone dear, poverty, or illness. Following this logic, only from the vantage point of hell would we find suffering endured on earth petty. From heaven, our being thankful that we aren't suffering anymore wouldn't dissipate that suffering. Nor would it make us stop wishing that others not go through such suffering, especially if we could prevent it. Suffering hasn't done anyone any good. Even if one alters one's life for the better, after some significant suffering, this doesn't mean that the suffering in itself was good: it means merely that people are so happy not to be suffering that they'll change their lives to try to avoid such suffering in the future. The mere fact that we are later comforted doesn't explain why it's there in the first place.

Besides, appealing to an eschatological justification begs the question. The topic is whether we have grounds to believe in a god and all god-accoutrements, and so bringing in one of the god-accoutrements (heaven) is already cheating. As Hume notes, for the evidence *at hand*, no hypothesis about a benevolent God is plausible.[15] For example, let's say that you enter a house and find a child battered and malnourished and chained in a small closet, while the parents are well-fed and unchained and unbattered. From the evidence at hand, you would think that the parents are abusive. To say, "Despite appearances, these are the best parents ever," you would have to do some fancy footwork. You would have to start with the assumption that these are the best parents possible and then come up with some account to explain away the counter evidence. Whatever elaborate theory you come up with, it will be based on the assumption that your pet conclusion is right, rather than allow for the evidence to direct you to the most fitting conclusion. If we allow the evidence to direct us, the suffering we observe in the world propels us to abandon belief in a metaphysical agent who cares to stop our suffering, knows about our suffering, and can stop our suffering. We cannot avoid this conclusion by simply presuming compensation will come to us. Nor would such compensation explain why God does not intervene, since good and able people still intervene even when they sincerely believe eternal compensation awaits every sufferer.

MORAL FORTITUDE

Not all suffering is the result of free will and this is the main problem with the free will defence. Suffering is too liberally applied. The moral development response handles this fact. Basically, we need a tough environment to "test" our mettle, to see if we are worthy of entering the Kingdom of God. In this sense, it isn't that we must suffer to get admittance into heaven, like some frat house initiation rite. Rather, by our dealing with suffering — both in us and perhaps more especially in our response to the suffering that we witness in others — do our moral sensibilities develop. We need to develop a moral stance to get into heaven. In this way, suffering is seen as a necessary step in God's overarching plan.[16]

This is the best response to the problem of suffering, but it falls short for all that. Consider first, the worry about why there is so much suffering — so much so, that it often incapacitates us, overwhelms us, as opposed to invigorates us. When the degree of suffering is more than we can psychologically handle, no beneficial effects on us can be expected — contrary to the claims of the moral fortitude defenders. If suffering were designed purely for our benefit, God would ensure that the suffering were not so excessive as to wipe out the good effects. We see no such restriction on suffering, however.

Ignoring the above, the moral fortitude defence reveals a misconception about morality. The claim is that suffering is needed in order to develop moral sensibilities. The alternative picture is that morality is developed to accommodate suffering. That is, absent suffering, there would be no need for morality. This may initially strike you as benefiting the moral development argument, but it really has the opposite effect. Many people like to think that morality is good *in and of itself*, that is, intrinsically.[17] To say that X is intrinsically good is to say that X is enjoyed for its own sake rather than for some other sake. For example, you may enjoy music for its own sake, not for what it can get you. Money, on the other hand, is typically enjoyed only for what it can get you, not for its own sake. In such a case, we say that music is intrinsically good, whereas money is instrumentally (or extrinsically) good. For you to say that morality is an intrinsic good, then, means that you enjoy being moral for its own sake, not for what it can get you. Notice that saying X is intrinsically good is *not* to say that X is *objectively* good. Do we enjoy music because it is good, or do we deem music good because we enjoy it? This question remains unanswered by saying merely that music is intrinsically good. People who proclaim morality to be intrinsically good typically mean that morality is objectively good. And for something to be objectively good is for that thing to be good independently of anyone's appraisal of it. This is an odd claim. Saying that music or a sunset would be enjoyable to anyone with ears and eyes and sensibilities like ours, whether or not such creatures ever existed, is not really to settle the issue, since it presupposes creatures *who find such objects enjoyable* ... and that's consistent with the subjective view.

The prospect of enjoying moral behaviour for its own sake — like enjoying a sunset for its own sake — strikes me as psychologically false, but even if it were true, it does not exclude the possibility of indoctrination. We are malleable creatures, after all, and can be made to enjoy things through proper training. Smoking a cigarette, for example, is deemed enjoyable to someone who has become addicted to it. Killing an unsuspecting Cree may have seemed an enjoyable and guilt-free act to a cowboy. Conversely, otherwise innocuous acts, like masturbation, say, have been deemed bad by some cultures. Anyone's guilt from masturbating, then, is due, not to the intrinsic nature of the act itself, but to the cultural norm laid over top of the act. This shows that the subjective feeling of guilt or moral righteousness is not necessarily an indicator of bad or good acts.

Saying, "I do good for its own intrinsic reward," apart from being psychologically displaced, is also theoretically problematic. If it is the doing good that I enjoy, does it matter whether what I take to be good really is good? And if it makes sense to ask this question, then we need a criterion for determining whether an act is good, independent of our intrinsic enjoyment of it. Conversely, if one enjoys doing good acts *because* they are good acts, the criterion to distinguish good acts must be understood independently of one's intrinsic enjoyment. That is, I would need to first know what act is good, then do that act, and then feel good about it. Hence, my determining what act is good must be independent of my feeling good about doing it. The determination must be made independently of any intrinsic rewards.

Meanwhile, we have plenty of evidence that morality is *instrumentally* good. Given the surfeit of suffering, abiding by certain social norms may be worthwhile if it has the effect of diminishing as much as possible our rampant suffering. Following rules of helping others and not harming others will certainly help lessen suffering.

Consider the concept of fairness: making sure that everyone has enough. If the world were abundant with food and shelter and clothing and spouses, and whatnot, we would never require this notion of fairness.[18] No one would be in need. Or, consider the specific moral rule: don't hit people over the head with hammers. But, if we were so constituted, like rams perhaps, that hammers hitting our heads felt nice, did us a favour, then that particular moral rule would not have been developed.

In this way of thinking about morality, morality is simply one of the many *tools* that humans have devised to help them navigate their social existence.[19] But, if there were no suffering in the first place, then this particular tool wouldn't do any good. Without suffering, we wouldn't develop this moral concept. Why would anyone think this bad? It shows that we develop morality in order to survive in a resource-limited, hostile world. Remove the hostility and suffering: we remove the need for morality.[20]

Consider a can opener. A can opener is useful for us, given that we have cans to open. But, if there were no cans, or if all cans had pull tabs, then we wouldn't need a can opener, nor would we miss can openers. It would be peculiar for anyone, other than can opener manufacturers, to say, "You can't get rid of cans, because then you would have to get rid of can openers!" That assumes that cans are needed given that we have can openers.

Or, if you prefer, consider medicine. Medicine is a great way to relieve sickness. But, if we were never sick, we would not need medicine. Saying that we need sickness in order for us to have medicine, or cans in order for us to have can openers, gets things backwards. Similarly, saying that suffering is needed to have morality gets things backwards. Pointing out the benefits of a moral response to suffering fails to dispel the problem of suffering.[21]

SUMMARY

The fact of suffering in the world is inconsistent with a view of an omniscient, omnibenevolent, omnipotent Supreme Being. This leaves one free to believe in a non-supreme god. What good that will do, I leave up to you.

II

OMNIPOTENCE

An attribute of a being is a trait ascribed to that being. An attribute of Samson was his long hair. Another was his strength. Typical attributes ascribed to God include great power, great intimate knowledge about your thoughts and deeds, and great goodness. If God is defined as a being with specific attributes, and those specific attributes are impossible, or self-contradictory, then God, so defined, cannot exist. Atheists point out that many of the particular attributes normally ascribed to at least the Judeo-Christian God are, indeed, impossibilities. We've seen in the previous chapter that something having the attributes of omnipotence, omniscience, and omnibenevolence is inconsistent with the existence of suffering. In this chapter, I shall look at the problem that omnipotence raises all by itself.

For many theists, though not all,[1] God is thought to be omnipotent. That is, God is all powerful. If God is all powerful, there is nothing that God cannot do. His power is infinite. There are no limitations. To find anything that limits God's power would mean that God is not, after all, omnipotent.

We will have to qualify this sense of omnipotence below, but for now, this is the meaning of putting *omni* and *potency* together. And the reason that people would think of God in these (or suitably qualified) terms follows from thinking of God as more praiseworthy than anything else. If power is praiseworthy, more power is more praiseworthy. If God is the most praiseworthy thing, take any praiseworthy attribute, God has to have that attribute to the utmost degree. This is why Anselm defines God as being greater than anything that can be conceived. Aquinas determines that anything that we can praise must have its root in a being most praiseworthy, and the only thing that can satisfy this condition for all time is something that is infinitely praiseworthy. If we admire power, then God's power must be absolute. If we admire purity, then God's purity must be absolute. If we admire dancing, we can praise Shiva, etc. The problem, though, is that it seems quite simple to show that God cannot be omnipotent — at least in the unqualified sense. The analogy of a stone is often used to demonstrate this. The argument is called *the paradox of the stone*.

THE PARADOX OF THE STONE

Can God create a stone so heavy that He cannot lift it? If the answer is "Yes," then here's something that God can't do: lift this particular stone. If the answer is "No," then here is something that God can't do: create this specific stone. Either way, God's power is limited. Ergo, God cannot be omnipotent.[2]

So goes the famous paradox of the stone. Has it convinced anyone? No. It seems too pedantic, disconnected, petty. But really, despite its simplicity and its seeming irrelevance, it should convince us of the general claim: infinity ascribed to an attribute belonging to an agent is untenable.

There are common theistic defences of God's omnipotence against the paradox of the stone. I shall explore three. The first redefines the notion of power. The second claims that the stone paradox is itself paradoxical thus nullifying any of its import. The third is a familiar appeal to the fact that God is beyond our understanding, and so what appears impossible to us needn't be an impossibility for God. None are successful.

NO IMPOSSIBLE POWERS

Aquinas tried to prevent paradox-of-the-stone type rebuttals in the thirteenth century. For him, the term "power" referred only to possible things.[3] One's not having the power to do impossible things is no limitation on one's power. Being omnipotent, then, is not to imply that one now has the power to do impossible things. Rather, of all things possible to do, an omnipotent being can do them. Impossible things are not intended to be on the list. Pointing out God's inability to create a stone too heavy for Him to lift is like saying that God can't create a square circle. These are impossible things. Being unable to do impossible things is not a limitation on God's power. Therefore, God's omnipotence is not hampered by such fanciful objections.

The problem with this response is that the definition of "omnipotence" dissolves into the following: a being is omnipotent if it can do all and only those things that it can do. Even a limited God is still more powerful than we are, presumably, but this definition of omnipotence can't let us infer even that. It's too weak. *We're* omnipotent by this definition. So are snails. A snail can do all and only those things that snails can do. True, a snail can't lift my coffee cup, but since that's impossible for the snail, it doesn't count as an impediment to the snail's omnipotence.

The obvious rejoinder is that the snail's inability to lift my coffee cup is a physical impossibility, not a logical impossibility. When Aquinas ruled out impossible things, he didn't mean *physically* impossible things; only *logically* impossible things. We don't want to say that a being is omnipotent if it can do all the things that that being can do. To correct the above misapprehension, Aquinas claimed that a being is omnipotent if it can do all the things which are "possible absolutely." This is a cumbersome way of speaking. In philosopher's terminology, a being is omnipotent if there is no *a posteriori* possible act it can't do. Or put negatively, omnipotence is not hampered by an *a priori* impossibility.

As discussed in Chapter 5, the distinction between *a priori* and *a posteriori* judgements is that between pure reason and empirical observation. *A priori* knowledge concerns logical, mathematical, geometrical, or definitional derivations. A judgement based on empirical observation of some sort is *a posteriori*. That my coffee cup is yellow is an *a posteriori* judgement. In Hume's terms, an *a priori* judgement is one in which its contradiction is necessarily false. For example, we define a bachelor as someone who is unmarried. That a bachelor is married is a contradiction in terms. Whether Joe is a bachelor, on the other hand, is an *a posteriori* claim, for Joe's not being a bachelor is a logical possibility. But, a bachelor's being married is not a logical possibility. It is not "possible absolutely." A snail's lifting my coffee cup, on the other hand, although not possible in fact, is possible absolutely, i.e., it is a logical possibility. In Hume's terms, its contradiction (a snail lifted my coffee cup) cannot be ruled out independently of experience: it is a logical possibility; hence, it is an *a posteriori* judgement.

I hope the distinction that Aquinas was getting at is now clear. Aquinas can allow for a snail's inability to lift a coffee cup as an infringement on the snail's power, since whether a being can lift a coffee cup is an *a posteriori* judgement, not an *a priori* judgement. Only *a priori* impossibilities do not count as hampering one's power.

Of course, if a snail's inability to lift a coffee cup is *a posteriori*, why isn't God's inability to lift a stone also *a posteriori*? The short answer is that it *becomes a priori* when embedded with the first part: the creation of a stone too heavy to lift. If one can do the first part, by definition one cannot do the second part. Conversely, if one can (always) do the second part, by definition one cannot do the first part. Hence, the creation of a stone too heavy to lift is a contradiction in terms, and hence, an *a priori* impossibility. Since a being's power is not limited by *a priori* impossibilities, God's being unable to create a stone too heavy for Him to lift is no limitation on His power, hence not a refutation of His omnipotence.

Has this gone too fast? I think it has. The snail's being omnipotent is not ruled out by such reasoning. Can an omnipotent snail create a coffee cup too heavy for it to lift? Since this, too, must be an *a priori* impossibility, this test is insufficient to rule out the snail's omnipotence. What has happened is simply that God is so defined as being able to do whatever God can do, and anything that God cannot do will simply be defined as an impossible thing given the definition that God is omnipotent.[4] But this simply begs the question. We define God as being able to do anything, and any task that God cannot do is ruled as inadmissible to showing that God cannot do everything. Whatever God can't do is simply defined as those things which involve contradictions. For after all, it is a contradiction for a being who can do anything to be unable to do something.

Let me rephrase this last point, for I fear it is opaque. On the assumption that God is omnipotent, the phrase, "a stone too heavy for God to lift," becomes a contradiction, an *a priori* impossibility. Similarly, on the assumption that God does not hate children, the phrase, "God hates children" becomes a contradiction, an *a priori* impossibility. But, if our task was to question this very assumption — perhaps we wonder if God does hate children — then telling us that it is impossible for God to hate children, given the assumption that God does not hate children, is not going to move us. Similarly, once we *assume* that omnipotence is a self-consistent concept, any evidence that it collapses into a self-contradiction must *ipso facto* be dismissed. But, such an observation hardly ends the discussion. What we are interested in is whether the concept of omnipotence makes any sense. Relying on the very assumption that it makes sense in order to defeat any counterclaims against its making sense is uninteresting. When we start with the definition of God as being able to do anything, any counter case will, *by definition*, be ruled out, since it would entail an *a priori* contradiction. Omnipotence is "saved" by mere definitional fiat.

Imagine if I claim to be the handsomest man alive. If you accept the assumption that I am the handsomest man alive, you can dismiss the large array of handsomer men, for it would contradict the assumption you take as true; ergo, the contrary evidence must be false. This is perfectly fine logic. What it is not, however, is a good argument.

Note that my objection is not saying that God's omnipotence cannot be proved — which, even if true, would not show that God's omnipotence is self-contradictory. Rather, the objection is that in order to avoid the contradiction inherent in God's omnipotence, the definition of omnipotence has been made into a question-begging loop.

TWO IMPOSSIBLE ACTS ARE EASIER THAN ONE

Another response to the paradox of the stone is possible. It is similar to the reply to Zeno's paradox. Zeno refutes motion. It is, accordingly, impossible to cross the room, for to do so, you would first need to cross halfway, but to do that, you'd have to cross half that distance, but to do that, you'd have to cross half that distance, etc. Since distance is infinitely divisible, the distance you would have to cross even to raise your foot is infinite:

ergo, you could never cross the room, let alone even start your journey. One answer to Zeno is to walk over and bop him on the head. A more civil answer is to point out that you can cross an infinite distance if you had infinite time, and since time is itself infinitely divisible, you have infinite time.

This trick may also be applied to the paradox of the stone. It goes something like this: Yes, it is impossible for God to lift that particular stone. But since God can lift any stone, it is also impossible for God to have created such a stone in the first place. So assuming that God is faced with a stone that He created that he can't lift, we already have proof of God's having done one impossible act. If God can do one impossible act, why not another?[5]

I like this sort of response. I feel as if I've fallen into Lewis Carroll's rabbit hole. The problem, though, is that the conclusion is that God can lift the said stone. That would be the performance of the second impossible act. But given this second impossible act of God's lifting the said stone, the first impossible act is mis-described: God did not create a stone too heavy for Him to lift. And not creating something too heavy for Him to lift is not a logically impossible act. I too don't create something too heavy for me to lift. I do that every day. Defenders of the paradox equivocate.

MORTAL COMPREHENSION

Imagine telling someone that a snake has infrared vision, and that this person retorts that infrared vision is impossible because it is outside of our range of experience. You wouldn't be convinced. Similarly, we could say that our mortal ability to conceive of infinite powers is thwarted by our limited nature. That we find a logical problem with omnipotence, thereby, does not show that omnipotence is impossible. It simply shows that we are too insignificant to comprehend God's omnipotence.

The reply seems fine for what it accomplishes. It does not accomplish anything, though. The argument can be used by atheists to show that speaking about God's omnipotence remains incoherent. To assume that God really has omnipotence is what is shown to be an impossible inference given our limited, mortal understanding. It hardly supports the grand claims of the theists. Instead, the conclusion is that we cannot say that God is omnipotent.

To think that we can still assert God's omnipotence (or any attribute) is to sneak in a question begging assumption of the most venal kind. The defence of omnipotence amounts to the following:

Impossible acts are easy to do for impossible beings.

12

OMNISCIENCE
AND FREE WILL

THE BASIC PROBLEM

If God is omniscient, then we can have no free will. Conversely, if we do have free will, then God cannot be omniscient. This is the basic problem with ascribing omniscience to God and free will to us. First, I shall make explicit why free will and omniscience collide, for it may not seem obvious. Part of this will involve making a distinction between two conceptions of free will: libertarian and compatibilist. The problem under discussion applies only to the libertarian concept. Secondly, I shall provide the basic theistic objections followed with an account of why those objections fail. As usual, a theistic out is to accept either (or both) that God is not omniscient, or that we have no libertarian free will.

To know something X, entails that X is true. There is more to the criteria for knowledge than truth, but the belief's being true is a necessary condition. If you believed what is in fact false, we cannot say that you *knew*. You thought X was true, or you thought that you knew X, but you were mistaken. If I know that a mushroom is on my plate, it is true that a mushroom is on my plate. If it is false that there is a mushroom on my plate, then it is false that I know there is a mushroom on my plate. While knowledge entails truth, the reverse does not follow. If X is true, it doesn't follow that we know it. There may be mushrooms on my plate, perhaps my mother slipped some in there, but it does not follow that I know that. My mother is hoping I don't know it. My telling you that knowledge entails truth is important for explaining why free will and omniscience collide. But we also need to be clear about the concepts of omniscience and of free will.

Omniscience entails knowing everything. Everything entails knowing future actions as well as present and past actions. If I know that a mushroom is on my plate, it is true that a mushroom is on my plate. If I know that a mushroom *will* be on my plate, a mushroom *will* be on my plate. If God is omniscient, there is nothing that God does not know. As with omnipotence, we might have to qualify God's omniscience a bit. For example, God may know that I'm afraid of dogs, but can God know my fear? Wouldn't such knowledge entail that God could be afraid? But we cannot imagine God being afraid. Moreover, most people who believe that God is omniscient mean only that God knows all *relevant* things, not necessarily *everything*. According to the anthropologist Pascal Boyer, almost all religions believe in a deity or spirit who knows all *strategic* information about everyone.[1] That is, although God may not know how many hairs are on your head,[2] He knows what you did last night. Even three-year-old children think of God as being omniscient. (Of course, they also think that their parents are omniscient.[3]) So let us accept that God's omniscience is limited to knowing the kinds of things that you do or can do. If you murder someone, God knows that. If you are charitable, God knows that. Whether we think God knows non-strategic information is not our concern in this chapter.

To believe in free will is to believe that not all of our actions are causally determined. We are not robots. We are not programmed. We sometimes make decisions that are not — at least obviously — the result of brainwashing or coercion. Free will can be understood in two different ways, though: a libertarian and a compatibilist way.[4] To be a libertarian about free will is to assume that free will is a metaphysical thing in us. We have free will like we may have the chicken pox. And it is this thing that we have inside us that enables us to rise above sociological and psychological and maybe even biological factors. For example, while many people succumb to mob mentality, a person with free will can nevertheless rise above such social-psychological pressures. While biological urges may impel us to have sex, a person with free will, may nevertheless resist such a biological temptation. Whatever free will is, the fact that we can rise above causal influences makes the hypothesis of free will seem plausible. One's actions are libertarian-free to the extent that your internal motivations are not causally determined. This is often indicated by exclaiming that one really could have done otherwise.[5] When I choose pear over peach, libertarians want to say my action is independent of the internal factors that have conditioned me to prefer pear over peach. I am not a robot. I really could have chosen peach instead of pear despite my preference for pear over peach.[6]

Determinists are the ones who say that some explanatory causal account can be offered for all human actions, just as some causal account can be offered for any physical event. If something blows up, we don't say, "Well it was free to blow up." Rather, we give the causal account of why it blew up. Similarly, we can give a causal explanation for why the person who rose above mob mentality did so, and we can give a causal explanation for why the person who resisted sexual urges did so. Such accounts may have something to do with their conditioning. If there is really no causal explanation for why someone did something — imagine I threw a pickle jar at you *for no reason* — you wouldn't normally say, "Malcolm must have free will," you'd say, "Malcolm must be insane." Since science teaches us that everything has a causal explanation, it would be inexplicable to exclude human actions.[7]

Compatibilists, like determinists, are suspicious of metaphysical properties. If we can explain human actions without appealing to metaphysical properties residing in humans, then leave such properties out. But with the libertarians, compatibilists believe speaking of free will has use. Imagine Beethoven hands over his money because a gun is aimed at his head, while Haydn hands over his money because he wants to be charitable. Neither the determinists nor the libertarians are able to explain the difference in these cases. To say, as the determinists would, that both are equally unfree is to miss a use that free will has: namely to distinguish actions that are externally coerced from actions that are not. Libertarians have trouble in explaining why Beethoven's action is unfree, so long as the internal metaphysical property isn't harmed by the external contingency of the gun. After all, he *could* have refused to hand over the money. He *could* have chosen death instead. To say he couldn't do otherwise would rule out our saying that martyrs act on free will. But surely martyrs' actions are free in the libertarian sense. Neither libertarians nor determinists can make a distinction between cases with external constraints and cases without. The fact that they can't seems to favour the compatibilist rendition of free will. The compatibilist notion of free will focuses strictly on external factors. By doing so, compatibilists make no appeal to any internal metaphysical property, nor do they doubt that one's internal reasons, principles, desires, and motivations themselves have some causal explanation.[8] That internal motivations may be causally determined is compatible with the determinists. Your internal motivations may well have some causal explanation, but you're still deemed free if no external constraints exist.[9] That compatibilists can call some acts "free" (those with no external constraint) is compatible with the libertarian view.

My task here is not to sway you toward one view or another. It is to note that only the libertarian view of free will conflicts with God's omniscience. There is no conflict in God's knowing what you will do tomorrow if everything you do is determined. Your knowing what your clock will do tomorrow does not conflict with the fact that the actions of your clock are determined. And since compatibilism speaks of free will in a way perfectly compatible (hence the name) with determinism, compatibilism, too, is not inconsistent with omniscience. But the libertarian view is.

To clearly see why libertarian free will (L-free will) conflicts with omniscience, I shall use Nelson Pike's example of Jones mowing his lawn. If Jones mows his grass at Time 2 (T_2) and God is omniscient, then God knew at Time 1 (T_1) that Jones would mow his grass at T_2.[10] But if God knew at T_1 that Jones would mow his grass at T_2, then Jones's mowing the grass at T_2 was already true at T_1 (because knowledge entails truth, recall). But, if what Jones would do at T_2 was already true at T_1, then it is false that Jones could have done otherwise at T_2. It is false, for if he could have done something different, we would not say that God *knew* that that is what Jones would do. We might *predict* what your friend will do in the future, but we cannot technically say that we *know* what your friend will do in the future given future contingencies. But future contingencies are things that God knows as well. Not being able to do otherwise at T_2 entails that Jones was not L-free to mow his lawn. Since this reasoning is true for every single action of every single agent (given God's knowing *everything*) there can be no such thing as L-free will if God is omniscient. Conversely, if Jones did L-freely mow his lawn (as he might believe), then God cannot be omniscient. Or, if a necessary attribute of God is omniscience, admission of L-free will is an admission of the non-existence of God.

WEAKENING KNOWLEDGE

Many find the above argument unconvincing. For example, the North African theologian Augustine (354–430), the Roman scholar Boethius (480–524) and the German logician Leibniz (1646–1716) to name a few, all suggested ways in which free will and God's omniscience were compatible. Augustine, as do many, wonders how our merely knowing what another will do can impede that other's free will.[11] We are free so long as no one impedes what we will. If Jones's will is to mow the grass, God's knowing that does not prevent Jones from mowing the grass any more than Smith's knowing that Jones is mowing the grass impedes Jones's free will. Therefore, Jones is free to mow the grass. If Smith locks Jones up in her garage, however, this would prevent Jones from mowing the grass. In this case, Smith's action impedes Jones's free will. Knowing that something will occur and forcibly preventing something from occurring are wildly different things. Free will restrictions can be sensibly applied only to the latter.

My knowing what you will do, then, cannot undermine your free will. If I know you hate mushrooms, I know you will decline a plate of mushrooms if offered. If I know you love your mother and are appalled at even the suggestion of harming her, I know you will not intentionally harm her. If I know that Jones mows his lawn every Sunday during the summer if it isn't raining and it's a non-raining Sunday during the summer, I know that Jones will mow his lawn. Such knowledge needn't undermine Jones's free will. He can still mow his lawn. We are creatures of habit, and the more we know someone, the more we can accurately predict what that person will do. Few would imagine that such prediction undermines their free will. To think otherwise is to imagine that free will demands complete non-predictability. It is to think that an act governed by free will is entirely random, an act without any reason whatsoever. But that's a recipe for madness, not free will.

Part of this argument amounts to accepting the compatibilist conception of free will, and to the extent that it does is to resolve the difficulty with omniscience. If theists do wish to take this route, however, they could no longer appeal to free will to resolve the problem of suffering (not that it did them any good, anyway). The reason for this is that the compatibilist sense of free will admits that the internal motivations (to cause harm to others, say) does have a clear causal explanation, which would seem, certainly from the L-free will perspective, to undermine moral responsibility. Also, under a compatibilist notion of free will, prayer would be a useless exercise. How can one petition for internal change when internal factors are determined. Perhaps God is powerful enough to change past factors, thus altering those internal conditions that determine our actions, but this forgets that prayer itself would be due to internal factors that have full causal explanations. If Haydn gets to heaven, say, *because* he petitioned God, and Beethoven fails to get to heaven *because* he failed to petition God, yet their reasons for praying or not praying are themselves fully determined, then the concept of divine desert dissolves.

Ignoring that, the common appeal to prediction misses the point. The problematic concept here is not free will, but knowledge. Specifically, the part of omniscience that mucks things up is foreknowledge. When we accurately predict what our friends will do based on our knowing what our friends *have done*, we do not (or should not) say that we *know* what our friends will do. We say we can predict with a fair degree of accuracy what they will do. This doesn't count as *knowledge*. It counts as *prediction*, even justifiable prediction. Recall, knowledge entails truth. But prediction does not entail truth.[12] A good prediction does not entail that the predicted future event is true. It entails only that there is good reason for supposing *now* that the predicted future event will transpire. It may have been a good prediction *even if it turns out to be false*. But to *know* something entails that it is true. We cannot say we knew X even if it turns out to be false. We would say we *thought* we knew X. If our prediction turns out to be false, however, we can still say we had good reasons to predict that event. Thus, to know a future event entails that that future event is true. If an action is true, the action occurred. But if an act occurred, we cannot speak of it as being a future event.[13] An occurred event can no longer be made not to happen. (Our interpretation of the event may change, but the factual element of the event cannot.) Thus, I can say that I know Jones mowed his lawn *last* Sunday. We might like to imagine that Jones *was* free last Sunday to mow or not to mow his lawn, but — given that he did mow the lawn last Sunday — he is not free *now* to have not mowed his lawn last Sunday. That is an act he cannot change. Given that he did mow his lawn, we cannot say it is now an act he cannot do. The truth of the act is set. One is not even compatibilist free to make a true fact untrue.[14]

I am not saying that *because* Jones-now can't undo what Jones-past did, that therefore Jones-now, let alone Jones-past, has no L-free will. That doesn't follow in the least. What I am saying is that God's relation to Jones's future is the same as Jones's relation to Jones's past. That's the meaning of God's having foreknowledge — something we don't have. But if God has foreknowledge, then what occurs in the future is already true today. For that matter, it was already true at the beginning of time. Just as Jones is L-unfree to change what he did last week, Jones is L-unfree to change what he will do next week, so long as God knows future events.

To summarize, our loose sense of knowing what Jones will do next week is not technically knowledge, since we cannot now say that a future event is true. Being that it isn't knowledge, our sense of predicting future events has no impact on the concept of L-free will. But that would not show that *knowing* future events would have no impact on L-free will. And that is the situation for an omniscient being — a being who has not only past and present knowledge, but future knowledge as well. If Smith believes that Jones will mow his grass, we don't presume that Smith's belief is *necessarily* true, whereas God's beliefs are necessarily true. Our accurate predictions of others' future events does not undermine others' L-free will, but that fact does not mean that God's knowledge of others' future actions does not undermine others' L-free will.

OUT OF TIME

In the response to Augustine, the concept of future knowledge is singled out as key. If God fore-knew what Jones would do, and given that knowledge entails truth, then Jones could not but do what he did, which is to say that Jones's action could not be L-free. Boethius's solution is to point out that it is incorrect to say that God *foreknew* Jones's mowing his grass. Foreknowledge entails temporality, but God is *atemporal*, or outside of time. God knows all *now*.[15] There is no past or present or future with God. He is outside of time itself. Thus, the problem between knowing and L-free will dissolves. Imagine the case where you watch Jones mow his grass. Since you are watching Jones mow his grass, you know that Jones is mowing his grass. But your knowing that Jones is mowing his grass does not undermine Jones's L-free will. Your witnessing Jones's action cannot in any way impede Jones's L-free will. Similarly, God's knowing that Jones is mowing his grass is like your knowing that Jones is mowing his grass. If Jones's L-free will is not impeded in your case, it ought not to be impeded in God's case. In this sense, God's *knowing* all is more like God's *seeing* all. So long as God is out of time, the L-free will omniscience problem dissolves.[16]

Whether God can be outside of time creates its own problems, something I shall explore in Chapter 13. Even if it were true, however, the problem does not dissolve. When I watch Jones mow his grass at T_2, I am not at the same time watching Jones mow his grass at T_1 and T_3, but God is.

Our knowledge of Jones's actions does not impede Jones's action, since our knowledge of Jones's action is temporally extensive with Jones's action. This is not the case with God's knowledge. Even though God is out of time, Jones is in time. As far as God is concerned all your actions have already happened. You know that it is senseless to say that you have L-free will *now* about your past actions. But your future actions are no different from your past actions from God's perspective. So, if you admit that you have no L-freedom to change the past, you should also admit that you have no L-freedom to change the future. In what sense do you have L-free will *now* about the future if the future is already itself now? Boethius may save omniscience by placing God outside of time, but not the concept of L-free will.

DIFFERENT NECESSITIES

Leibniz suggests that there are two kinds of necessity: hypothetical and absolute.[17] Hypothetical utterances take the form: "if one thing, then another thing," or, "if P, then Q." If such a proposition were true, then Q necessarily follows P. But admitting this is not to say that Q is necessary, since Q is conditional on the occurrence of P. If I jump in the water, I will necessarily get wet. But that truth does not imply that I will necessarily get wet, since it is possible that I won't jump in the water. My getting wet in this case is a *hypothetical necessity*, a necessary event conditional upon the occurrence of something else. An absolute necessity has no such conditionality. If Q is an absolute necessary truth, then Q will necessarily occur whether P does or not.

Given this distinction, Leibniz claims that absolute necessity interferes with L-free will, but hypothetical necessity does not. Moreover, omniscience entails hypothetical necessity only, not absolute necessity. Hence, omniscience does not interfere with L-free will.

Leibniz's reasoning goes as follows: if God knows at T_1 that Jones will mow his grass at T_2, then it is hypothetically necessary that Jones will mow his grass at T_2, but not absolutely necessary, since God's knowledge is still contingent on Jones's actually mowing the grass or not, an act that Jones has L-free will over. In other words, God knows that Jones mows because Jones mows, not Jones mows because God knows that Jones mows. Plantinga makes the same point.[18] If I know that Henry is a bachelor, it is necessarily true that Henry is a bachelor (given the meaning of knowledge) but it does not mean that Henry is *necessarily* a bachelor, for bachelorhood is still a contingent matter. My knowing that Henry is a bachelor does not mean that Henry cannot get married.

But Leibniz and Plantinga are wrong. Even hypothetical necessity undermines L-free will. The concern is whether Jones mows the grass with L-free will. The concern is not whether Jones's mowing his grass is conditional upon something else. Of course it is. It is conditional upon his having grass, his grass growing, his having a lawn mower, his living in a neighbourhood where social pressures push one to mow one's grass, to having a lawn rather than a field, etc. God's foreknowledge of all those contingencies is not to the point. Think of a rock rolling down a hill. Its continuing to roll is contingent on the rock being round enough, the hill being steep enough, gravity working today, etc. The mere contingency of the rock's rolling down the hill doesn't translate into the rock having L-free will. Hypothetical necessity impedes L-free will, for if the contingent conditions are in place, Jones *must* mow his grass, given that it is true he mowed his grass, otherwise God would not have known it. That Jones necessarily mows the grass given God's foreknowledge of the conditions that make Jones mow his grass means that Jones can't do otherwise — and this is so even when we admit that Jones's mowing the grass is only contingently necessary.

God's knowing all the causal explanations for every one of your actions including your future actions would not undermine your having compatibilist free will, of course, since all that it requires is that no external agency impedes your internal desires. Compatibilist free will allows for those internal desires to be fully causally determined, and hence knowable.

OTHER WORLDS

Plantinga wishes to defend Leibniz's position by an appeal to the concept of other worlds. If two worlds (W_1 and W_2) are exactly alike in every detail but one, we can get a better conceptual analysis of that one difference. In this case, we imagine two worlds identical in every facet except that Jones mows his grass in W_1 and Jones does not mow his grass in W_2. In both cases, God knows beforehand what Jones does. Thus, Jones in W_1 mows his grass at T_2 and God knows at T_1 that Jones will mow the grass in W_1 at T_2. Meanwhile, Jones in W_2 does not mow his grass at T_2. God knows at T_1 that Jones will not mow the grass in W_2 at T_2. This shows that there can never be a time where God would not know something, given his omniscience. It also shows that Jones may or may not mow his grass, depending on which world he L-freely chooses. This shows that although God's foreknowledge remains intact, Jones is still L-free to mow or not mow his grass. In other words, Jones's L-free actions are unaffected by God's foreknowledge.

The use of other worlds here is to help counter the claim that God could have a false belief if Jones really were L-free. For if God knows Jones mows his grass, and Jones really is L-free to mow his grass, it is possible that Jones does *not* mow his grass. But if it is possible that Jones does not mow his grass, then it is possible that God has a false belief. It is possible that God did not know something. But that would show that God is not omniscient. The other worlds scenario is intended to help clarify the fact that *whatever* Jones does, God knows it. Jones's being L-free to mow his grass does *not* entail that God has a false belief, for if Jones did not mow his grass, God would have known that. If Jones did mow his grass, God would have known that. God knows all, *whatever* Jones does. Hence, Jones's actions remain L-free.

The other worlds move is unhelpful. Whatever Jones does, God knew that beforehand. All that means is that whatever Jones does, Jones cannot but do that. All this shows is that there can never be a world in which Jones's actions are L-free. To avoid this dead-end, Plantinga would have to say that God knows all the possible ways the world can turn out (all the different worlds that could be), but not which of those worlds becomes actual (until it does), given that such a contingency depends on Jones's L-free action. But then God's knowledge is dependent on what Jones L-freely does. That is, given Jones's L-free will, God doesn't know something: namely which world will be actualized by Jones. This might save L-free will, but not God's omniscience. The other worlds detour hardly solves the problem, it highlights the problem.

SUMMARY

However one looks at it, omniscience and L-free will collide. Omniscience is not merely knowledge, but foreknowledge, and this is what rubs against L-free will. Theists need to reject omniscience or L-free will, or preferably both.

13

---∞---

TIME AND
IMMUTABILITY

PROBLEMS WITH IMMUTABILITY

God is sometimes deemed to be immutable. To be immutable is never to change. If God can change, then He is either changing for the better or for the worse. Being perfect to begin with, God cannot become better. For God to improve implies that God was not, at least originally, perfect. And even if God develops into perfection, once that God reaches perfection, no further development can occur. If God changes for the worse, then God is not merely no longer perfect, but could never have been perfect. His no longer being perfect is bad enough for those who believe that God's perfection is eternal. But for a thing to become worse implies that it was not perfectly made in the first place. It contained a flaw: the ability to become worse. A really perfect being should not be able to decay. Built-in obsolescence is a sign of imperfection. Given God's perfection, God cannot change. A perfect God must be immutable.[1]

So far so good? But here's the problem. A parallel argument may be given to show that a perfect God must *not* be immutable. If God were immutable, God would be (i) unable to create anything; (ii) unable to love us; and (iii) unable to know temporal things (hence, not omniscient).

Creation
To create, even out of nothing (*ex nihilo*) is to do something. But doing something involves change. But God can't change. He's immutable. In a trivial sense, if God creates something X, then God changes relative to X. If I create a bubble, prior to my bubble, I was bubbleless, and now I'm not. Such relative change is not a change in my intrinsic nature, of course, and so such relative change is not the problem. Let us allow an immutable being to change relative to changing things in the universe. If God is immutable in the intrinsic sense, then the problem concerns not so much *that* an immutable being creates, but *why*. Even if He could master the feat of creating something by doing nothing, *why* would He create something if He is

immutably perfect? Was He bored? Did He think something was lacking? But nothing could be lacking in such a perfect Being. Being immutably perfect as is, there could be no *point* to His creating the universe.

Love

For God to have personal relations with us, one would think that God needs to *feel* for us. But to feel for us, to feel for our plights, to feel differently if we praise his name or say his name in vain, to laud our virtues and rebuke our sins, God would need to *change* his emotional states consistent with the change in our fortunes or our deserts. Consider a parent's love of his or her child. If bad things happen to the child, the parent would feel bad. If good things happen to the child, the parent would feel good. If the parent's emotional state does not change along with the change in the child's fortune, we would not think the parent loves the child. Imagine the child is being eaten by a snake, and that there is no change in the parent's emotional state, though witnessing the event. Unless we can come up with some reasonable excuse, such as that the parent was in shock, we would not think that that person is a good parent. We would not think that the parent really loved the child at all. Love entails self-sacrifice. Such a selfless act entails modulating one's emotional state in accordance with the circumstances. Such modulation entails change. Yet if God is immutable, God's emotional states could not change with our fortunes. God would stand in relation to us as would a stoic: unattached, unemotional, unloving. Thus, if God were immutable, we would not believe that God loves us. We would find it difficult to imagine that He even cares for us.[2]

Time

Time entails change. Change is measured in time. If there is no change, there is no time. So a being who does not change is a being not in time. There are at least five problems concerning God's being outside of time. First, if God were outside time, there is no way for God to have any interaction with us, who are in time. For example, I cannot play billiards with David Hume given different temporal periods. Hume's being outside my time period is a sufficient reason for my being unable to play with him. So, if God were out of time, an implication of immutability, then God could have no interaction with us. Secondly, if God were outside of time, God could not create anything, for creation entails a before and an after. If *A* creates *B*, *A* precedes *B* in time. But if *A* is outside of time, then *A* could not create *B*, for *A* would then have had to have preceded *B* *in time*. The logic holds for God's creating time itself. Therefore, if *A* is outside of time, so is *B*, or *A* could not have created *B*. Since we're in time, either God did not create us or God is not outside of time. Thirdly, a being outside of time could make no sense of temporal propositions. Neither the claim that Adam *begat* Cain (Gen. 4:1), or that God "confounded the languages of people" *after* the Tower of Babel was started (Gen. 11:4–9), could make any sense to a being outside of time. One needs to know not merely the two events, but how the two events are temporally related. But if this is a proposition that an atemporal being cannot know, an atemporal being cannot be omniscient. The claim that God existed before Moses would be false or meaningless to God. But a believer in God cannot think such a statement false or meaningless.[3] Moreover, the concepts of promising and deliberation become nonsensical to a being outside of time. What would a promise *mean* to a god who is outside of our time? My doing X and my promising to do X are different things. They are different precisely because of time. I promise to do X before I do X. I can't promise to do X if I've already done X or while I'm doing X. But for an atemporal God, promising and doing would be simultaneous. Similarly, deliberation happens within time. To an atemporal God, Jones's deliberation about mowing the grass happens simultaneously to his mowing the grass, which happens simultaneously to Jones's being born which happens simultaneously to Jones's dying which happens simultaneously to Jones's decomposed body one hundred years after his death. If God cannot understand what a promise is, or what deliberation is, God cannot be omniscient. Fourthly, it is common to say of God that He is eternal. But eternality requires a concept of time. To be eternally outside of time is incoherent. The fifth worry harkens back to the problem of whether God loves us. If my child is innocently happy, I am happy. If my child is sad, or in pain, I am unhappy. That is because I love my child. But what would I do if my child were both happy and sad at the same time? I don't have any experience of that. I presume that I would be confused. But since all events that make us sad or happy occur to God simultaneously — and this is so for every single person ever alive and who ever will be alive, given that God loves us all, not just you — the emotional state of God must be too peculiar to match what we normally mean by love. A being in whom all emotional states occur at once and yet remains for ever unchanged is not recognizable to us as an emotional being at all. But if God loves us, God is an emotional being. If God is not an emotional being, God cannot love us.

The above points may not be decisive. It is common, for example, to cite the "space-time loaf" illustration to give an idea of how a being could be outside of time yet know what's going on in time.[4] Take all time-slices and arrange them in sequence so that they form a loaf, like a loaf of sliced bread. The slices of bread represent the various time slices. It's a big loaf, admittedly, but nothing prevents a being standing outside the loaf, yet seeing any one of the time slices from the same timeless advantage. In this sense, God can know that Jones mows at T_1 and T_2, just as easily as you can see a slice of bread on one end of a loaf at the same time as seeing a slice of bread on the other end of a loaf, or just as easily as you can see two neighbours mow their grass at the same time. I don't think that this analogy is quite right, however. It places God outside the space occupied by the objects He's viewing, but not clearly outside space itself, since God's vantage is still given a spatial direction. Similarly, it places God outside the time occupied by the objects that God is viewing, but not outside the constraints of time itself. Time is an *ordered* sequence of events. To know "before" and "after," God needs to have the time slices arranged in a time-specific order, and to know which direction "before" constitutes (to the left, say) and which direction "after" constitutes (to the right). The time slices have to be properly arranged and God must understand that arrangement for God to see that Jones is mowing at T_1 and at T_2 *and* that T_1 occurs before T_2. But once you model the *order* of time slices, you are modelling time itself. What is time but an ordered sequence of events? And so long as God can view the time slice pictures *in an order* — even an order dislodged from what we're stuck with — then God is not properly speaking outside of time. For God to be properly outside of time, the sequence must be unknown to Him. The time slices must be randomly shuffled. Only then can we properly speak of God being outside of time. But if the deck is random, God can know that Jones mows at T_x and at T_y, but God cannot have any clue whether T_x precedes T_y.

Perhaps I am wrong on the above account. Perhaps all that is needed is for God to be outside *our* time, and admit that this need not mean He is outside of His own time. As such, He could still understand the proper sequence, yet experience it all at once (our time). Time may be a crutch to us, a crutch that God does not need. The fact that a cripple needs a crutch does not show that God needs a crutch. The concept of time, like the concept of infinity, is perhaps too peculiar for us to ever grasp. When I try to comprehend spacelessness or timelessness, as when I try to grasp infinity, I only get as far as the point at which my synapses seem to explode. I shall revisit time below. For now, suffice it to say theists can go either way. Immutability seems both to be required and not required for a being who is perfect. A contradiction ensues. Theists have some explaining to do. Atheists can say, "See, the very concept of an immutable god is a contradiction in terms."

ANTHROPOMORPHIZING

The philosopher of religion, Charles Hartshorne argues that God is not immutable.[5] Immutability is *not* a feature of perfection. So, if God is perfect, God is mutable. For a being to be "perfect," all that is required is for the being to be deserving of the utmost respect and admiration. Since an immutable being would not be deserving of our utmost respect and admiration, ascribing immutability to God would *undermine* our notion of His perfection. Perfection in that sense is a purely formal, empty, abstract sense. But it cannot be applicable to a god we deem worthy of worship. A god that changes his emotional state in accord with our fortunes because He loves us is more perfect than a god who does not. Since God is deemed to be more perfect than less perfect, God must be mutable, not immutable.

Anselm takes a different route. His solution is to note a distinction between our sense of compassion and love and God's sense of the same things. Of course we will feel sympathetic suffering if our loved one suffers, but to expect God to be so dependent on such contingencies is to anthropomorphize God, to turn God into our own image. Anthropomorphizing God fails to recognize that we are made in God's image, not the reverse. For Anselm, God's compassion is absolute. Therefore, God must be immutable.[6]

Hartshorne's worry with this manoeuvre is that it admits that we simply cannot understand God's love. God's love would be wholly alien to love as we know it. But if God's love is not understandable to us, God Himself can't be understandable to us. Anselm would not deny the charge. For him, God is beyond our ken in every way. But Hartshorne finds such total dissociation between humans and God troubling. Anselm wishes to start with God's absoluteness, and throw everything out that doesn't fit with that. But nothing can fit with that, so we end up throwing out God Himself. If we begin with God's love, on the other hand, we must throw out any abstract quality that doesn't fit with that. From this vantage, abstract qualities of absoluteness and infinities are what go.[7]

Anthropomorphizing God solves the contradictions inherent in ascribing abstract qualities to God, but it leaves open the charge that we are not worshipping God anymore; we are worshipping merely an idol of God. We are left with the realization that the concept of God cannot be known with any certainty. Theists seem to accept that as par for the course. Atheists think that this admission is far more damaging than theists allow. It is imprudent to believe a proposition the content of which you admit you do not know. To say, "I believe in God, but don't ask me what God is," raises no eyebrows. But if you were to say, "I believe in X, but don't ask me what X is," we would think that you do not understand the meaning of belief. This is why Hartshorne, among others,[8] prefers to believe in a loving God, not an abstract, ineffable God.

TIME REVISITED

The conflict between Anselm and Hartshorne partly revolves around the troubling aspects of time. Is it really incoherent to conceive of an eternal being outside time? McCann, for one, thinks not.[9]

First off, it is argued that since God created *everything*, then God created time itself. As a creator of time, God cannot be Himself bound by time. Secondly, we may admit the possibility of timelessly eternal states of affairs. Thirdly, the creation problem is supposedly solved because God creates the universe out of nothing, *ex nihilo*. If God were to create the universe out of already existing stuff, then God's creation must be accomplished *in time*. But since God created the universe out of nothing, it also follows that time needn't be a part of the process. Time is part of the created universe, and just as God is outside of the universe, God is outside of time. And fourthly, time is an illusion. That we *seem* to be in time is no more telling than that we *seem* to see yellow. But yellow is what *we* bring to our world, not technically in the world itself. Likewise, time is what we bring to the world, not in the world itself. It is a lens that we see the world through. There is no more reason to suppose that God is restricted by time than by our illusions.

There are difficulties with each argument, of course. First, even if we accept that God is the creator of time, it doesn't follow that He will necessarily reside outside of time. If I create a house, surely I can reside in it. That is, we can admit that God *was* outside of time, but is so no longer, or alternatively, *can* be in time if He so chooses, being omnipotent. Nothing prevents this possibility merely from conceding that God is the creator of time.

Secondly, I am not at all certain that we do accept the possibility of a timelessly eternal state of affairs. But even if we do, that would not imply that therefore there are temporally eternal *beings*. That is another matter.

The third argument simply says that a magical being can do magical things. But even granting impossible acts to an impossible being, it would not prove God's atemporality. For if God can create the universe *ex nihilo*, we can conceive of the state of affairs *before* the creation, and a state of affairs *after* the creation, even if prior to the creation no such conception of time were possible.

And lastly, the possibility that time is an illusion to us would not settle the conflict concerning God. If we are forced to see the world temporally, whereas God is atemporal, we can never hope to get an accurate picture of God. This does not resolve Hartshorne's problem.

SUMMARY

The complexity of understanding God as perfect creates difficulties for conceiving God at all. Atheists need not resolve the problem. Theists argue between themselves on these points. My role here is to point out that whichever route the theist takes, incoherencies abound. All such incoherencies dissolve, however, with the dissolution of our belief in a god.

14

IS GOD LOVE?

My very first philosophy class occurred in a CEGEP in the west end of Montreal.[1] Our teacher asked us to stand in the middle of the room. Once this was accomplished, those who believed in God were asked to move to the left side of the room. Those who did not believe in God were asked to move to the right side of the room. I found myself with one other student on the right side of the room. I remember he wore white overalls. Perhaps they were in style once. The teacher asked us to reconvene in the middle of the classroom. Now he divided us up once more. Those who believed in love were asked to move to the left side of the room. Those who did not believe in love were asked to move to the right side of the room. Now only one person stood on the right side of the room and it was the guy in white overalls. I thought to myself, "Geez, that guy just doesn't believe in anything." As far as I was concerned, this undermined his stance on belief in God. I fully expected that he would receive some sort of flak from the teacher or the other students. To my surprise, they turned on me for being inconsistent.

Perhaps it was that incident that drove me to philosophy. I knew at the time that it was not inconsistent to believe in love yet deny God, but I was too young to be able to articulate it. Love is certainly a difficult concept to nail down, but I knew that I loved my mother, and my father, but not so much my brothers at the time. I was less certain about my love toward a sample of my female peers, but love needn't be an all or nothing affair, so I was confident enough that love existed, whatever it *really* was, and I was also confident that none of that love seemed to require my believing in metaphysical agency.

True, it says in the Bible that God is love (1 John 4:8) and this is where the confusion arises in others. If it were true that God is love then I cannot reject one and accept the other. That would be incoherent. Analogously, if unicorns were cows, I could not consistently reject the existence of unicorns while accepting the existence of cows. But there is nothing incoherent in refusing to equate cows with unicorns. Merely because the Bible says God is love is hardly confirmatory. It is that equation I reject.

DIFFERENT KINDS OF LOVE

When pressed, people are wont to distinguish kinds of love. The love of one's parents, the love of one's children, and the love of one's siblings are all different from each other, yet different again in kind from sexual love. And love of objects is different from love of beauty or love of justice. And both of these are different yet again from love of humanity or love of life. And perhaps love of God is yet another kind of love, one that theists hold to be the supreme kind of love.

Given these different kinds of love, it is possible that my concept of love is different than the concept of love in the statement, "God is love." If so, my believing in love but not God would not show that God is not love. When theists say, "God is love," perhaps they mean one sort of love. When I say I can love without God, I am, perhaps, referring to a different sort of love. If so, my humble counter misses the mark. Presumably sexual love (*eros*) is not the love that theists mean to emphasize, and love of friends (*philia*) is a bit too weak. A love of one's child is pretty powerful, and this fits the analogy that God is our father. In this sense, it is easy to imagine that God loves us in the way that we love our children — only infinitely more so. But this nice thought doesn't *equate* God with love. When a theist says, "God is love," or "God loves me," she is not intending to say, "God is God," or "God Gods me."

But if God's being love is not the sort of love that we experience, what meaning could "God is love" have for us at all? Theologians like to clarify things for us by speaking of *agape*.[2] *Agape* is distinguished from other kinds of love by its essentially selfless character. The Christian paradigm is Christ's gift of His life for the redemption of sinful humanity. So when theists purport that God is love, presumably they mean that God is *agape*. My love of my mother, for example, does not require my abandoning atheism, but that is because the type of love is quite different. What I need to do is experience *agape* and see if that is possible without my also experiencing God.

Now I am in a tougher spot. If I claim to experience *agape* without experiencing God, I may be accused of mistakenly believing that I'm experiencing *agape*, whereas in reality it must be something more earthly, mere *philia*. Conversely, if I fail to experience *agape*, this will be because I fail to admit God. My dismissal of the relation of God and love is now no longer such a simple task.

In fact, it is now an impossible task. This should not count in theists' favour. For comparison, let us say that Smith claims that a true feminist is one who is necessarily a lesbian. Let us next imagine that someone,

Jones, complains that she, Jones, is a feminist, although not a lesbian. Jones needn't have any issue with lesbians. Simply, she denies being one herself. Now if what Jones says is true, this will rebut Smith's narrow definition of feminism. But what if, instead, Smith merely asserts that, given Smith's definition, Jones is obviously not a feminist. What Smith is missing in his question-begging reply is that Jones is challenging Smith's definition. It does not count as an adequate reply to dismiss Jones's challenge by appealing to the original definition. It cheats, or, at any rate, misses the point. Smith fails to see that the disagreement is over the definition itself.

Similarly, a theist who rejects the charge that one can love, even of the *agape* kind, without belief in God is appealing to the very definition that is in doubt, and so misses the point. Definitions are not facts. They are concepts a community comes to adopt for practical purposes. And although the definitional association of God with love works fine for those who believe in God, there is nothing in the concept of love itself that forces atheists to also adopt that definition. Their accusation is that it is too narrow. There can be talk of love — even *agape* — without talk of God. This complaint is not dismissed by appealing to the theist's definition, since it is the definition itself that is in question.

Where does this leave us? Back where we started. My experiencing cows does not entail that I have experienced unicorns, *unless* I accept the definition that unicorns are cows. Nothing in the bare experience of cows, however, commits me to accept this stipulative definition. Similarly, my experiencing love — even deep, life-affirming love — does not entail that I have experienced God, *unless* I accept the definition that God is this kind of deep love. But such a stipulative definition is not forced on me merely by the bare experience of my deep love. Once this is realized, we see that our abandoning belief in God does not mean we also abandon deep love.

PART IV. FAITH

15

FAITH AND REASON

In Part II, we examined various arguments purporting to prove God's existence. Even if none of them succeeded — as I have argued — most people believe in God on faith, not philosophical argument. God is not something to be proved. Belief in God is a matter of faith. Atheists' attempts at discrediting proofs for God's existence are therefore of limited concern to theists. Many theists feel the existence of God in their very souls or hearts, and that is proof enough.

Is faith an adequate justification for one's belief in God, or is it — as atheists purport — a mere cop-out? In normal circumstances, merely because one feels conviction about something doesn't make that belief true. Just because you hope that you have the winning lottery ticket, for example, does not mean that you do have the winning lottery ticket. Even if, against the odds, you in fact did win, it is not your *hope* that made you win. Other than the superstitious, most of us realize this when it comes to secular matters. Atheists point out that since the faith response is insufficient in the secular world, it is also insufficient for our belief in God.

A first response is to point out that faith is not to be equated with mere hope. But to make this distinction stick, faith would need to be more like knowledge. Perhaps not a knowing *that* kind of knowledge, but at least a knowing *how* kind of knowledge.[1] Someone may know how to ride a bike despite being unable to explain precisely what it is one knows. But even then we can verify the claim to know by demonstration. What demonstration is available for faith in God? That you do good works might show your faith, but not that God exists.

From here, theists may respond in one of two general ways: either (a) make a case that faith is reasonable, after all; or (b) make the case that faith is better than reason. Option (b) admits that faith and reason part ways, but claims so much the worse for reason. This shows that a gap between the two hardly supports atheism. In this chapter, I shall examine the (a) camp. In the following chapter, I shall look at the (b) camp, referred to as *fideism*.

Proponents of the (a) camp believe that faith in God is not unreasonable. Arguments within this camp may be further divided into two groups. (1) Although an appeal to faith is an insufficient response for secular matters, it is perfectly adequate for one's belief in God. (2) Although faith is inadequate in certain secular cases, that does not show that faith is *always* inadequate. Faith is a sufficient justification for certain secular beliefs, and therefore it is (or can be) sufficient for one's belief in God. We'll call the first the *God Is Special* argument. The second, we'll call the *Secular Faith* argument. Neither argument succeeds. Let us see why.

GOD IS SPECIAL

The Argument

God is different than other things in every conceivable way. Therefore, how we come to believe in God should also be different than how we come to believe in other things. We come to believe propositions about the world through reason. Therefore, we should come to believe propositions concerning God through some other faculty: faith. Conviction of God's existence is established directly in the soul by God Himself. We do not come to accept God through mental calculation. Asking for justification of that belief is to assume incorrectly that the belief came through some mental feat. But this is not how it came about.

Analogously, if you see a shooting star, you feel justified in knowing that a shooting star passed. Your justification for the belief that there was a shooting star when you thought you saw one is nothing other than the mere fact that you saw one. Imagine, however, if someone replied: "Your seeing a shooting star is insufficient justification for me. Could you please provide some other justification that I would accept." If you accept the challenge, you are at a loss. There is now no shooting star. The fact that there is no shooting star now should not count against your having seen a shooting star, any more than your not seeing a dog now counts against your ever having seen a dog. Your interlocutor, however, seems to insist otherwise. That is why you are apt to think that she is simply nuts. There is no other justification for your having seen a shooting star other than the fact that you did in fact see it. Faith in God is a similar experience, save that you do not see God; you "feel" or "sense" God, or somehow experience God's presence, perhaps like my Port Eliza experience mentioned in Chapter 3. And that is all the "justification" you need. The fact that such faith is not sufficient for atheists or shooting star sceptics is, frankly, not your problem[2] — unless part of your faith mandates that you convert heathens.

The Rebuttal

Faith is an inadequate rejoinder to the fact that no argument supports belief in God. And this is so not for the simple reason that an atheist hasn't experienced a particular phenomenon that a theist has. Appeals to faith are inadequate because they beg the question. The premise merely repeats the conclusion. Justification requires that the premise be something *different* than the conclusion. If I say "*P*: therefore *P*," that's a perfectly valid argument, but also quite uninformative. The appeal to faith in the God is Special argument does no more. It amounts to saying, "I have faith, because I have faith." We *know* you have faith. That, presumably, is not in question. What is in question is whether what you believe on faith is true or not. The mere fact that Jones believes in God does not make the content of Jones's belief true. What we are interested in is whether or not the content of Jones's belief is true, not whether Jones *has* the belief.[3] To the extent that faith arises from some personal experience of "God," there is still a gap between the interpretation of that experience ("that confirms God's existence!") and the bare phenomenal event ("I seem to be experiencing God"). Appealing to faith doesn't close the gap.

Your having faith in God, however sincere, simply amounts to your believing in God. But you would not say, presumably, that God exists because you believe it so. Believing something is no guarantee that it is true. Theists try to correct this defect by claiming that this is good justification for God, since He is the sort of being that communicates directly with people's souls. Note, however, that this assumes that God exists. Since this was the very conclusion that theists were trying to give justification for, it is cheating to merely presume it. It begs the question.

Notice that we do not similarly beg the question in the case of the shooting star. When you ask me about the shooting star, I do not say it is true because I know it, let alone that it is true because I believe it, or sincerely believe it. Such a rejoinder is clearly inadequate because we all know that a proposition is not shown to be true *because* it is believed. And even if I cannot convince you that a shooting star has passed when I said it did, I presumably can get you to believe in shooting stars in general. Thus, my seeing a shooting star when you did not is already consistent with your framework of beliefs. With your believing in God, however, it is not a case of both of us believing in God, and your making the case that you just saw God pass this instant. Your claim about God's existence would be more like my claiming to you that I believe in fairies, even though neither of us have ever witnessed such things. The shooting star analogy is misleading.

A more favourable account of faith is one in which faith is seen as an *act of will* given: (i) an urgency to act; and (ii) a tie between the evidence *for* and the evidence *against* belief in a god.[4] In such a case, we cannot find fault with the decision. Flip a coin and go. Whether there is really an urgency to believe in God, or whether the evidence for and against belief in a god is properly deemed a tie are claims atheists reject. More to the point, atheists accuse the faithful of relying on their faith to determine both the urgency and the tie.

SECULAR FAITHS

The Argument

The second response is more sophisticated. Theists support their appeal to faith by observing that there are reasonable appeals to faith in the everyday world. In other words, even atheists rely on faith. For example, how do you know that your chair exists? Normal people will answer something like, "I see it," or "I can feel it." But if we ask, how do you know your perceptions are veridical (true representations of the world), normal people are at a loss of what to say. Our senses record to our brains certain images that we take to be true representations of the world. But are they? How would we know? We would have to examine what the world is *really* like, and then compare that with what our senses tell us. To compare what the world is really like, of course, must be done without the contamination of our senses. But to remove our senses is to remove *all* data. We would not get the true, undiluted picture of the world; we would get no picture at all. It would be like peeling a carrot to see what colour lies beneath the veneer of orange. We could not discover the "true" colour of the carrot by this method. Instead, we would keep peeling until there'd be no carrot at all. Similarly, empirical reason cannot answer the appearance/reality question.

But do we give up our belief in chairs? Do we give up trusting our senses? Of course not. We believe that the chair exists roughly as we perceive it. We admit that we have no indubitable proof upon which to base this belief, but it is the bedrock of our belief in science. Science is predicated on trusting (generally speaking) our senses. Science is predicated on confirming or disconfirming data based on empirical observations. But it cannot employ its own method to confirm whether empirical observation ultimately provides us with a true picture of the world. It carries on, though, *as if* it were so. In other words, science proceeds *on faith*.

Normal people believe that the chair exists independently of our senses, and that the chair is roughly as we perceive it. We maintain this belief *without proof*. We maintain this belief by a form of faith. If it is permissible to believe in science on faith, then surely it is permissible to believe in God on faith.[5]

We also have faith in our friends and neighbours. If we didn't have faith that our neighbour was a nice guy, we would certainly treat him differently. Treating him as if he were mean-spirited will likely make him treat you a little differently, too. His retaliatory treatment of you will probably entrench your belief that he is mean-spirited after all. This is a sort of self-fulfilling prophecy. Treating someone well rather than badly will increase the chances of that person treating you well. Only through faith can friendship exist at all.[6]

Related to having faith in your friends is your having faith that other people have minds.[7] We see behaviour in others and ascribe a mental state. For example, when a rock lands on your toe, you feel pain (a mental state). You also scream, hold your toe, jump up and down, etc. When you drop a rock on Emma's toe, say, you notice that she behaves similarly. She holds her toe, jumps up and down, screams, etc. So, given that the outward behaviours are the same, you naturally infer that Emma has similar inner mental states — the feeling of pain in this case — to you. But is there any guarantee that Emma, let alone anyone else, is not an automaton programmed to behave *as if* she has a mind? No. You don't see Emma's mind. You only see her behaviour. The worry does not concern whether we ought to infer mental states in others. Of course we should. We make such inferences all the time. The worry concerns whether we have rational grounds to do so. And, so the argument goes, we don't. That others have minds is an assumption that we take on faith.

And anyone familiar with sports psychology also knows the power of faith. Fear and doubt will impede performance. Confidence and faith enhance it. Is a golfer's faith that she will rip a drive over two hundred yards of water reasonable? It is not backed by evidence since it concerns a future act. For that matter, there is plenty of evidence of one's drives not going as planned. A prudent golfer will more likely recognize that the odds may not be in her favour. But thinking along those lines will more likely make one's muscles tighten, will impede fluidity, and thus *cause* the ball to plop into the water. To avoid that, the golfer must have faith that she can hit the shot before she hits it. William James noted the phenomenon. Imagine being trapped on a cliff and one's only hope of escape is to leap across a chasm.[8] Without the faith that one can do it, one will be stuck "shivering on the brink."[9] The mind is a powerful tool when it operates on faith. Are faith and confidence in sports unreasonable? Hardly. The results speak for themselves.

True, relying on faith may be unreasonable in some circumstances. W.K. Clifford imagines such a case.[10] A ship owner is told his ship is unseaworthy. Nevertheless, he has faith that the ship will not sink, and sends it off with passengers for another Atlantic crossing. The ship sinks, killing all aboard. The owner's "but I had faith" cannot absolve him of gross negligence. But pointing out cases of unreasonable faith does not mean that relying on faith is always unreasonable. Trusting our senses, trusting our friends, trusting that people have minds, trusting in our physical abilities are four cases of reliance on faith in the everyday real world that seem perfectly reasonable.[11] Faith in God is claimed to be reasonable in similar ways.

The Rebuttal

Atheists can accept the reasonableness of secular faith. All they need deny is that belief in God is analogous to reasonable secular faith. We can show that by looking at each of the four analogies cited above: sports psychology, friends, other minds, and material objects.

Believing that one can hit a drive two hundred yards over water, or that one can jump a chasm, is not unconnected to evidence. But belief in God is unconnected to evidence. I cannot jump fifteen yards across a chasm merely by having faith. A beginner golfer cannot hit her drive two hundred yards merely by having faith. Confidence is one thing; overzealousness another. Confidence has to be in line with experience. One's confidence in one's ability to hit a golf shot or leap a chasm is based on past experiences of golf shots and leaps. To make the analogy work, our faith in God would have to be based on past experiences with God. But the appeal to faith is based on the recognition that we have no past experiences with God.[12] Therefore, the faith found in sport psychology has no bearing on faith in God. There is no prior experience with God to make the analogy stick. Faith in God is not dependent on experience or physical possibility. So, while we can agree that the faith found in sports psychology is reasonable, the comparison to faith in God does not hold.

One's faith in friends cannot support one's faith in God for two reasons. (1) We base our secular faith on evidence. Generally, we withhold faith in convicted felons and rapists and idiots. We proffer it conditionally to strangers who appear normal. We extend it freely to those with a proven reputation of fair play. None of this evidential support is available in our faith in God. It is to be given purely without evidence (and, in the case of the problem of evil [Chapter 10], counter to evidence!). (2) Besides, it is not one's faith that God will react kindly to you that is in question. It is whether or not God exists at all. This is not the sort of doubt that you have about your neighbour. You may doubt whether he is someone to be trusted, but few of us doubt whether he exists. Once you accept that God exists, go ahead and have faith that He will be kind to you, or that He does His job well. Similarly, go ahead and have faith that your pilot will do his job well, or that your friends will be kind to you. But the analogy can't show that it is thereby not unreasonable to have faith in God's *existence*.

And faith in other minds differs from faith in God. For one, the other minds argument presupposes a folk-psychology notion of mind: that the mind is a real entity hidden from external view, a ghost in the machine. Those who reject such a notion — and there are many[13] — will find the analogy between belief in other minds and belief in God totally useless. Even accepting the folk-psychology theory of mind, the other minds argument still fails. I know that Emma exists and infer that she has a mind. I infer that Emma has a mind based on Emma's behaviour being similar to my behaviour when I attribute my behaviour to the supposition that I have a mind (perhaps itself a wrong inference). However problematic such mental state ascriptions are, with God the case is wildly different. With God, *two* inferences are being made: first, a mental state, and second, an existing being to house that mental state. So the analogy is inapt. Barrett anticipates this objection. People have bodies which we observe, God does not. But we can infer mental states without recourse to observing bodies. We do it all the time, for example when we talk on the phone.[14] Hearing a voice, however, is still a case of having empirical support of an existing entity. It's not that we hear God talking to us, and infer a mental state. We also infer that God is talking to us.

Now we come to faith in our senses.[15] Belief in material objects is reasonable in ways that belief in God is not. Simply put, we cannot help but believe in the existence of objects independently of our senses. Even the sceptic will jump out of the way of a train. Our senses, after all, are our sole windows to the world. Calling our senses untrustworthy leaves us with no guidance whatsoever. Our senses present to us what we deem is real. We would still so deem this even if it were all illusion by some standard wholly alien to us.[16] That is so because we simply have no choice. What we *mean* by reality is what our senses reveal to us as real. Even if this were all illusion, one big solipsistic sleeper,[17] we still make a distinction within this illusion between dream and waking life, between illusion and reality, delusion and sanity. And it is for this reason that we have "faith" in our perceptions of material objects. To believe otherwise is insane. Sensory faith is reasonable because its opposite is unthinkable, or at least, unliveable.

To not believe in God's existence, however, is not unliveable, let alone unthinkable. We can survive quite well without belief in God. Belief in God is not a necessary belief in the way that our belief in our senses are. The world's events are adequately and more simply explained without the hypothesis that God exists. So faith in God cannot be reasonable *in the same way* as faith in material objects, or faith in our senses, or faith in science. The analogy between sensory faith and religious faith is therefore untenable.[18]

CONCLUSION

Atheists do not find the faith claim very convincing. This is so whether we understand faith as a kind of willing, a kind of trust, a kind of steadfast opinion, or a kind of self-imposed rule that governs one's interactions with the world.[19] It is often said that atheists *would* believe in God if they had that special feeling. Perhaps many would, but it is irrelevant. It would not change the fact that feeling is an inadequate justification for belief in God. Telling me that you have faith in God's existence is simply another way of telling me that you believe God exists. I already know you believe that. What I don't know is whether your belief is a true belief. The feeling, after all, can be explained by your insecurity, your fear of a meaningless existence, or your hopes of a world better organized and more just, or the prospect that your belief happened to have been sufficiently reinforced by your parents and peers, or a variety of other error theories. Faith that God exists is not evidence of God's existing. We know that you have faith. Whether you epistemically ought to have faith is what we're wondering about. And this is not settled by appealing to your faith. On that point, Aquinas was right.[20] Unfortunately, Aquinas was wrong to think that the evidence favoured theism, but that returns us to Part II.

16

FIDEISM

In the previous chapter, we dismissed the argument that faith in God is reasonable. Some philosophers — albeit not so many theologians — have rejoiced in this finding, since, to them, something's being reasonable is a mark against it. Reason is a constraint on living. Reason is a constraint on forming a personal attachment with God. Arguments that revel in the unreasonableness of faith are referred to as *fideist*. Religious truth, if such a thing is to be accepted at all, must be accepted on the basis of faith in divine revelation, not reason.

Fideist arguments may be divided into two varieties: those following Kierkegaard and those following Wittgenstein.[1] A third group may be said to follow Tillich, but I shall reserve my discussion on Tillich for the next chapter.

KIERKEGAARDIAN FIDEISM

Kierkegaard is an existentialist. Minimally, that means that he is one of those thinkers who recognize that the most important questions in life concern who we are, what we ought to do, who we ought to become. These are matters that we are absolutely free to decide. With such freedom comes the angst of the decision and living with the decision. It is one thing to follow the crowd, another to live authentically, autonomously. Living autonomously, though, carries with it the burden of being solely responsible for your actions, your beliefs, your values, your life. With the weight of such responsibility comes trepidation, fear, angst. There are two ways of making decisions: an objective way and a subjective way. Objectivism demands impartiality. This is fine for the domain of science. If we want to know how heavy a rock is, we can be impartial. But for the questions that matter to us, who we are, or who we ought to become, or what we ought to do, impartial objectivity cannot help us.

Consider the question of death. Objective thinking can tell us about death. My mother is dead. She died of heart failure. These are facts, but the facts alone cannot speak to my subjective experience of those facts. Nor can an impartial view on death get at what really matters to me: *my* death. What is *that*? With such existential questions, we aren't concerned with objective truth: we're concerned with subjective truth.

A desire to live religiously is a free commitment. But faith is objectively uncertain. There is risk. Rational knowledge about the objective truth of God is inconsistent with a proper religious attitude. Faith requires risk. Evidence would destroy risk and thereby would destroy faith. Faith and reason are necessarily opposed.

Faith and morality may even be opposed. Kierkegaard uses the story of Abraham and Isaac (Gen. 22:1–12). God tells Abraham to kill his son, Isaac. If anything is immoral, it's killing your son. But Abraham's faith in God is so overpowering, he is prepared to violate common moral values. He is ready to violate his love of his son. He is ready to violate everything except his faith in God. To Kierkegaard, this story highlights the utter paradox, the utter absurdity, the utter irrationality of faith.[2]

For this reason, then, the truth of theism is not Kierkegaard's concern. Rather, the focus should be on a personal relation to God.[3] Such an attitude seems right — *so long as one is already convinced of God's objective existence*. And herein lies the problem. As put, what Kierkegaard asserts is disingenuous. Kierkegaard claims, "Because I cannot know God objectively, I must have faith."[4] We would not think it so clever to say, "Because I cannot know objectively that a Martian visited me in my undergraduate days, I must have faith it did." Compare someone's saying, "The truth of Martians visiting earth is not my concern, it's my personal relation with Martians that matters to me."

Of course, if *A* has a relation with *B*, that presupposes the truth of *B*'s existence. It is one thing to say, "I don't care to explain to you why I take God's existence to be true," and another thing to say, "Whether God really exists or not is irrelevant to my faith." The first presupposes the existence of God, and that's what atheists doubt. The latter is simply false, since God's existence is necessary to have a relation with Him.

Or is it? Does Kierkegaard really not mind having faith in something non-existent? Imagine if Tom loves Jane, but Jane does not love Tom in return. Is Tom in a relation with Jane if his love for Jane is unrequited? As far as Tom is concerned, his love of Jane may completely consume his life. That she is not in love with Tom, has in fact had a restraining order put on Tom, would be irrelevant to Tom's phenomenological experience. Could we properly say that Tom is still in love with Jane? Or might we suggest that he is not really in love; that he is in some other psychological state? In any event, would it be proper to say of Tom that his love of Jane is all that matters and whether or not Jane returns his love is irrelevant to Tom? Surely that is far-fetched.

Or, consider Dante's love of Beatrice. In the early fourteenth century, Dante Alighieri wrote *The Divine Comedy*, a trilogy including *The Inferno*, *Purgatory*, and *Paradise*. Dante also wrote an earlier work of sonnets and lyric poems called *La Vita Nuovo* (1292). In both works, the characters Dante and Beatrice appear. Dante is Dante, of course, and Beatrice is modelled after a real woman named Beatrice Portinari. There is little evidence that Beatrice even knew that Dante existed, and it would appear that Dante was well aware of that. From *La Vita Nuovo*, we learn that Dante first saw Beatrice when they were both nine (at any rate, Dante was nine, and the presumption is that so too was Beatrice). He did not see her again until they were eighteen, whereupon an introduction of sorts was made, and Beatrice indicated "disapproval" of Dante. They never met again, unless you count the appearance that she made in Dante's dream seven years after her death. That vision is claimed to have inspired Dante's great work, *The Divine Comedy*. Though Dante's love was unrequited, that did not diminish his love for her. And perhaps Dante's love so clouded his mind that he did not even have an accurate picture of who Beatrice really was. In that sense, Dante didn't love Beatrice: he loved Beatrice*. Beatrice* may well have never existed. That would have no bearing on Dante's psychological state. But it would make us wonder whether Dante's love was really directed at Beatrice. In any event, we could not imagine that Dante would be indifferent to Beatrice's loving him back (although had she loved him back, he might never have written *The Divine Comedy*).

After all, one may love a phantom. In *that* sense, Kierkegaard may wish to speak only of the great psychological phenomenon of having a personal relation with God, *whether or not God exists in fact*.[5] This makes sense, but it can hardly bode well for theists. It would mean that God may be a figment of the imagination. This is hardly the sort of move that can support theism.

For Kierkegaardians, the issue is decision, not belief.[6] To believe in God requires evidence. But waiting for evidence nullifies the relation. Saying, "I won't love you unless you love me back first," is not the best approach to love. Similarly, it is not appropriate to come to God only on the basis of objective facts. Demanding objective proof demeans the subjective experience, and *that* is where true faith lies. One must, thereby, simply decide. *Just do it*, as Nike's motto advises us. Of course, this couldn't rule out deciding *not* to believe. One could just as easily do that. It would be inconsistent for Kierkegaard to say that deciding not to believe in God is no good. If this were so, then one can decide to believe or decide not to believe with equal freedom — and, presumably, both are thereby subjectively true, or can be, if so decided. This makes the concept of "subjective truth" uninteresting. If *P* and *not-P* are both subjectively true, the concept of subjective truth doesn't hold much meaning. "Subjective truth" simply means that the belief held by a subject is believed to be true by that subject.

Kierkegaard extols the merits of unconditional love. We needn't disagree with him about that. It would be conditional love to love someone only if that person loves you first. It would be conditional love to love someone so long as that person remains physically attractive, or financially solvent, and these seem to be cases of lesser love, if they even count as love at all. But we don't want to take the concept of unconditionality too far. It is reasonable to restrict your love to existing persons. Saying, "I will love Pat on the condition that Pat exists," seems perfectly fine, even if the need to say such a thing rarely comes up. Conversely, "I will believe P independent of the evidence for P," seems perfectly insane. That it's your subjective choice is irrelevant to our epistemic appraisal of such a choice.

For Kierkegaard, knowledge, or important knowledge, concerns inward reflection. Knowledge must relate to the knower. This highlights his emphasis on subjective truth, which he pits against staid, sterile, objective truth. Normally, we don't make this dichotomy. We don't speak of knowledge as being either subjective or objective. We admit that it is both. Knowledge must, of course, relate to the knower. That needn't be denied by "objectivists." When we say, "Knowledge is justified true belief," the emphasis that it must be a *belief* entails that if I know X, I *believe* X. If I don't believe X, then it can't be the case that I *know* X. But my simply believing X doesn't mean that I know X. Kierkegaard seems to be confusing a necessary condition for a sufficient condition.

We could, instead, assert that Kierkegaard is not confusing the basic definition of knowing, but *altering* it. If so, *his* sense of "knowing God" is *our* normal sense of "believing in God." But the fact that Kierkegaard believes in God is not what is in doubt.

WITTGENSTEINIAN FIDEISM

Wittgenstein reminds us that language is a convention and limited. Meaning is interwoven with practice. To understand a word, or sentence, is to know how to use that word or sentence. But how we use words is contingent on the way that we happen to carve up the world. Nothing dictates that we must carve up the world one way rather than another. There is no totality of facts to which our meaning must conform. There is no value-free natural science. We define meaning according to the particular rules of a particular practice — our language game. But nothing dictates that that practice — or game — is the only way of doing things, that those rules are the only ones that could be applicable. Take, for example, the following symbol used to give direction:

Is this an arrow telling us to go to the right, or is it the side view of an eye socket with a line indicating the direction in which the eye is looking, i.e., to the left? Which way it tells us to go depends on the governing convention in place.[7] To say one is wrong, the other correct, is to misunderstand. Right and wrong only make sense from within a specific convention. They cannot be used across conventions. Similarly, atheists and theists don't really contradict each other. They play different games. A move in one game (such as, "God doesn't exist!") cannot be compared to a move in another game (such as, "God exists!") any more than we can usefully compare a king's move in chess with a king's move in checkers.

Concerning the metaphysical, language is especially inept. Metaphysical concepts cannot be put into words. There are two ways to go from here: (i) follow the default model of reasonable belief and conclude that any existential claim that cannot be put into words is not reasonable to believe; (ii) accept that a real phenomenon is not accessible by conventional language. Fideists opt for (ii). For them, the metaphysical makes itself manifest. That is all the evidence required. To ask for evidence for the manifestation is to play the wrong game.

To say words are meaningless is, perhaps, too strong. For certainly theists speak to theists about their metaphysical beliefs. But language use, Wittgenstein points out, is like a game. Permissible moves within one game needn't be permissible moves in another. And any similarity of moves across games, a bishop's and a checker's move, for example, has only surface similarity. Analogously, the language that atheists speak has only surface similarity to the language that theists speak. But to say that one is better than another, or that one better captures truth than the other, is as senseless as saying the bishop is better than the checker. There is simply no argument for comparison at all.

This does not mean that anything goes within any given language game. We judge whether a chess move is good or bad, legal or illegal, from within the game of chess itself. Likewise, we may assess a theistic doctrine from within theism itself. All Wittgenstein is saying, so far, is that the assessment cannot be done externally to the given language game. Judging whether faith is reasonable, then, cannot be a matter for atheists to decide. They speak a different language.

Dialogue ends when someone plays the Wittgenstein fideism card. Atheists appraise religion by rational standards and find that religion fails — but what are rational standards? Are they not themselves biased and indefensible? What we have left are two language game bubbles each right by its own standard and — supposedly — no hope of appealing to an overarching standard to appraise which standard is better. Religion has not won here — rather, conversation ceases. It is as if, while playing a video game, to avoid trouble we push a suspend animation button. The machine freezes. We have not lost, but nor can we continue playing.

The fideist move is more than unhelpful; it is disingenuous. The claim is that we have two separate bubbles. From one bubble — the rational — we get the belief that there ought to be a way of deciding between language games. From the other bubble — the fideist — we get the belief that it is impossible to decide between language games. But how could a Wittgensteinian make such a conclusion without being able to access the other language game? From within its own bubble, it could not possibly speak about something outside itself. At best, a Wittgensteinian would have to remain agnostic concerning whether one language game can critically reflect on another. The proper conclusion is that a possibility of communication must be left open, not closed.

For Wittgenstein, if Jones says, "I'm sick because I'm being punished for my sins" and Smith says, "I'm sick, but it's because of germs," there is no contradiction. On the one hand, that is true. There is nothing in what Smith says that rebuts what Jones says. Compare Jones's statement, "I passed the test because I studied hard," and Smith's claim, "I passed the test because I was lucky." We would not imagine here any contradiction either. But what if Smith, instead, says, "You're wrong; sickness is caused by germs, not by sin." Are we not now to take Smith's claim as a contradiction of Jones's claim? Wittgenstein appears to say no, for it would entail standards of one bubble game applied to another bubble game.[8] Likewise, Jones may say, "God exists," and Smith may say, "God doesn't exist," but there is no contradiction here either ... so long as we interpret the first proposition as "Jones believes God exists," and the second proposition as "Smith believes that God doesn't exist." But to pretend that therefore the two propositions, "God exists" and "God doesn't exist," don't contradict each other is to have a peculiar view of what contradiction means. To say that these two speakers are playing different games stretches matters beyond sense.[9]

As far as reasons for being sick, we might think that the implications of the beliefs may count in favour of one belief over another. If a random sample of sick people eat well, wash often, take antibiotics, and recover, while a random sample of sick people merely pray and don't recover, we might think that that sort of evidence should count in favour of Smith's hypothesis. But according to Wittgenstein's non-contradiction hypothesis, no evidence can count in favour of one over the other.

Statement A contradicts statement B if and only if, (i) A and B can't both be true, *and* (ii) A and B can't both be false. In the case of "God exists," and "No, He doesn't," this condition appears to be met. The only way it would not be met is if the meaning of a term has somehow shifted in the two statements. Perhaps "God" and "He" do not refer to the same entity. Perhaps existence means one thing in the first statement, and something else in the second. In either case, we would then say, the two statements do not contradict each other. This, roughly, is what the Wittgensteinian fideists assert. But can such an assertion hold?

According to the Wittgenstein adherent, D.Z. Phillips, God's existence cannot be a fact, not because God does not exist, but because people approach facts neutrally.[10] From a neutral stance, to believe X means that one is prepared to believe not-X. But those who have faith are not prepared to not believe in God. Nor do the faithful approach the concept of God neutrally.

This sentiment captures, I think, the insular bubble approach to faith in God (what I shall call non-falsifiable in Chapter 20), but it seems idle for all that. It doesn't reveal that theists and atheists are not engaged in a factual dispute. It reveals only that (some) theists are unwilling to entertain the possibility that their sincerely held belief is false. But we already knew that. And unwillingness to entertain the possibility of one's belief being false is not normally something to be recommended. Why are fideists allowed this sort of escape?

Besides, it doesn't seem true that all factual beliefs are treated neutrally. It is a fact that my mother died. I am not neutral about that. Nor am I prone to believe it false. Given my understanding of the world, I cannot help but believe it to be true and it would take a whole lot of fancy footwork that I can't even imagine to get me to change my mind on that. But it is a fact, nonetheless. I don't say, given my non-neutral subjective feelings about my mother's death, that therefore my mother's death is not an objective fact. Commitment to a fact does not mean that it isn't a fact. And as a fact, it is subject to some kind of test.

The possibility that God doesn't exist can't be declared simply to make no sense. It makes perfect sense to atheists. All it means is that it makes no sense to someone who is committed to believing it would make no sense for it to be false. But what does this tell us? Absolutely nothing.

17

ULTIMATE CONCERN

In Part IV of this *Primer*, we have been addressing the problems with faith. But faith is understood in different ways. We examined views of faith consistent with reason, and views of faith wildly discordant with reason. A third way of understanding faith is to see it as simply independent of reason. Paul Tillich belongs in this latter group.

For Tillich, faith is the state of being "ultimately concerned."[1] Our "ultimate concern" is that which determines our being: the reality, the structure, the meaning, and the aim of our existence. An ultimate concern is unconditional, total, and infinite. Faith is not a dogged refuse-to-believe-the evidence kind of wishful thinking. Nor is faith the result of calculated reason. Those who understand faith as either counter to or in accordance with reason make a mockery of faith. To ask whether faith is reasonable, as I have been asking, is simply to confuse levels of experience.

ONTOLOGICAL, NOT COSMOLOGICAL

Tillich prefers the phrase "Ultimate Concern" to "God," since, for Tillich, the latter term is made out to be an object, out there, not something manifest, here and now. Tillich blames the cosmological school of Aquinas and Descartes for that. They conceived God as a thing that you can come to know through reason. It puts "God" on a par with a stone or a star or a sturgeon — a mere thing, a mere object. (A mistake pantheists have taken to an extreme.[2]) To Tillich, the best reply to this way of looking at God is atheism. The cosmological approach *kills* religion.

Tillich resurrects the ontological approach. In this sense, God is not something to deduce or infer. Doing so divorces us from God. The *immediate* knowledge of the Absolute is destroyed. From the cosmological approach of Aquinas, we get the definition of Faith as a "low degree of evidence,"[3] as epistemically weak. From the vantage of the ontological approach, however, God is being itself.[4] And faith is the act of being "immediately aware of something unconditional."[5] We are aware of God through our whole being. God is already present to us as the *ground* of our own being. In that sense, God is not a thing that we may know or fail to know; rather, God is being itself. God is that in which we necessarily participate by the very act of existing. In other words, God is our *ultimate concern.*

"Is it reasonable to have faith?" is a question for the cosmological school. It is a senseless question for the ontological school. Similarly, asking, "Does God exist?" is a question for the cosmological school. For Tillich, God is *beyond* even existence.[6] If God *exists*, then God cannot be existence itself.[7] Since God is the *ground* of existence, it is a category mistake to suppose that God *exists*. Existence is too limiting for God. God is greater than even existence.

Tillich provides an analogy between God and light.[8] Everything that we see requires light, yet we often fail to notice the light. Instead, we pay attention to the objects made visible by the light. Treating light as a thing to be illuminated alongside of sticks and stones will fail miserably. Similarly, looking to find God as one would look to find a stick or a stone will fail. God is being itself and we sometimes fail to notice this by focussing only on objects. Tillich believes that the ultimate concern is self-evident, however. As he says, we are immediately aware of the unconditional — *if we turn our minds to it.*[9]

THREE AMBIGUITIES

Three ambiguities confront us when we shift from talk of God to talk of ultimate concern. When one has an ultimate concern, we can speak about the state of being ultimately concerned, as well as the thing about which one is ultimately concerned. (Tillich would not like my use of "thing" here, but I mean it as a grammatical indicator only.) Thus, the first ambiguity concerns which of these two Tillich means. For clarification, let us call the state of having an ultimate concern the *verb*, and the thing about which one is concerned the *noun*. The official line, then, is that faith is the verb, God is the noun. It is important for Tillich that both noun and verb components are evoked.[10] Like Buber (who urges an I-Thou, rather than an I-It, relation with God), Tillich wishes to emphasize the personal relation that the faithful have with God and to avoid treating God as a mere thing.[11]

But settling the ambiguity between verb and noun does not resolve two other ambiguities: whether we consider the verb component or the noun component, an ambiguity exists concerning whether the ultimate concern is subjective or objective. Consider first the question from the verb (or internal) perspective. When Tillich speaks of the ultimate concern as verb, is he speaking only of the state of being concerned, or of the state of being concerned about the proper object? In other words, is it possible that although I think I have an ultimate concern, I may be mistaken — much as we may wonder whether someone is in love merely because she thinks she is in love. Whether the verb is subjective or objective is the second ambiguity.

The third ambiguity concerns how we ought to interpret the noun. Is the external status of the ultimate concern as noun subjective or objective? Does the noun itself count as an ultimate concern merely because it seems so to you? Or, does Tillich mean that there is really only one thing that deserves the credit of being named the ultimate concern? If the latter, presumably only a god would count.

At first glance, it may appear that the second and third ambiguities are the same. They do both involve a choice between subjective and objective conceptions. And if the verb is interpreted objectively, then the noun will necessarily be objective too. But if the verb is subjective, the status of the noun is not determined. It may be either subjective or objective. For example, if being in love is defined subjectively, you may be in love with someone who neither loves nor respects you. In such a case, your friends and family would wish that you were not in love. This is different from saying because the object of your love is objectively unlovable, you are not really in love, despite your thinking you are. Similarly, one may really have an ultimate concern in an objectively non-ultimate thing. This is different from saying that since the object is not an objectively ultimate concern (as noun) you cannot possibly have an ultimate concern (as verb) in it, despite your thinking so. For example, let's say what I deem my ultimate concern is to make money. In such a case, do we say that I am really in a state of being ultimately concerned (subjective verb) and that therefore money really is my ultimate concern (subjective noun)? Or do we say that, although money is my ultimate concern (subjective verb), money is not really an ultimate concern (objective noun)? Or do we say that, given that money is obviously not a proper ultimate concern (objective noun), people can never really be in the state of having an ultimate concern, if they think that money is their ultimate concern (objective verb)?[12]

I do not mean to imply that Tillich does not resolve most of these ambiguities. I mean to point them out and warn against equivocation. Tillich admits that one can have an ultimate concern in the wrong thing: a false idol. This is the danger of faith: to elevate the merely conditional to the status of the unconditional.[13] If Tillich meant that the ultimate concern as noun were purely subjective, he could never speak of having an ultimate concern in the wrong thing. This, therefore, resolves the third ambiguity. Your ultimate concern as noun may turn out to be, not properly speaking, ultimate at all. The ultimate concern as noun is objective.

It still leaves open the second ambiguity: whether or not the verb of being ultimately concerned is subjectively or objectively determined. For our purposes here, this second ambiguity is less worrisome. What is important is that the ultimate concern can be both noun and verb, and although we may understand the verb subjectively, we can never interpret the noun to be merely subjective (see Table 17.1). People are concerned about many different things (success, country, art, science, money, sex) and some of these subjective concerns seem to be "ultimate" to them. Presumably, they would be mistaken. Since we can get our ultimate concerns wrong, it seems to very much matter in what I place my ultimate concern. The verb is the faith and the noun is the proper object in which to place one's faith. That is, there can only be one real ultimate concern as noun ... presumably God.

Table 17.1: Three Ambiguities

AMBIGUITY	RESOLUTION
1. VERB OR NOUN	BOTH
2. VERB: SUBJECTIVE OR OBJECTIVE	?
3. NOUN: SUBJECTIVE OR OBJECTIVE	OBJECTIVE

THE PROBLEM

We have seen Tillich's reasons for speaking of ultimate concern instead of God. And we have seen how at least the first ambiguity inherent in that switch is intentional. By conjoining the verb with the noun, the concept of ultimate concern elucidates more clearly the personal relation that the faithful have with God. But the danger of equivocation is too great. There is something too facile in claiming that God is the ground of being and anyone who recognizes being, thereby recognizes God. Is it useful to say that an atheist is experiencing God when she's experiencing being?

Let us grant that in the very act of existing, you must have an ultimate concern, and that is the meaning of faith. If so, it is nearly impossible not to have faith so long as you are alive. This is why it is sometimes said that atheists reject atheism by living, by caring about things, by having ultimate concerns.[14] Such remarks equivocate, however. It would be closer to being true if the ultimate concern involved only the verb, or the noun, as purely subjective. But we have seen that that cannot be how Tillich imagines it.

Atheists may believe in ultimate concerns as subjective verbs, but never as objective nouns.[15] That is, atheists can allow for persons to fashion their lives around what they take to be of ultimate concern to them. Atheists can do so without thereby being committed to believe that the thing in which they have an ultimate concern is real in the objective noun sense, let alone fit for being deemed an ultimate concern for everyone, let alone fit for being an ultimate concern even for the person herself. However much Tillich wishes to avoid treating God as a thing, we cannot forget the real distinction between having an ultimate concern as verb and having an ultimate concern as objective noun. Our question is whether Tillich hopes to move from the verb to the noun without further ado. And now that we have seen Tillich's resurrection of the ontological model, the answer is obviously, "Yes, he does so hope."

Resurrection of the ontological model resurrects all its problems as well (see Chapter 5). Nothing in the definitional move alone ("God is the ground of being") can affect the inference that God thereby *is*. Tillich's "solution" simply begs the question. Why define God as "the ground of being"? *That* question is not answered by merely reasserting it.

Another worry concerns Tillich's claim that the ultimate concern is *immediate* without interpretation or inference. Whatever underlying immediate experience there is, it must be metaphysically neutral enough to allow different theistic interpretations as well as even atheist interpretations. It is not obvious that the immediate experience, the bare bones ultimate concern, is religious. And this shows that religious interpretation is not mandated by the experience itself. The unmediated experience may be too banal, too neutral, too atheistic for Tillich's use. For example, what prevents me from understanding the ground of being as nature, not God? Why hijack my neutral interpretation to satisfy a preconceived religious interpretation?

Besides, although the experience is immediate, Tillich notes that one may get it wrong. This shows that the immediacy of the experience carries no special weight. One may immediately see ghosts, or mirages, or have other hallucinations. One may experience these things with one's whole being. Fear of ghosts, for example, is an immediate whole-being feeling. To say, "Yes, I really experience fear," is one thing. To say that the fear is due to really encountering a ghost is another. Likewise, to say, "Yes, I really experience a presence of God," is one thing. To say that therefore the presence is really real, another. That is what I mean by complaining that we cannot move from the verb (believing) to the existence of the noun (the thing believed) — however much supporters of the ontological argument wish for it to be so.

18

PO-MO THEO

I have so far neglected postmodern theologies (po-mo theo). I will partly rectify that here. I face a difficulty, however. Whatever I say about postmodernism must be problematic, since postmodernism is, at least partly, a critique of any pretension to assuming that language can signify distinctly and atemporally. Meaning and truth are themselves meaningful only within a specific world. No such world view can be maintained without question-begging, however. Since this is (roughly) the postmodern critique, criticizing postmodernism by appeal to conventional concepts will miss the point.

Still, one has to start somewhere. When I speak of postmodern theologies, I will speak of the views of the German philosopher, Martin Heidegger, the French deconstructionist, Jacques Derrida, and the French Christian philosopher, Jean-Luc Marion. All three criticize certain standard approaches to theology, and some of these criticisms echo the complaints of atheists. But they do not settle on atheism; they strive for a deity that is beyond the limiting circumference of analytic discourse. Postmodern theists are similar to fideists in rejecting traditional notions of reason as being sacrosanct and foundational. My general complaint, as you shall see, concerns their presuming the existence of a being that they feel unable to grasp through analytic methodologies. Postmodern techniques cannot *generate* that belief. But I am getting ahead of myself.

Heidegger, Derrida, and Marion do not wish to think of God as an abstract entity, a thing unto itself.[1] Heidegger is especially bothered by this manoeuvre, thinking it thereby objectifies God, makes of God a tool to be used for our own ends. It is bad enough to use people for our own ends, but to use God this way is even more heinous. Martin Buber makes the same point.[2] The important aspect of God does not concern His attributes, nor even His existence, but the personal relation God forms with you. Speaking of God generally misses the point. Talk of God treats God as an "it," an object, an object to dissect. But, to use Buber's terminology, God is a "Thou." The atheist's conception of God may well be dead, non-existent, but that's not the real God anyway. They have simply missed the boat. God is the eternal Thou!

Buber invokes the mysticism found in the anonymous fourteenth-century spiritual guidebook, *The Cloud of Unknowing*.[3] The author of this work notes that if God is greater than can be conceived, any conception must thereby fall flat. And if we pray to a god of our own conception, we are doing no better than praying to an idol. We should give up speaking about God entirely. We must remain silent. Heidegger appears sympathetic to such mysticism when he accuses theists of assuming that God can be captured by human understanding.

The Cloud of Unknowing regress makes sense. What doesn't make sense, however, is how anyone can believe in a being the conception of which is, by definition, impossible to believe in. For whatever you believe is by definition false. Notice it isn't merely that your belief is indeterminate. Since God is defined as being beyond your conception, any conception you have will necessarily fall short. *The Cloud of Unknowing* regress should lead to agnosticism, at best, not theism.[4] For an illustration, consider the following: I believe that there is a monkey in a box. You provide a cogent, articulate argument that there is no monkey in the box. Rather than concede to your argument, imagine I say, instead, that language and empirical evidence are obviously too limited since they do not support my belief about the monkey in the box. You would think I were a lunatic. It's precisely because language and empirical evidence do not support my particular belief that I should give up my belief. The leap into mysticism from the "language is poor" premise is unfounded.

On the other hand, recognizing that God will always be above full human understanding need not mean that we can have *no* understanding of God. I do not know how my television works, but I know *that* it exists. So the postmodern critique of theism may not really apply to most kinds of theisms. Its main target appears to be Hegel who brashly proclaimed that absolute knowledge *is* possible, and that such absolute knowledge would include full knowledge of God. For Hegel, Christianity is the "perfect religion," because only in it is God presented as He is in reality: namely, the "infinite, absolute end in itself."[5] For Hegel, such a being is fully ascertainable by reason. Postmodernists have no such faith in reason or any pretensions to objective truth, to something's being revealed as it is in itself. And this critique should apply to Hegel's hyperbole, as well. Even in heaven, the knower will invariably impede the knowing.

Derrida, too, rejects notions of absolute truth and unambiguous meaning.[6] Some philosophers distinguish truth from absolute truth. Of course, if *P* is true, it must be absolutely true, since truth is a discrete value, not a continuous one. In this sense, adding "absolute" in front of truth is mere redundancy, like adding absolute in front of pregnant. If one is pregnant, one is absolutely pregnant. But most who speak of absolute truth do not intend the qualifier to be merely redundant. There is a metaphysical connotation that is being invoked, and that extra non-relative bit is indeed suspect. I presume that the deniers of absolute truth conceive of truth as being necessary, not merely contingent. "There is a piece of lint on my sock," may well be an absolute truth (if it is true, it is absolutely true, not partially true), but it is certainly not a necessary truth. Its truth is merely contingent. Something's being necessarily true is a matter for *a priori* claims.[7] It is correct to say, "Two plus three *necessarily* equals five." It is not correct to say, "A piece of lint is necessarily on my sock." Since I do not equate "truth" with "necessary absolute truth," I can reject any pretensions to necessary absolute truth without rejecting any pretensions to truth. But others *define* truth as being necessarily absolute. It would appear that that is so with Derrida, for he does not think it untoward to reject truth after he has rejected absolute truth. This is not simply an aside. It underlies my main complaint with the postmodern movement. They are right that there is no such thing as an absolute, necessary *a posteriori* truth. But *a posteriori* truths have never been deemed to be absolute or necessary. So to reject absolute truth is not to reject (*a posteriori*) truth. To reject truth entirely, thereby, is to cling too tightly to the very concept of truth that they had just rejected. But let me continue.

For Derrida, knowledge is impacted, to say the least, by one's language (whether oral or written). Language is not simply a vehicle to detail a true proposition, but it defines truth in the telling. Language constitutes the very objectivity that we come to label in the world. Meanwhile, language is relative and flexible. Hence, the meta-concept of objectivity is likewise relative and flexible. Concepts such as truth and meaning belong in this flexible, relative, domain, yet they mean to apply outside that domain as well, which is impossible.

For Derrida, all we can know, if that term can be used at all anymore, is whatever is immediately present to us. There is an Eastern flavour here. Rid one's mind, be here now. Such sentiments echo the Zen notion that you already are the Buddha. It is only your mental constructions that prevent you from such insight.[8]

Finding Derrida an ally of Zen may seem troubling to some,[9] but Derrida is adamant that pure presence, if it is achievable at all, is to have no reference to anything outside itself in semantic space or time. If such a stance were possible, we could speak of it either as the unification of self and other, or the dissolution of self and other. And to that extent, this captures the mystical elements looming in Buber, or Meister Eckhart, or Rudolf Otto.[10] (For more on mysticism, see Chapter 21.) But if we do not reach such unification, or such dissolution, a spatial and temporal differentiation exists — what Derrida calls the *différance*. In Heideggerian terms, it is hubris to believe that one can stand face to face with being.

Postmodernists object to the reduction of God to purely human conceptions (what Heidegger identifies as "onto-theo-logy"). God is above all that, and needs to be freed from such constraints. To highlight the differ-

ence between postmodern and traditional theisms, Marion makes an analogy between icon and idol.[11] An idol is worshipped for what it is, not for
what it signifies. An icon is an avenue to something else, something beyond.
We have the icon to speak about, but what we really mean to get at is that
which "transpierces" the icon. With idols, on the other hand, we've come
to a full stop. This is what makes idolatry bad. It mistakes the signifier for
the signified. This is Marion's analogy to highlight the difference between
postmodern theology (icon) and onto-theo-logy (idol).

Following the postmodernist bent, what we get is a rejection of standard theological discourse that attempts to tell us what God is, or even
that God is. Atheists can agree, but postmodern theology still believes that
there *is* something beyond the icon that *is* being signified; otherwise they're
not theists. It is difficult to know upon what that supposition is based. Is
being here now sufficiently theistic? Can an atheist not be here now? Can
an atheist not be present in Derrida's sense? Too often people assume without question that an atheist cannot have a mystical experience. But this is
presumptuous. I argue that they *can* have the experience; they simply do
not *interpret* it in any religious or even metaphysical sense. For example,
I can have a déjà vu experience without thereby believing that I have just
circumvented time. I shall, however, leave *this* part of my discussion to my
chapter on mysticism (Chapter 21). For now, let me return to my monkey
in a box.

A MONKEY IN A BOX?

Let us imagine that there is a dead monkey in an opaque box. You stand
outside of the box. You are unable to open even a peep hole of the box.
Let us also imagine that the monkey has recently died and so not only is
there no monkey noise emanating from the box, nor is there, as of yet,
any dead monkey odour. Your basic empirical apparatus has, thereby, no
way of inferring that there is a monkey in the box. There is no reason for
you to suspect that a monkey is in the box. Let us imagine that the box
is unlabelled, or although it says "Dead Monkey," you are sceptical for it
could be a name and not a description. Or perhaps there is even a picture
of a monkey on the box, but this is not sufficient for you to be convinced,
or even suspect, that there is a monkey in the box, since you have seen a
picture of a zebra on a box that contained no zebras. But since there really
is a dead monkey in the box, your rigid reliance on available empirical
data precludes you from accepting a true belief. So far, this represents a
possible position of the atheist. The atheist cannot gather enough evidence
to believe in God, so deems it reasonable to not believe in God. The atheist prefers a false negative to a false positive. The atheist may be wrong.
Atheists are (or can be) fallibilists (see Chapter 1).

So here is one kind of mistake to make *vis-à-vis* beliefs concerning the monkey in the box: falsely believing that there is no monkey in the box. There is another kind of mistake to make: falsely believing that there is a monkey in the box. Two kinds of true beliefs are possible: believing that there is no monkey in the box when there isn't, and believing that there is a monkey in the box when there is. This is the usual demarcation. Postmodernists highlight yet another kind of mistake. Those who believe rightly that there is a monkey in the box may be further divided into two camps: those who believe that they have a fair representation of that unseen monkey, and those who do not believe that they necessarily have a fair representation of the unseen monkey in the box. The postmodernists complain that traditional theists fall into the first category — and all those in the first category are mistaken. Although they rightly believe that there is a monkey in the box, their belief about the monkey fails to map onto the real monkey in the box.

Imagine that the picture on the box is a picture of a brown monkey, whereas the monkey in the box is a black monkey. Those who believe that they know that there is a monkey in the box with certitude on the basis of the picture are, according to the postmodern critics, confusing the picture for the real monkey. Like the atheists, they too have a false belief. Yes, what they say has some semblance to what is true (for there really is a monkey in the box as far as postmodern theists are concerned), but their mental image of the monkey in the box does not really match the real monkey in the box. They believe in a false monkey. They are worshipping a false idol.[12]

So far, then, we have now seen three kinds of mistakes concerning the monkey in the box: (i) falsely believing that there is no monkey; (ii) falsely believing that there is a monkey; and (iii) falsely believing that there is one kind of a monkey when there is another kind of a monkey. For that matter, there is also the inadequate justification charge: one can believe truly but unjustifiably so. In that sense, I may believe that there's a monkey in the box for inadequate reasons (I had a dream about it, for example) or I may believe that there is no monkey in the box when there isn't simply because I refuse to believe in monkeys at all. My belief about there not being a monkey in the box in this case is true, but it is only circumstantially true, or true by luck, not justifiably true. But the postmodernist critique concerns the third option. What are we to make of it?

The postmodern theists discussed seem to know that there is a dead monkey in the box. They are lucky that way. They are unwilling to claim that their representation of the dead monkey is in any sense like the real dead monkey. But given the disconnect between signifier and signified, from where does their confidence arise concerning there even being a signified? The exercise that the traditional theist and atheist are engaged in concerns how anyone can come to know if "God" refers to anything real at all. Postmodern theists' refusal to answer that question (since it entails

succumbing to a logocentricism that they reject) can hardly count as illuminating. At best, we should expect agnosticism. But even then, we can
point out (as I've done in Chapter 1) how agnosticism ignores the concept
of the burden of proof.

SUMMARY

Postmodern theists maintain that the concept of God is problematic only
due to the paucity of language combined with the limitations due merely
to the arbitrary imposition of Western empiricism. Words carry mundane
denotations; yet religious language is meant more figuratively and symbolically. Attempts to pin it down to the mundane denotations as atheists are
wont to do, thereby miss the point. Atheists are like those literalists who
fail to appreciate poetry.

On the other hand, avoiding criticism of the theory by hand-waving
gestures toward our impoverished language doesn't answer the central
question: How do you know that God exists? To that question, an appeal
to faith merely translates into repeating that one believes that God exists.
Because atheists needn't doubt that postmodern theists believe in God, the
postmodern diversion is useless.

19

PASCAL'S WAGER

Blaise Pascal suggests that it's a better bet to believe in God than not to believe in God.[1] He admits that we cannot know for sure that God exists, that the proofs for God's existence fail. So your belief in God is more a matter of faith. But Pascal believes that you have a good reason to have such faith. Basically, if you believe God exists and He does, then you win. If you believe in God's existence, and God doesn't exist, there's no great loss. If you don't believe in God, but God exists, you lose. If you don't believe in God and God doesn't exist, no great gain. Add up the various options and you'll see that believing is a better bet than not believing.

Consider if God exists and is roughly like what Christians say He is. Then, if you believe in Him, there will be great return for your investment. Sure, you'll have to go to church, and help out your neighbour, and not swear, but the rewards of heaven will outweigh all those inconveniences. Of course, if God doesn't exist, then you don't get any reward. The cost to you is that you could have been having affairs, say, or watching football rather than going to church, and swearing without fear of damnation, and stuff like that. But the rewards of heaven far outshine the paltry and ephemeral rewards of earth.

Meanwhile, if God exists and you remain either a sceptic or an atheist, the penalty is hellfire.[2] That's really bad. So, if God exists, it is certainly better that you believe in Him even without any other reason for doing so. Of course, if God doesn't exist, there's no punishment for being an atheist. But wouldn't it be more rational to avoid a worst case scenario? Wouldn't belief in God be a good bet? Table 19.1 offers the basic outcomes.

Table 19.1: Basic Matrix

	BELIEVE	DON'T
GOD EXISTS	HEAVEN	HELL
GOD DOESN'T	SMALL LOSS	SMALL GAIN

To understand where Pascal's argument goes astray, we need to put some values in the various boxes. We will note worries about the arbitrariness of these values below, but for now, let's say, on a range from +100 to -100, successful entrance to heaven earns +100, and hell gets -100. Let's say the small inconvenience of believing equals -10, whereas the earthly benefits of not believing earns one +10. Yes, these are arbitrary, but the point is simply to show that heaven is way better than hell and also better than any earthly gain one may reap from not believing in God. And whatever the costs of a non-hypocritical religious lifestyle, it does not compare to the costs that one would incur in hell. Given these payoffs, we can now sum up the two columns, as shown in Table 19.2.

Table 19.2: Raw Values

	BELIEVE	DON'T BELIEVE
GOD EXISTS	100	-100
GOD DOESN'T	-10	10
SUM	90	-90

Given these figures, and the assumption that the higher payoff is better, it is more reasonable to believe in God than to disbelieve in God. This is Pascal's point.[3]

TWO PROBLEMS

Many theists dislike Pascal's wager. It seems far too secular a reason to believe in God. The impetus for believing in the above matrices can be transcribed as asking, "What's in it for me?" Surely, this is not the right sentiment to have when approaching God. In fact, it seems the complete opposite of what attitude one should take. Had Pascal published his *Pensées* during his lifetime, he would surely have been excommunicated.[4]

Such an attitude is unfortunate. Pascal was adamant in clarifying that he was offering merely a foot in the door approach for atheists and agnostics. He supplemented his theory by suggesting that, in time, habit would inculcate the correct attitude.[5] In this sense, Pascal was an early behaviourist. Aristotle, too, took this approach to ethics. If you do as the virtuous do, you will, in time, come to be virtuous.[6] Neither Pascal nor Aristotle confused *doing* with *being*. Excommunicators, unfortunately, are rarely able to pick up such subtleties.

More problematic, however, is that probabilities are missing. Pascal asserts that since God either exists or doesn't exist, the odds of God's existing are 50–50. Nothing of the sort follows. Since my lottery ticket is either a winner or a loser, I cannot therefore assume that the odds of my winning are 50–50. Far from it.

Pascal's intended audience, recall, were atheists. Theists didn't need an argument to believe in God; they already did.[7] Atheists would never put the odds of God's existence at fifty per cent. Atheists will not believe that the existence of God has the same probability as the non-existence of God. Rather, they say that the evidence is insufficient to support the claim about God. For them, even asserting a ten per cent chance of God's existing is too high. But, even a ten per cent chance of God's existing is sufficient to alter Pascal's conclusion. Multiplying the values from Table 19.2 above with a ten per cent probability of God's existence reveals that belief in God is *not* a reasonable bet. The higher utility is garnered by *not* believing. This is captured in Table 19.3.

Table 19.3: With Probabilities

	BELIEVE	DON'T BELIEVE
GOD EXISTS	100(.1)	–100(.1)
GOD DOESN'T	–10(.9)	10(.9)
SUM	–3.5	3.5

Similarly, without taking the odds into effect, Pascal's reasoning would tell us to buy a lottery ticket. Since the payoff is so high (say $100.00) and that you lose next to nothing in buying a ticket (say $2.00), it is reasonable to buy it (see Table 19.4).

Table 19.4: Lottery without Probabilities

	BUY	DON'T BUY
WIN	$100	$0
DON'T WIN	–$2	$0
SUM	$98	$0

Since $98.00 is better than $0, you should buy the lottery ticket. Something's gone wrong. We now know that what has gone wrong is the failure to take the probabilities of winning into account. This is rectified in Table 19.5.

Let's say that the probability of your winning is one in a thousand. Typically, the odds are much worse, but this will do. Since $0 is better than –$1.99, you should *not* buy the lottery ticket. In fact, given these values, you stand to lose close to $2.00 every time you buy a lottery ticket. How else do you think lotteries stay in business?

Table 19.5: Lottery with Probabilities

	BUY	DON'T BUY
WIN	98(.0001)	0(.0001)
DON'T WIN	-2(.9999)	0(.9999)
SUM	-$1.99	$0

DEFENDING PASCAL

To be fair to Pascal, he avoided — or tried to avoid — my charge about probabilities. To show where Pascal failed, I inserted some admittedly arbitrary values. One might complain that the cost of theism is not negative even if God doesn't exist. Religious belief may provide meaning in one's life that is otherwise absent.[8] Likewise, one may argue that I have overvalued secular living. Why is swearing or having an affair given a positive utility? Others may complain that it is impossible to place any value on happiness or well-being. Conversely, or additionally, one may complain about such an exceedingly low probability of God's existence. Surely no theist would accept that at the outset. The inherent vagary in calculating the payoffs for Pascal's wager suggests that my argument above has been too quick.

I shall not linger long with these sorts of objections, since it turns out that they support the atheist's case. They show that we need to come to an agreement about the values before we can rely on Pascal's wager, but since agreement on the values is exactly what Pascal's wager was intended to help solve, Pascal's wager is hopeless. That is, his argument was to convince the atheist to believe in God. But the atheist first needs to accept the probabilities of God's existence to be high enough for the calculations to work in favour of belief. If the atheist already believed that, she wouldn't be an atheist in the first place.

Perhaps for that reason, Pascal himself did not worry about the above charges. Instead, he threw in a mathematical trick. Heaven, he said, could not be given any finite number, for it surely would always be above that. Instead, heaven was *infinitely* good, while hell was *infinitely* bad.[9] If heaven is awarded an infinite positive number, while hell is given an infinite negative number, then whatever other values we cook up, and whatever probabilities we assign (so long as they're greater than zero), it won't matter: it will always be better to believe. A fraction of infinity is still infinite.

Given our acceptance that heaven is infinitely great, and hell infinitely bad, Pascal's argument succeeds. But another response is appropriate at this juncture. The belief that heaven is infinitely great, or for that matter that heaven even exists, is contingent on my believing in God. Belief in God and belief in heaven are a package deal. For me to believe in heaven requires my belief in God. But Pascal's argument for why I should believe in God requires my belief in heaven. We've gone in a loop. My belief in

God was what Pascal's wager was supposed to lead me to. But it does so only so long as I believe in God in the first place. The failure remains.

To be clear, Pascal's wager does not convince atheists because atheists would need to first accept preliminary suppositions about God's existence. This is unlikely. It is for that reason that Pascal's argument fails to be convincing for atheists. That it convinces theists, on the other hand, is uninteresting and, at any rate, not Pascal's stated objective.

—∞—

NON-FALSIFIABILITY

FLEW'S GARDEN

Imagine that two hikers come across a garden in the middle of the woods. One hiker, the believer, suggests that there must be a gardener around. The other hiker, the sceptic, doubts this. There is no sign of any habitation within a day's hike. So, unless the gardener comes in by helicopter, the garden is more likely a freak occurrence of nature. The two make a bet. To test the gardener hypothesis, they set up camp and wait. No gardener comes. The sceptic wants the believer to pay up, but the believer suggests that they have not waited long enough, or perhaps that the gardener has been scared away by their presence. The sceptic notes that the garden is in the same pristine shape that they found it, so either the gardener is invisible or this is the work of nature. The believer opts for invisibility. Being invisible is still more probable to the believer than that the garden gardens itself. To test this further hypothesis, the hikers set up an invisible electric fence. The fence electrocutes some rabbits, but no gardener. Again the sceptic asks the believer to pay up. The believer suggests another hypothesis: namely that the gardener is not only invisible, but able to detect and avoid invisible fences. The sceptic is now thoroughly annoyed and demands: "What evidence would definitively count against your theory?" The believer retorts, "Nothing at all!"

This little story was used by the British philosopher, Antony Flew.[1] The lesson is the same as I gave when I spoke about the monster under the bed in Chapter 1. Whenever the appeal to faith means no more than that the faithful are unwilling to change their belief in God *no matter what*, they have ventured into the realm of the *non-falsifiable*.

A belief in God need not be non-falsifiable. A person might admit that if certain of her prayers are unmet, her child's recovery from illness, say, she will abandon belief in God. In such a case, her belief in God is falsifiable. Notice that her child's recovery cannot count as verifying her belief in God's existence, since the child may have recovered notwithstanding God's non-existence. Of course, in this example, the child's non-recovery may not itself count as proof of God's non-existence, any more than the child's death would count as proof of the mother's non-existence, or the mother's non-love. Our concern is not with what counts as *good* falsifiability tests, but simply to note that sometimes people admit *no* falsifiability tests. The charge of non-falsifiability applies only when the faithful are unwilling to admit that anything can count against their faith in principle, so committed are they to God's existence.[2] A non-falsifiable hypothesis about God (or anything) is not deemed false, but *vapid*.

This is the argument, anyway. Below is my attempt at backing it up. To do so, first, I shall divorce the falsifiability criterion from logical positivism. Then, I shall explain how falsifiabiltiy is a crucial criterion of scientific method. Then, I shall raise standard objections to the criterion of non-falsifiability. Lastly, I respond to those objections. In the end, I hope to vindicate Flew's basic worry: religious claims that cannot be tested are as vacuous as horoscope predictions.

NOT LOGICAL POSITIVISM

Flew's basic claim is that many (perhaps even most) faith claims are non-falsifiable and that is a bad thing. The concept of non-falsifiability, however, is connected to a now defunct school of thought called *logical positivism*. Logical positivists suggested that non-falsifiable claims were neither true nor false, but *meaningless*.[3] Many have found such definitional fiat puzzling. "God is love," may be a proposition with an empty referent, but to call it as meaningless as "Juniper silent noises silverly," is a bit odd. My intent here is to use the principle of non-falsifiability *without the logical positivist baggage* — at least as far as that is possible. Specifically, I shall not speak of falsifiability as a criterion of *meaning*. Instead, I shall understand falsifiability as a requirement that specific kinds of hypotheses be *testable*.

When we are confronted with a claim, and our concern is whether or not to believe it, we naturally consider whether any counter evidence to the claim exists. Thinking along these lines is to use the falsifiability criterion. And we do so without accepting (let alone acknowledging) logical positivism. If I say, "My cat has fleas," you understand that some investigation of the cat may be in order. You understand roughly what conditions would support the claim. You see fleas on the cat, perhaps. Likewise, you understand what conditions would count against the claim. You see no fleas on the cat after close inspection, for example. If I say, "I am the greatest golfer ever," you understand that my claim should be consistent with my shooting very low scores. If bogeys and double bogeys are the norm for me, this should count against my claim. If I say, "God is love," you are entitled to wonder what kind of test is needed to decide the matter. If I reply that no test is appropriate, I have entered the realm of the non-falsifiable.

FALSIFICATION AND VERIFICATION

When an hypothesis predicts something and it does not happen, we normally count this as evidence against the hypothesis. If the test was well conducted, we call the disconfirming result a case of *falsifying* the hypothesis. Perhaps the test was not well constructed. It may be prudent to vary the conditions a little bit to rule out the possibility of experimental contamination. But so long as the experimental conditions were well applied and well adhered to, the principle of falsifiability pertains. A claim that is *non-falsifiable* is one in which nothing would count against the claim even in principle. That is, the conceptual framework is such that *whatever events happen in the world*, the hypothesis would not be disconfirmed.

The phrase, *even in principle*, is an important qualification. Sometimes we cannot imagine something's being false. "It snows in Saskatchewan at least once during a given year," for example, is a statement that we can't practically conceive of as being false. But it is falsifiable: hence, non-vacuous. That is, we know what *would make the claim false*: namely, that it doesn't snow in Saskatchewan during a given year. Perhaps global warming will make that counter condition true. But a claim that cannot be shown to be false *even in principle*, will deny the possibility of even *conceptual* counterfactuals.

For illustration, consider Freudian psychoanalysis. Freud proposed a complicated conceptual structure that was used to explain human behaviour after the fact, but not to predict very specific things in advance. A mother's neglect may cause later psychological malaise in the child, but not necessarily autism, for example, or kleptomania. The theory could explain everything, but it was precisely this property that made it scientifically empty. Consider the hypothesis that Hector has developed a rash because he has repressed a sexual desire for his mother. If Hector says, "Yeah, I do have sexual fantasies about my mother, how did you know?" we have confirming evidence. If, instead, Hector claims that he never had this sexual desire, and is, frankly, offended at the wild accusation, the Freudian response is: "See: you've repressed your sexual fantasies, and the result is your rash." However implausible the theory, Hector will feel stymied, since whatever evidence he offers will be interpreted as confirmation of the Freudian hypothesis. But it is precisely because everything can be interpreted as confirmation — and nothing can count against it — that renders the hypothesis empty.

The recognition that *falsifying* theories is a necessary move in scientific methodology was defended by Karl Popper.[4] He recognized that a scientific hypothesis should be testable. What distinguishes science from pseudo-science is that the former is testable, the latter is not. If a hypothesis is really true, then testing it won't show it to be false. It may fail to show it to be true, alas, but it won't show it to be false, whereas testing a false hypothesis may well show it to be false. If so, we have a reason to abandon or modify our wrong belief. This is good news — so long as we prefer to hold beliefs that are more likely true than false.

The emphasis on falsifiability need not be at the exclusion of verification. We can certainly verify particular judgements, like "The pickle is on the plate," just as we can verify that God exists (perhaps post-death). The pickle hypothesis is verified if we observe a pickle on the appropriate plate. When we verify universal statements, like "All pickles are sour," we do so by verifying a bunch of particular cases and generalizing from there. Popper's point is simply that in scientific method, verification alone is not sufficient.[5] If enough evidence points in favour of the hypothesis, *and none sufficiently against it*, we can count the hypothesis sufficiently verified. Not merely do we want to see a bunch of cases where pickles are sour, we want to find no cases where pickles are sweet. Similarly, when assessing any causal claim, that A caused B, say, we need to do two things. We need to (i) set up cases of As occurring, and see if Bs come about, and (ii) set up cases where As do not occur, and see if Bs also don't occur. If A does cause B, we expect to find Bs in condition (i), and no Bs in condition (ii). If that is the result, we can say our hypothesis is confirmed, or verified (all else being equal), and if either condition fails (no B in (i), or a B in (ii)), we say the hypothesis is disconfirmed, or falsified. "Pickles are sour" and "God loves us," should both be testable in this kind of way. If no possible event could, even in principle, count against God's loving us, then "God loves us" is non-falsifiable.

Notice that, "God exists," *can* be verified, at least post-death.[6] But this doesn't get us anywhere, since I can similarly verify "A magic monster exists under the bed." If it's there, I'd see it. This shows that verification is only half of the picture. Not finding such a thing is due to the magical nature of the beast, after all. While we can admit that "God exists" is verifiable (though not verified), we can point out that "God exists" is not falsifiable, for God's absence is not generally taken to falsify the hypothesis that God exists. And while God's existence may be verified post-death, God's non-existence cannot be (if nothing at all exists after death). To modify Epicurus's observation, where death is, a falsifier is not.[7]

The demand that a claim be falsifiable is crucial if we want to judge whether we should or shouldn't accept the claim. Claims should be subject to some kind of test, at least in principle. If a claim is not falsifiable, it is not testable. Non-testable claims are as empty as horoscopes: vacuous predictions about which any event would count as satisfying. Falsifiable claims, on the other hand, are courageous: they boldly make predictions that others may debunk. They boldly proclaim the exact kinds of events that would disconfirm their hypothesis, and these are events that can happen — events that, if they happen, others can clearly recognize their happening. When I say, "Pickles are sour," I imply that the next pickle you eat will taste sour to you. If I say, "God loves you," presumably I imply something. What? Without clear, falsifiable predictions, the hypothesis is as uninspiring as someone yawning.

OBJECTIONS

Most find the pronouncement, "'God exists' is vacuous," not only offensive, but clearly wrong.[8] As Hick remarks, nothing is more meaningful than faith in God, and so any theory that says otherwise must itself be vacuous.[9] I shall ignore such heartfelt question-begging complaints, and focus instead on the following five objections, all aimed at the criterion of non-falsifiability: (i) even scientists' pet hypotheses are non-falsifiable in practice; (ii) some non-vacuous and true claims are non-falsifiable; (iii) while universal claims are falsifiable, but not verifiable, certain particular claims are verifiable, but not falsifiable — yet non-vacuous and often true; (iv) the presuppositions of science are non-falsifiable; and (v) the criterion of non-falsifiability is itself non-falsifiable, so is self-defeating.

(i) The shift to falsifiability suggests that scientists are ready to reject their own theories at the drop of a hat. Scientists are people, however, and are as much subject to bias and vested interest as the rest of us. Since reputation often hinges on the success of the scientist's research, it is unlikely that she will be willing to simply discard her theory after it has been deemed false. Scientists may be impurely motivated. They may be motivated to get grant money, they may have invested years of their lives, and their careers may be on the line. To think that they will simply discard their theory over a single contradictory result is naïve. Even without imputing improper motivation to these poor overtaxed scientists, there may be other very legitimate reasons making scientists loathe to reject their theories. The methodology itself may have been flawed. If so, it would be too quick to assume that the theory is wrong. It is prudent to first wonder whether the experiment itself was contaminated in unknown ways. How do we rule out these alternative explanations? The answer should be obvious: by doing more studies, not by abandoning one's hypothesis. And it is this frank admission that appears to undermine the claim that science, unlike faith, is falsifiable. Science claimed that although we cannot verify theories, we can at least prove a theory false by a single disconfirming bit of information. We have seen that there are plenty of exceptions to this rule. Because of these imperfections in many experimental situations, people complain that science isn't as open to refutation and testability as the dogmatic non-scientific explanations that they were intended to replace.

(ii) Consider the proposition, "There are three consecutive '7's in the decimal configuration of π."[10] One would say that this is a non-vacuous proposition. That is, we can certainly understand it to be true. We would know how to confirm it if we saw it. But it is not falsifiable. Our failing to see three "7"s in whatever configuration of π we examine would not show that there are not three consecutive "7"s in the decimal configuration of π. This is because the decimal configuration of π is infinite. Our failing to find it among our *limited* configuration would not show that it does not occur somewhere in the infinite configuration. So here is a claim we admit to be non-empty, yet non-falsifiable. This shows that the non-falsifiability criterion does not define emptiness. On the same lines, we can ask whether probability statements are falsifiable. Take flipping a fair coin. We say it has a fifty per cent chance of landing heads. But on any actual trial of even one thousand throws, we wouldn't actually bet on exactly fifty per cent heads coming up. If we did, we'd commit the Gambler's Fallacy. ("The last ten tosses came up tails, so the next toss *must* come up heads to even things out.") So, the probability claim of 0.5 odds is non-falsifiable, yet not vacuous.

(iii) Universal affirmative statements (All *A*s are *B*s) are falsified by particular negative statements (Some *A* is not a *B*). Similarly, universal negative statements (No *A*s are *B*s) are falsified by particular affirmatives (Some *A* is a *B*). But what falsifies particular statements themselves? The official answer is universal statements. "There is one apple that is rotten" is falsified by observing the entire set of apples in the universe and finding none that are rotten. But our ability of examining every member of a set is often impractical, if not impossible. All we can usually accomplish is the observation of a subset. But "There is one apple that is rotten" is not falsified by "Here are a bunch of non-rotten apples," since the two propositions are perfectly compatible. If the number of apples is not specified, find all the non-rotten apples you want, you won't have falsified the claim any more than a particular affirmative verifies a universal affirmative. And, to make matters worse, if a non-falsifiable claim is used to falsify a universal statement, then how can the universal statement itself have been falsified? So here are a bunch of cases where perfectly sensible claims about particular things — claims that we would say are non-vacuously true — are non-falsifiable.

(iv) All of science is based on the following claim: "Every effect has a natural cause." The claim is not falsifiable. If anything happens for which a scientist cannot find a natural cause, we do not expect the scientist to say, "Gee, there must be a supernatural cause for that!" We expect more prudence. We expect the scientist to say, "I don't know what its natural cause is, but I do not abandon my belief that it has a natural cause." To make matters worse, all of science is predicated on precisely the claim that everything has a natural cause. It's on the basis of that supposition that scientists start looking for the particular cause. Thus, it is not merely a particular claim that science accepts that is non-falsifiable. Rather, since the claim, "every effect has a natural cause," is crucial to science — since science is predicated on that very claim — we are entitled to say that *science itself* is non-falsifiable. If faith in God is non-falsifiable, so what? It's in good company, company that includes science itself.

(v) Is the falsifiability theory itself falsifiable? The answer is obviously "No." For anything that would count as disconfirming the principle of non-falsifiability would have to be something that is (a) non-vacuous, yet (b) non-falsifiable. But such a combination is precisely what the theory of non-falsifiability denies can ever come about. If anyone suggests a candidate, for example, "God loves us," rather than disconfirming the principle of non-falsifiability, non-falsifiable proponents will say, "The counter example does not count, for, being non-falsifiable, it must therefore be empty, as the non-falsifiable criterion dictates." This is question begging. And once we admit that the theory of falsifiability is itself non-falsifiable, its own criterion renders the falsifiability criterion vacuous. Therefore, we have no reason to give the falsifiability criteria any more attention: it is self-refuting.

REPLIES

(i) The first complaint about the foibles and biases of scientists is not a philosophical complaint. Nothing in accepting the biases and limitations of experimental conditions rules out the principle of non-falsifiability as an ideal, any more than pointing out how many practising theists are hypocritical shows that theism is wrong. The practical remedy to the above complaint is to note that science is social.[11] We do not deem the findings of one study to be conclusive. Other scientists — with different biases — will have to replicate those findings first. Alternatively, the original findings will be disconfirmed through further study by other scientists with different biases. In this sense, competition among scientists helps combat bias in the long run.[12] Bias, though ineradicable within any given experiment, can be mitigated by the social aspect of science. Repetition and diversification of testing methods is exactly what scientists employ to determine whether a theory has been falsified or the experiment contaminated. If they can't tell, they certainly don't assume the theory has been verified. They keep tinkering. This is exactly Popper's point: both verification and falsification are needed before any hypothesis can be affirmed, and it is this two-tiered testing method that religious hypotheses frequently ignore.

(ii) Concerning the second complaint, we need to note the difference between *a priori* and *a posteriori* claims, as discussed in Chapter 5. An *a priori* claim is one in which the truth or falsity of the claim is based purely on its analytic content. If Boris is married, we are entitled to infer that Boris is not a bachelor. We are entitled to that inference without knowing Boris personally. Nor do we make that inference because of our experience with people who are married. It is not a judgement based on a survey of how many married men are also non-bachelors. We know the inference to be true merely because of definitional fiat. Being a bachelor *means*, among other things, being unmarried. We are entitled to make the inference purely on analytic grounds. There is no recourse to experience once the concepts are understood. The truth or falsity of *a posteriori* claims, on the other hand, is determined by experience. To determine whether Boris is a bachelor or not, you have to know something about Boris. You have to get outside the purely analytic endeavour of word parsing. You have to get outside the purely conceptual world of logical relations. You have to go out into the world and discover something about Boris, the person.

Given the distinction between *a priori* and *a posteriori* claims, we can now stipulate that the non-falsifiability criterion is meant only for *a posteriori* claims, not *a priori* claims. Each of the counter cases above show *a priori* claims being non-falsifiable. They do not give cases where *a posteriori* claims are non-falsifiable. Defining whether there are consecutive "7"s in the decimal configuration of π might seem like an experiential thing, like walking in the woods and looking for three mushrooms in a row. It is not, though. It is a case of an *a priori* calculus. It is a purely conceptual affair. It is the same thing when we determine that a fair coin has a 0.5 probability of coming up heads on a toss. This number isn't determined by a survey. No government grant for a large-scale survey of coin tosses was needed. The probability is determined by dividing the number of possible sides that a fair coin can land on in a single throw by the total number of sides that the coin can land on: i.e. ½, or 0.5.[13] This is simple arithmetic. Purely *a priori*.

A priori claims are different kinds of claims than *a posteriori* ones, and require different kinds of assessment. The non-falsifiability charge is intended to apply only to *a posteriori* claims. Existence claims, like "This apple is rotten," or "It snows in Saskatchewan," or "There is a bunny rabbit in the bushes," or "God exists," are *a posteriori*. The claim about three consecutive "7"s in π is *a priori*. That *a priori* claims may be sensibly non-falsifiable does not show that *a posteriori* claims can be sensibly non-falsifiable. True, there are some who suggest that "God exists" is *a priori* — Anselm and Descartes, to name two — but this requires the ontological argument to work. As we noted in Chapter 5, however, it doesn't.

(iii) Saying "The cup is on the table" is falsified by finding no cup on the table. The worry about falsifying particular statements, then, is a worry about falsifying a certain kind of particular statement. Presumably the open-ended kind, like "There is a bunny rabbit in the bushes," or even more open-ended, like "There is a bunny rabbit somewhere in the world," or even worse, "There is a bunny rabbit somewhere in the universe at some time." The more open-ended the particular statement, the more difficulty we have with falsification. Taking the last example, our never finding a rabbit in this world would not falsify the statement. Similarly, my not finding a bunny in the bushes may be due to my not looking in the right bushes, as opposed to the statement's being false. Once we recognize that the open-ended particular statements may be (technically) non-falsifiable, this should count in favour of non-falsifiability. For objection (iii) to work, we need a sensible particular claim that is non-falsifiable. Instead, we discover only the horribly vague, open-ended sort of propositions count as non-falsifiable, and this strikes me as exactly right.

True, if an open-ended statement is based on statements we know to be true, like bunny rabbits exist, we may fail to see the vacuousness of the expanded, open-ended version. To highlight the worry about open-ended utterances, imagine if I say, "There is a unicorn somewhere in the universe at some time." In such a case, our not finding a unicorn in our world in our time frame would not count as falsifying the utterance. But now we see that it is precisely because the utterance is too open-ended that it renders the utterance useless.

This shows that the principle of non-falsifiability does apply to particular statements as well as to universal statements, *so long as we limit our searching parameters*. The non-falsifiability charge against the particular claim about the rotten apple succeeds only so long as the number of apples referred to is infinite. But the statement, "There's a rotten apple in this bushel," is falsified by finding no rotten apples in that bushel. Likewise the claim, "There is a monster under my bed," is falsified by finding no monster under the bed, so long as we limit the concept of monsters to non-magical and visible varieties. The claim, "There's a magical monster under the bed that will avoid detection," is not falsifiable, since non-detection no longer counts as refuting evidence. That is why the claim is vacuous. That is why the claim, "There is a magic apple somewhere in the universe" is also vacuous. It is too open-ended. That we have a criterion to complain about such claims seems right, not wrong.

To reiterate — for I think this point important — a particular statement *is* falsifiable so long as the set of places in which we are allowed to look for the object in question is limited. The more open-ended the particular statement, the more non-falsifiable it becomes. For example, after we've exhausted the bushes and find no bunny rabbit, we can say that the claim about a bunny rabbit in the bushes has been falsified. But if we say that a bunny rabbit exists somewhere, our not finding a bunny rabbit in the bushes would not count as falsifying the claim. For that reason, scientists (or those who recognize the importance of scientific method) would like the speaker to limit the set of places for us to look. If the speaker is saying anything at all, she needs to go out on a limb a little bit: to specify some condition which — if not met — would make the speaker herself change her mind about her particular claim. If the speaker is unwilling to do that, then we can complain about non-falsifiability.

So, to that extent, if we treat "God exists" as a particular claim, we can still complain about non-falsifiability if the speaker is unwilling to limit the confines of her search for such a creature. Finding no inference to

God from either the ontological, the cosmological, the design, or the moral argument, makes one wonder what *would* count against the hypothesis, and it is precisely here where at least some faithful say, "nothing at all." It is this refusal that renders the utterance as empty as those horoscope predictions: "You may meet a stranger." This is not to say that horoscope predictions are *necessarily* non-falsifiable. A falsifiable prediction may have been formulated so: "Today you will form a new friendship with a twenty-three-year-old red-headed woman who knows how to play the violin." That's saying something; the former isn't.

If we say, "A rabbit exists," our finding a rabbit would verify the utterance and we need go no further. This isn't a counter to Popper's demand that we need to both verify and falsify a statement, for in this case, finding a rabbit does two things: it discounts any cases of not finding a rabbit (it falsifies any counter claim), as well as verifies the particular statement. That a single confirmation does the work of two criteria is exactly what we'd expect with particular statements. The non-falsifiability worry, then, comes with claims that cannot, in fact, be verified. Only those ones can't be falsified. So, all non-falsifiable particular statements will be false particulars. The fact that the falsifiability principle cannot support our belief in false particular statements strikes me as being a plus for the falsifiability principle.

(iv) If Hume is right, the claim that everything has a natural cause, is neither *a priori*, nor *a posteriori*. It is an inference that we make based on the best evidence, but at the same time it is an assumption that we rely on to defend our continuing to search for natural causes of various effects. The hypothesis, "God exists," is claimed to be similar. The similarity is strained, however. The differences are stark.

First off, the arguments for God being the best explanation are extremely weak. The evidence for naturally caused events tends to be strong. For example, the hypothesis, "Gee, that stray baseball must be what broke my window," can be replicated by throwing baseballs through windows. The claim, "It thunders because God is angry," cannot be replicated, since we do not have access to God's being angry: we only have access to thunder. Moreover, we can use the presumption that everything has a natural cause to predict things. "Gee, if I throw this baseball, I bet the window will break." But claims about God have no such predictive value. The hypothesis "God loves you," can't be used for anything. It tends to be maintained even if really bad things happen to you (recall Chapter 10). The claim, "Sally loves you," on the other hand, can be used for certain kinds of predictions. She will be happy at your happiness, she will be sad at your sadness, she will not intentionally run you over with her car. "God exists" is nothing like "every thing has a natural cause." Reliance on the former doesn't do anything. Reliance on the latter we can use. We can predict things with it. We can shape our world by assuming it. The presumption of God's existence does none of that.

After finding both the broken window and a strange baseball in my living room, I *could* instead assume that both appeared coincidentally together for no known natural causes. It might *look* as is if the baseball caused the window to break, but maybe the two are completely separate events. *This* kind of belief, this *denial* of the supposition that everything has a natural cause, is more like the rigid belief in "God exists." The cherished belief is simply superimposed over the evidence. The belief is held independently of any evidence, and this excessive tenacity is what makes the utterance empty.

Secondly, and more importantly, to say that, "Everything has a natural cause," is non-falsifiable, is to rely too heavily on Hume's analysis of induction. True, my not witnessing today the sun's rising tomorrow, means my claim, "The sun will rise tomorrow" is not itself a simple observation. But it is *based* on past observations, and if these are not allowed to count for anything, then there can be no distinction between good and poor inferences. Under Hume's analysis, my inferring that the sun will rise tomorrow based on countless reliable past observations is on a par with someone inferring that farmers wear plaid because they have seen a single farmer wear plaid. If we allow for induction, the claim "Everything has a natural cause" is more likely true given that everything we've ever witnessed had a natural cause, and that we have found no non-natural causes to date, though we may have found some causes unexplained. Given this background, the reasonable inference is that all things have natural causes. To disallow this move based on Hume's overly stringent criterion of "verify" is idle.

(v) Lastly, we come to the self-refuting charge levelled at the non-falsifiability criterion. A response similar to (ii) applies here as well. The non-falsifiability principle is the following: "*A posteriori* propositions ought to be falsifiable in principle." This proposition is not itself a descriptive *a posteriori* proposition. It is a normative principle governing *a posteriori* claims. This doesn't mean it can't be falsified. It does mean that the falsification process is different. For an analogy, consider the following two statements:

(1) Speeders ought to be ticketed.
(2) Speeders are ticketed.

The first is a normative claim. The second is a descriptive claim. Finding an unticketed speeder refutes (2) but not (1). Demanding that the discovery of an unticketed speeder ought also to refute (1) is to confuse levels of discourse. Saying this does not mean that we can only test descriptive claims, not normative ones. We do test normative claims: only what we're testing has to be unpacked first. Proposition (2) is confirmed or refuted by observation. We see speeders not ticketed, or we see speeders ticketed. Confirmatory observation also occurs in (1), but not directly. We cannot observe the ought. Rather, we need to understand the reasoning given for (1) first. Perhaps what we desire is safer driving conditions. And perhaps we believe that speeding increases accidents. So to decrease accidents, we should try to decrease speeding. To that end, we suggest ticketing speeders. Now each of these components of the ought statement can be falsified. Perhaps we don't want safer driving conditions, all things considered. Perhaps speed is not the main cause of accidents. Perhaps ticketing is not a way of reducing speed. While normative claims are not falsifiable the way descriptive claims are falsifiable, when the reasons are suitably specified, they are falsifiable just the same. Something similar may be said with the falsifiability criterion itself.

The falsifiability principle is an outcome of certain background assumptions, particularly the desire to hold warranted beliefs. If your goal is to have warranted beliefs, and it is impossible to have warranted beliefs of non-falsifiable *a posteriori* claims, then you ought to endorse the proposition: "*A posteriori* propositions ought to be falsifiable in principle." Just as it is possible one does not want safer driving conditions, one may not desire warranted beliefs. To the extent one doesn't, the falsifiable principle will not apply. It is not making a descriptive statement of fact. It is a normative utterance concerning how we ought to handle descriptive statements. The claim, "God exists," on the other hand, is not intended as a normative claim. It is intended as a descriptive statement about the world.

SUMMARY

The principle of non-falsifiability is intended as a way of distinguishing testable *a posteriori* claims from non-testable *a posteriori* claims. Non-testable *a posteriori* claims are deemed vacuous, in the sense that they convey nothing. One might as well have sneezed. Faith in God is often (perhaps very often) a non-testable *a posteriori* claim. If nothing is allowed to count against God's existence, saying "God exists," tells us nothing more than that you believe in God.

The standard complaints against the principle of non-falsifiability confuse practice with theory (i), or confuse *a priori* claims with *a posteriori* claims (ii), or confuse unspecified particular claims with specified particular claims (iii), or conceive of verification of any inference as impossible (iv), or confuse normative claims for descriptive claims (v). The claim "God exists," is an *a posteriori*, particular, descriptive claim, like "A bunny rabbit exists in the bushes," and thereby is non-vacuous only if we can understand what would show the claim to be false. So long as the faithful are unwilling to allow anything to show their claim to be false, they are not saying anything much at all. Flew's objection stands.

PART V. IMPLICATIONS

MYSTICISM

A mystical experience is often interpreted as an encounter with the divine or the sacred. Given that definition, if a mystical experience happened, then there must be something divine or sacred. Otherwise it could not have occurred. Mysticism, then, stands as testimony against atheism. Atheists need not deny mystical experiences, however.[1] Atheists need only point out the gap between the bare experience and the interpretation of that bare experience. Before I elaborate, let me review what is commonly said about mystical experiences.

COMMON COMPONENTS

Various scholars have examined diverse mystical reports across cultures and historical periods and have singled out a number of commonalities.[2] Such cataloguing portrays mysticism as an ineffable, ephemeral, life-changing experience of being one with the universe. Typically, mysticism is understood to reveal reality, not cloud reality. This means that what we normally take as reality, mere appearance, is now seen as a false front.

Ineffability
There is, foremost, an ineffability. The person who has had the mystical experience admits the difficulty in putting the experience into words. The experience transcends normal discourse, normal experience, normal dichotomies. Since language is dependent on those normal experiences and normal dichotomies, language is ill-equipped for the task.

Noeticism
William James claims that mystical experiences are noetic. That is, they arouse purely the intellect, not the emotions or the body. Martin Buber disagrees. They are essentially ineffable, and therefore cannot even count as noetic. For Buber, noeticism entails some kind of solution, but mystical

experiences are not solutions to intellectual conundrums. Mystics may feel "salvation," but not find a "solution."[3] For Buber, even calling the experience an "experience" is misleading. Rather, the mystic receives a presence.[4] And that presence permeates the perceiver, permeates the universe, permeates both seer and seen.

Union/Communion

A person having a mystical experience "sees" or "feels" or "comes to recognize" a communion or union with the universe. There are differences between whether mysticism is perceived as a union, or a communion, and I shall explore those differences below. But basically, a mystical experience is commonly recognized as involving a dissolution of subject and object, me-it relations, and everything is perceived as one unified whole.

Ephemerality

However wonderful, the mystical experience is ephemeral, or transient. The very act of recognizing that one is having a mystical experience is sufficient to kill it. It brings one's consciousness back into the mix, but mystical experiences are all about removing one's consciousness. This also explains why mystical experiences are ineffable; they occur beyond consciousness; and effability involves consciousness. Since consciousness is so hard to avoid in humans, the mystical moment is fleeting, and the "normal" world comes crashing back with all its dichotomies and segregations.

Appearance and Reality

Mysticism takes a stand on the reality-illusion dichotomy. What we take to be real is illusion. Mysticism provides a glimpse at the real reality. This is in contrast to materialist reductions: what you see is pretty much all there is — or, more guardedly, all you can ever claim to know.

Lasting Effect

Those who experience a mystical event tend to be deeply moved afterwards. Mere hallucinations or dreams, for example, however moving during the experience, do not move the experiencer after the fact. The experiencer recognizes the difference upon waking, and moves on with life. Not so those who have had a mystical experience. For them, they have had a glimpse at reality, and are no longer fooled by the "waking life."

Lesser Mysticism

Lastly, and perhaps more contentiously, is the prospect that mystical experiences have degrees.[5] Athletes periodically "get in the zone," and this depth of concentration may be described as a "baby" state of mysticism. During accidents, persons sometimes experience a slowing of time. In my case, a truck grill was coming at me at 120 kilometres an hour, but as I sat in the backseat of the spinning, out-of-control car, there was nothing I could do.

I braced myself, and waited. The scene occurred as if in slow motion. I felt peace and tranquility despite the full recognition of my imminent death. Once the car finally veered into the ditch, everything sped up faster than normal as if to try to recover from the rift in time. Then I was in shock from the excess adrenaline, like being hung over after too much stimulus. Such phenomenological descriptions of accidents are common.[6] Such adrenaline states may be a preliminary form of mysticism. (For more on brain states, see Chapter 24.) And sometimes persons, for whatever reason, simply "space out." They stare off in space and are unreceptive to being called, or tapped on the shoulder. Nor are they in deep concentration. They cannot say that they were thinking of anything at all. They are in a no-mind state, almost a trance. Again, this sense of consciousness removal may be at least one of the preliminary stages of mystical experience. Similarly, those experiencing sensory deprivation, or those on certain hallucinogenic drugs, just as much as those meditating, may all be experiencing varying degrees of mysticism.

These are the usual traits noted by the experts. Let's examine some of them a bit more closely.

CONTENT

The content of a mystical experience tends to be described either as a union with the divine, or as a communion with the divine. The difference may appear subtle, but the former veers from standard religious tenets. If I am in union with God, then I too am God. For some theists, such a sentiment is sacrilegious, although perfectly consistent with Zen Buddhism.[7] Others describe the ecstatic state not as a union with the divine, but a communion. Independently of the sacrilegious component, the other distinction in the union-communion debate concerns personal identity. Those who describe their mystical experience as a communion with the divine maintain their personal identity. There is an experience that happens to *them*. Admittedly, they are transformed. They are born again. They are renewed, yet still remain themselves. On the union side, even personal identity is transcended. Above I said, "I too am God," but this presupposes that there is still an "I." The notion of an "I" belongs in the dichotomous world left behind.

Rudolph Otto maintains that there is another distinction to be made within the union camp. Some mystical experiences are introversions, whereas others are extroversions. For introverts, the facade of the universe dissolves along with the experiencer. You dissolve. The universe dissolves. What is left? Absolute nothingness. For an extrovert, on the other hand, the universe and the self cohere as one. The ocean is you; you are the ocean. One does not experience nothingness. Rather, everything is one. In

Martin Buber's terminology, there are "neither things nor beings, neither earth nor heaven — but everything is included in the relationship."[8]

Thus, variations in mystical content may be put in terms of number: zero, one, or two. Eastern accounts of mystical experience tend to be of the union type: either zero or one. Western accounts of mystical experiences tend to be two: a communion between self and the divine. This distinction is important. We can wonder, are the three kinds of mystical experiences different, or are they fundamentally the same? If they are different, is one better, more advanced, than the other? After all, if going from a diverse number of things to two is an improvement, wouldn't the higher step be to go to one; and then to go to zero? Or — and what I take to be more likely — are they really the same experience and the only difference occurs in the cultural interpretation imposed on it after the experience? If this latter is the answer, the existence of mystical experience is hardly a concern for atheists. Atheists need only deny that the experience is a union or a communion with a real divine. Rather, it is a neurological phenomenon that can happen to anyone and is no more informative than a random dream, or tea leaf residue. That is, we have an experience, and our culture partly determines how we best interpret that experience.[9] Admitting the role of interpretation undermines the claim that mysticism is evidence against atheism.

METHOD

There is some dispute over how to properly achieve a mystical experience. Some suggest it may happen spontaneously; others suggest that it can happen only through proper rituals. What counts as a proper ritual itself will vary. Some suggest that drug use can count, while others firmly denounce the idea. Concerning whether drugs can offer a door to the mystical realm, there are three possible answers. (i) No. Drugs cause hallucinations, not access to reality. The drug state is purely subjective, not so mystical states. (ii) Yes. Both give access to the "other" realm. The other realm is a reality hidden by our normal perceptions, and any way of escaping our normal perceptions will provide a window to the other realm — whether through religious training, secular meditation, or a quick chemical fix. (iii) Yes, but not because both give access to a real state, but because both are simply subjective states of mind. The difficulty with option (i) is that the reports of non-drug induced mystical states seem pretty similar to reports of drug-induced states.[10] To call one subjective and the other not cannot be based on the evidence. It would seem to be simply a bias. For example, Copleston rejects the notion that drugs can be an avenue to mysticism, since only the mystical state, not the drug state, brings with it a sense that what one is experiencing is objective.[11] Contrary to Copleston's belief, however, those who take drugs claim that there is very much the sense that what one is experiencing is objective. Drug states, like mystical states, carry with them their own reality: a reality that is described in remarkably similar ways as non-drug mystical experiences. Perhaps, then, a mystical state is like a magic eye poster. At first look, a magic eye poster is simply a lot of abstract squiggly lines, but looked at in the right way, a three-dimensional image appears. Some seem to see the three-dimensional image right away, without any preliminaries. Others seem to need some sort of guidance: "Stare at this spot for ten seconds." Some can see it while on drugs; others cannot. And then there are a few, like me, who seem unable to see the three-dimensional image no matter how hard they try.[12]

At least with a three-dimensional image, we can compare responses. If someone on drugs stares into the magic eye poster and sees a spaceship, while a sober person sees, instead, a tall ship, we might suggest that drug ingestion is not a good method for magic eye poster viewing. But if they both see the same thing, then *how* one comes about seeing the three-dimensional image becomes less relevant. Whether one sees the image by using drugs, or by staring, or by chanting first is irrelevant to whether or not one sees the objective image lurking beneath the abstract swirls. With mystical experiences, however, it is not quite so easy to solve. For it is not that one finally "sees" an object. What one experiences in a mystical event is difficult to put into words. As ineffable, it transcends words. As a result, one may protest that if one had a mystical experience the wrong way, one is not having a *genuine* mystical experience. One is having some other sort of experience; but not the real deal.

If you seem to have had a mystical experience and someone tells you that you did not because you did not take the right steps beforehand, or, conversely, that you did not renounce your previous way of life afterward, how can you respond to this charge if you believe it to be wrong? Unlike the magic eye poster, you cannot say, "But I saw the tall ship. It had three masts. The waves had white caps." And then they could say, "No, the water was calm, and there were five masts." Or if you say, "But the universe was me, and I the universe, and all was one," and they say, "Yes, you say that, but did you really *feel* it. It's not there in your eyes." You would feel that these are fairly subjective charges. Even if they were right, how could they know? Wouldn't that be like their telling you what you really dreamed about last night, despite your assertions to the contrary?

To say, "You cannot have had a genuine mystical experience if you remained an atheist," is, to use Chapter 20's terminology, non-falsifiable. The counter evidence (an atheist having a mystical experience) is ruled out *in principle*.

SELF-CONFIRMING

How can we know that reports of mystical experience are to be treated differently from illusions, delusions, and hallucinations? Why give mystical reports any credence at all? One answer is that, mystical events carry with them their own self-confirmation.[13] Of course, so too do illusions, delusions, and the like. One could not be deluded if, while being deluded, one knew it was mere delusion. Nevertheless, many mystics cite the experience itself as self-confirming. Bertrand Russell warned us about such things.[14] We can never judge the truth of a belief by the belief itself. The fact that you believe X can never be what makes X true, if it is true. All that can be said is that it is true that you believe X. Presumably, *that* is not in question. What is in question is whether what you believe is likely to be true or not. We can never judge veracity of an internal state by that very internal state alone.

To elucidate, Russell makes a distinction between two sorts of knowledge claims: (a) *knowledge by acquaintance*; and (b) *knowledge by description*. Knowledge by acquaintance is an awareness of an internal subjective state: "I am in pain"; "I am nauseous"; "I am in love"; "I believe in God." These things are true merely on the grounds of their being so experienced as true. But knowledge by description is knowledge of the external world, and is not true or false merely on the grounds of one's internal state. Despite my belief that *P*, the truth of the matter may well be not-*P*. Thus, while it may be true that Thomas believes that God exists (knowledge by acquaintance), it doesn't follow that therefore Thomas holds a true belief (knowledge by description).

Given the above, to speak of the certainty and self-authentication of mystical states is merely to speak in the realm of knowledge by acquaintance. We need not doubt that the speaker believes she has experienced a mystical state. Our real question is not answered by acquiescing to that. What we want to know is whether the mystical experience has any relation to how the world really is. And to believe it does *ipso facto* is to illegitimately move from knowledge by acquaintance to knowledge by description. That one experiences what one interprets as divine can never by itself legitimate the divine, any more than an experience of a mirage fifty yards away legitimates the existence of water fifty yards away.

William James, by the way, admitted as much. He concluded that mystical experiences seemed veridical for the persons experiencing them (i.e., knowledge by acquaintance), but could not be authoritative for outsiders (i.e., knowledge by description). James didn't stop there, however. He speculated that it "must always be an open question whether mystical states are windows to a more extensive and inclusive world."[15] But this is a bizarre inference. It would seem to make sense only if we presuppose the legitimacy of a divinity accessible through mysticism. But we were supposed to be led to this belief by examining something about mystical experiences themselves. What we find, instead, is simply this self-confirming certainty of those experiencing it. To follow James's inference would commit us to give credence to all sorts of illusions, delusions, and hallucinations, since they, too, carry with them their own self-confirming bias. As noted earlier, those deluded do not believe that they're deluded; otherwise they would not be deluded.

JUDGING BY THE EFFECTS

One answer to the above worry is to note that those who have had mystical experiences change their lives. Those who have been merely duped by hallucinogens, illusions, or delusions do not (usually) alter their lives because of the experiences. Thus Copleston, for example, suggests that we can judge the veracity of the experience by its effects: "[W]hen you get an experience that results in an overflow of dynamic and creative love, the best explanation of that ... is the actual existence of an objective cause of the experience."[16]

But this stretches things. For one, that people change their lives due to their having had a mystical experience shows merely that they were genuinely affected by the mystical experience. We need not doubt that. This doesn't show that the experience was veridical.[17] It shows merely that they think it real. Again, we needn't doubt that. Those convinced of being abducted by aliens change their lives too. They don't relish being branded as "crazy," yet they feel compelled to tell and retell their story. If we are allowed to determine the veracity of events by how much they changed a person's life, then alien abductions should be accepted as fact. Moreover, it is not the case that all persons who have had mystical experiences have altered their lives. That it happened to St. Francis of Assisi or to Mother Teresa is not informative. That it happened to a large number of people is not informative. One would have to conclusively show that it happened to all persons having a mystical experience. The danger here is that one (Copleston, for example) simply *defines* a genuine mystical experience as one which alters the experiencer. If your life was not altered by the experience, then that experience was not genuinely mystical. But now the argument has collapsed upon itself. If a genuine mystical experience is defined as one in which the experiencer alters her life, we have ruled out, *a priori*, the possibility of having the experience without the life-changing effect.[18] But then the emphasis on effect is merely a definitional ploy. It cannot count as empirical evidence.

CONCLUSION

Mystics claim that the mystical state gets at the *real* reality that lies beyond the penumbra of appearance. Part of the appeal of such a claim is that under normal psycho-physical states, we confront a gap between the appearance of reality and reality. I see what appears to be a rock, but is the rock really as it appears to me? I can never know, since all I can go by is what the rock appears to me to be. The rock-as-it-appears-to-me and the rock-as-it-really-is may be perfectly aligned (we assume so, naturally), but we can never *know* whether that's so. If normal perception can fool us, it is possible that an altered perception may bridge the gap, that we may see things as they really are. This is the role of mysticism: to bridge the gap between appearance and reality. Unfortunately, such an argument doesn't go far enough. Mysticism is itself a perceptual stance, and as a perceptual stance, it confronts the same appearance-reality gap. If one doubts that normal perception gets at reality, why should one believe that an altered perception gets at reality any better? We simply exchange one matrix for another.

Mystical experiences may be no more than psycho-physical states. This is more easily admitted if we accept James's claim about lesser mystical events. But as psycho-physical states, there is nothing necessarily revealing about a *real* reality beyond the reality perceived under normal psycho-physical states. In other words, atheists can accept mystical experiences without thereby believing in some sort of god, let alone believing in anything supernatural.

22

———— ∞ ————

GOD AND MORALITY

It is common to believe that a world without God is a world without morality.[1] As the saying goes, "If God is dead, everything is permissible."[2] Such a sentiment can backfire, however. Since we do have morality, therefore we do have a god. This is a looser rendition of Kant's and Aquinas's argument visited in Chapter 9, and is as inadequate, but for different reasons.

Notice that in the moral argument (Chapter 9), the critique against Kant entailed denying that there exists a *summum bonum*.[3] Similarly, one might be tempted to deny that there exists a morality. Those who deny the existence of morality are called nihilists. But an atheist need not be a nihilist. Importantly, one can reject the existence of a *summum bonum* without rejecting the notion of morality.[4] The argument in this chapter is to express why we can accept a morality without accepting the existence of a god. Morality and God are completely independent subject matters. Talk of one has no bearing on talk of the other. So I shall argue.

MORAL PRINCIPLES

Let's say that I'm one of those people who do not want to do anything immoral. And you tell me that doing X is immoral. I may still do X. This isn't because I lied about not wanting to do immoral things. Rather, it's because I may disagree with your version of what's immoral. Apart from your telling me what's moral and what's immoral, you have to justify your distinctions in terms that I can reasonably endorse. Given disparate religions, and different religious interpretations within religions, it would be better if the appeal to moral restraint could be resolved without needing to defend one's metaphysical conceptions. In other words, it is more likely that we can universally agree that torturing children for fun is a bad thing to do without needing to agree on which religious interpretation is the correct one, or which religion is the correct one, or whether any religion is correct. But if competing theists and atheists alike can all see that torturing children for fun is immoral, then the recognition of immorality is independent of religious dogma.

Besides, appealing to God in resolving moral disputes is ineffective. Perhaps you are opposed to murder because one of the ten commandments tells you so. What kind of a reason is that? It might be fine for the non-autonomous, but are we really afraid that we can find no reason to forbid murder unless we are told by some authority not to murder? Shouldn't we be given more credit than that? After all, assuming God exists, one would expect that such a being would give the commandment against murder for a reason, and it shouldn't be that hard to figure out what that reason likely is. Presumably it has something to do with violating the principle of not doing stuff to others without their consent.[5] Alternatively, it might be: Don't do that which would undermine society if everyone does it. We — or non-masochists, anyway — could even agree on a negative version of the golden rule: *All else being equal, don't do to others what you would not like done to yourself.* Agreeing on a moral rule that is proclaimed in a religious text doesn't show that God is necessary for morality. Atheists need not reject everything that religions say; only the main tenet that there exists a metaphysical being who has the attributes that religions associate with God. People may differ as to what the underlying reason should be, but the point here is that a theist and an atheist can engage in a moral discussion at this level without ever having to come to an agreement on whether God exists, let alone what the best interpretation of God's will is.

This is the main point of what is referred to as the *Euthyphro argument*, named after Plato's dialogue, "Euthyphro."[6]

THE EUTHYPHRO ARGUMENT

Euthyphro is on his way to prosecute his father for murder. It turns out that one of their labourers got drunk and slit the throat of one of their domestics. The father bound the drunken murderer and tossed him in a ditch to remain there until the authorities arrived. Unfortunately, the drunken labourer died while in the ditch. (It is unclear to me how long he remained in the ditch: a couple of hours, overnight, a couple of days, a week?) In any event, Socrates was surprised that Euthyphro would accuse his father of being a "murderer" under these circumstances, let alone prosecute his father even if he did deem him a murderer. Euthyphro defends his actions by saying that he knows what is pious, what is holy, and what is just. That must be grand, thinks Socrates, to understand something so important. Perhaps Euthyphro could enlighten humble Socrates. Euthyphro says that is easy to do: "What is pleasing to the gods is holy, and what is not pleasing to them is unholy."[7] This is the reasoning ethical theists use when they claim that what is moral is what God loves, and what is immoral is what

God hates. All very nice, so long as we know what God loves and what God hates. If we know that, we'll be on the right track. Alas, how could mere mortals know such matters? But this isn't the worry that Socrates raises. He goes deeper. Even if we all agree on what God loves and what God despises, a problem remains.

To paraphrase that problem, Socrates asks Euthyphro, "Is murder immoral because God hates it, or does God hate murder because it is immoral?" Such a question annoys Euthyphro who believes Socrates is saying something bad about gods. But the question simply reveals that talk of God is irrelevant to talk of morality, not that God does not exist. This is an important distinction. Of course in this book the arguments are against the existence of God, but the moral argument is maintaining that God exists *because* morality exists, and to defeat that argument, it does no good to point out that God does not exist (a premise that theists won't accept) and nor need we hold the untenable position that morality does not exist. Instead, the argument is defused if we show merely that there is no necessary connection between God's existence and morality, and that is what the Euthyphro problem reveals. Let's clarify why.

First off, we may note that God either exists or doesn't exist. There is no other option. Meanwhile, morality either exists or doesn't. Thus, we have four possible states of affairs: (a) God exists and morality exists; (b) God exists and morality doesn't exist; (c) God doesn't exist but morality exists; and (d) neither God nor morality exist. If options (b), (c), and (d) are true, then of course the moral argument will fail to show that God exists. The moral argument for God's existence requires condition (a). The Euthyphro argument reveals that even if (a) holds, the moral argument would *still* fail. Let's see why.

Socrates's question reveals a dichotomy. It would appear that either: (i) God created morality, or; (ii) God merely abides by morality. If God merely abides by morality, then there is a problem for religion. God was supposed to have created everything. If He didn't create morality, this would be peculiar. And if God didn't create morality, then of course morality is justifiably divorced from talk of God. So option (ii) is not favourable to the moral argument for God's existence.

That's why option (i) is usually deemed preferable. But if God created morality, a further dilemma awaits us. Either (i.a), God created morality for no reason at all, or (i.b), for some reason. Choosing (i.a) entails that moral rules are arbitrary. Our morality happens to say, "Don't murder people." Perhaps God could have said, "Don't ride bicycles," or as in Deut. 22:11, "Don't wear a garment made of linen and wool." These are absurd if taken as moral rules, obviously. But why are they absurd? It wouldn't be absurd by proponents of (i.a) for (i.a) implies that the only reason that X is moral is because God says so. Asking why God said so is totally irrelevant. Therefore, we would not be able to make any moral distinction between any of God's decrees. Eating fish on Friday, say, is on a par with killing people for fun on Thursday. Understanding this implication makes God a bully, and morality totally arbitrary.

Under (i.a) God punishes those who disobey His rules, yet He imposes such rules arbitrarily. If *this* is your picture of morality, nothing more than a whim imposed by a bully, then that kind of morality would dissolve once the bully dissolved. If the bully demands that you hand over your lunch money, you have to hand over your lunch money. There is no other reason to hand over your lunch money to the bully except that he demands it and threatens you with some sort of punishment should you fail to comply. That is why, if you remove the bully, you remove the need to hand over your lunch money. Apart from the presence of the bully himself, there is no other reason to comply with the dictate. But moral rules are not typically thought of that way. We believe that we have reasons to be moral *even if we won't be punished by someone for disobeying them.* But version (i.a) cannot get at this aspect of morality. It is not surprising, therefore, that version (i.a) is neither palatable to God, nor to morality. Surely, God is not a bully, and surely, morality is not arbitrary.

That is why (i.b) seems the preferable option. We like to imagine that the rule against murder, say, is not arbitrary. We like to presume that there is an underlying reason behind that moral dictate: a reason that, if we knew about it, would make sense to us. And this returns us to my point above. Even accepting that God exists and created morality, that would not mean that morality would pass out of existence if God happened to die, or never existed. This is because God created morality for a reason, and presumably that reason would remain whether or not God remained.

The only way this conclusion could be challenged is to suppose that the *reason* would die along with God. But there is no justification to suppose this. Let's imagine God decrees assault to be immoral because it causes pain to the assaulted. If God dies, we would not imagine pain to die along with God. The assaulted will still feel pain whether God is dead or not. Pain and causes of pain will still exist whether or not God does. If moral rules are guides to help reduce pain (at least minimally) then those rules would still make sense whether or not God exists.

In other words, whether God exists or doesn't, and whether God created morality or didn't, we would still have a reason to create and abide by moral rules if merely to help reduce pain. If God created X for a reason, and that reason still applies, we have a reason to create X even if God were to have died, or had abandoned us, or never did create X. It is no problem for atheists to accept that if God did exist, He would have created morality. But this doesn't mean that He did. It only means that we recognize that it is reasonable to create a morality, whether God created it or not.

Once we adopt (i.b) then, we admit that there must be a reason for God's choosing these particular moral rules. And once we emphasize these reasons, or principles, nothing prevents an atheist from accepting those principles — as long as they really do count as reasons to be moral. That is why atheists needn't deny morality when they deny God's existence. They can still see that living in a society that forbids murder, rape, assault, and theft, say, would generally be better than living in a society without such restrictions. This is so even if you think that morality is more than mere restrictions against assault (that it also has something to say about charity, say), so long as you think that rules against assault are a necessary part of morality. After all, whatever it is that you want to do, including being charitable, you're more able to do it without a knife in your back.[8] One needn't believe in a god to believe the truth of this.

The moral argument for God's existence fails if we select option (i.b). There is no necessary connection between believing in the merits of morality and believing in God. Therefore, if God is dead, it would not follow that everything is permissible, since permissibility may simply be a social convention that we find useful to impose. Our interest in the question, "Why be moral?" goes beyond the answer: "Because God says so," for we still want to know, *why* He said so.

What follows from the Euthyphro argument is that the moral argument for God's existence requires our accepting (i.a). That is, we would have to conceive of morality as a set of arbitrary demands of a bully God. If you don't conceive of God as a bully — and few, if any, do — this shows that morality cannot be a mere dictate of God. But only if you think morality is dependent on God in this arbitrary way would morality disappear at the disappearance of God, just as the reason to adhere to a bully's whim would disappear at the disappearance of the bully. Precisely because we find (i.a) untenable (i.e., God is not a bully), we find that God is not needed for morality — that morality is independent of belief in God. Choosing option (i.b) recognizes that God is not a bully, and that God imposes moral strictures for non-arbitrary reasons. And as soon as we admit that, we recognize that those reasons should remain whether or not God does. We accept morality because we believe that life under a moral structure is better than life under an amoral structure. We accept the cost of abiding by morality for the benefits that a moral system can provide us: minimally, peace and security.

INNATE MORALITY?

The Euthyphro argument is sometimes condensed to the simple observation that not all atheists are immoral, and therefore we don't have to believe in God to be moral. I hope a review of the argument above shows that this simplifies matters too much. Someone may insist that even atheists are children of God and thereby have embossed in their souls the distinction between right and wrong.[9] The Euthyphro argument, in other words, shows only that atheists can be moral (or simulate morality), but it doesn't show that morality is not from, nor dependent on, God. In other words, atheists may do the right thing, not because of their post-hoc rationalizations, but because God still guides their hands whether or not they know it.

For this sort of argument to work, it must be demonstrated that morality is the kind of thing that is writ in our souls, and is so writ whether or not we recognize it. A variety of interpretations are possible concerning what it means for morality to be embossed in our souls in this matter. Teasing these apart will reveal that thinking morality is innate is a useless idea.

Consider first the distinction between thought and action. If anything is innate (and I make no such claim), grasping or sucking reflexes should count. Minimally, then, talk of innate traits fits with action, not thought. But moral action is not innate in the way that reflex actions are innate. Reflex actions are pretty universal and happen without reflection, whereas there are too many immoral actions by too many normal people, and many moral actions occur after reflection, not without reflection. One may try to save innate morality by speaking, instead, of an innate *disposition* to act morally. A natural impulse, say, always moves us in the right direction, but selfish interests sometimes get in the way and prevent us from doing the right thing. This explains both the reflection and the lack of universal action without abandoning the concept that a moral sense is innate. In many cases, however, moral phenomena seem to go in the opposite direction: I have an urge to steal, to strike, to harm, and through reflection come to decide that I had better not. To say that sometimes I have natural moral tendencies is not saying that I have no natural immoral tendencies. This shows that to determine whether a particular tendency is moral or not, I can't appeal merely to the fact that I have the tendency. Morality is an ascription that we make *about* our natural tendencies. Tendency to aggress: bad. Tendency to be kind: good. But to determine that one tendency is good, another bad, is to appeal to something other than the mere tendency itself. Moral sense is not something that is revealed by simply looking at our natural tendencies. It is not a matter of navel-gazing.

One can try to save the matter by saying that most normal humans have at least the capacity to make moral decisions and from this infer that moral capacity must be innate. But we also have the capacity to kill, to steal, to assault, to harm, so that too must be innate. But if capacities to be moral are innate alongside capacities to be immoral, the concept of "innate" does nothing.

In fact, this has long been recognized in the philosophy of biology. Take the pink colour of flamingos. This seems to be "innate," since pinkness is both species specific and universal among flamingos. But it turns out that the pinkness is due to an alpha- and beta-carotene rich diet.[10] If the trait is due to diet (like obesity, say), it seems a stretch to call it innate. One might suggest that the trait to have that diet is innate, or that the trait that such a diet has such an effect may be innate, but then the concept of "innate" amounts to being a trait that is relatively insensitive to variations in the environment that do not affect it.[11] To avoid such platitudes, biologists avoid the term entirely. Instead, they speak of canalization, or species-specific traits, or generative entrenchment, or genetic traits, or common environmental effects, etc.[12]

To think of morality as innate in terms of behaviour is out, then. What about understanding knowledge of right and wrong as being innate? Is the knowledge of good and evil etched in the epistemic portion of our brains? We supposedly ate the fruit from the tree of knowledge of good and evil, after all (Gen. 2:17, 3:6). Thinking of moral knowledge as innate, however, is ambiguous and teasing apart the various interpretations reveals that the concept is too muddled to be of any use. Consider the following three claims:

(a) We know only that X is wrong. We don't know why X is deemed wrong, nor do we necessarily endorse the view that X is wrong.

(b) We know that X is wrong, and we know the reason for X being wrong, but we don't necessarily endorse that reason.

(c) We know that X is wrong, and we know the reason why X is wrong, and we endorse that reason.

Only (c) is a true ascription of moral agency, presumably. We don't think of moral agents as being simple rule-followers. Moral agency isn't merely following the rules. Moral agents follow the right rules *for the right reason.* Knowing the right reason, they are also able to reflect on whether stated rules are in fact moral. Merely because society tells you that you morally ought to catch and return runaway slaves, for example, doesn't necessarily mean that that society is giving us a *moral* rule, at all. Mere rule-followers may often do actions that moral agents do, but they will also be more likely to turn in runaway slaves.

For our assessment of "moral," agents must not only know the rules and the reasons for those rules, but *endorse* those (right) reasons. This is what differentiates the (c) group from the (b) group. If one doesn't endorse the reasons to be moral, one won't likely be moral, and the "knowledge" will be useless. Consider, for example, a recreational golfer who, while knowing she ought not to improve the lie of her ball before she hits it (when not on the tee or green), improves her lie just the same, even unabashedly so. Her knowing the rules and the reasons for the rules doesn't impact her adhering to the rules. Mere knowledge doesn't translate into action.

When we speak of someone who is moral, we don't mean to imply that the person knows the rules and knows the reasons for the rules, but isn't motivated by those reasons. So when we speak of moral agency, we mean to invoke situation (c). To return to our theme, no one will say that morality is innate in sense (c). Not everyone is motivated to be moral, and even fewer are moral all the time.

And when people invoke innate morality, they also don't mean it in sense (b). People argue all the time about the reasons to be moral. Even when we agree that murder is wrong, there is little agreement on *why* murder is wrong. Kantians appeal to deontological reasons, utilitarians offer teleological accounts, virtue theorists suggest that to be so motivated to murder is a symptom of deviation from mental well-being. Contractarians suggest that it is unlikely that a reasonable person would, under normal circumstances, agree to be murdered. Countless other accounts may be offered. My point is not to say which is the right view, but to point out that the long-standing disagreement on what the right view is makes it highly improbable that knowledge, in sense (b), is innate.

The above said, it is questionable whether anyone actually would satisfy sense (b). To *know* the reason for saying that X is immoral should also entail being motivated to not do X ... so long as the reasons apply in the case at hand. Take speeding. If the reason against speeding is the increase in odds of accidents to speeders, then, so long as you don't like accidents, you ought to be motivated not to speed. To speed anyway is either because you don't think that the odds are high enough, or you think that the odds don't take into account variance in types of speeders. Perhaps only reckless speeders get into accidents and you don't deem yourself reckless. Or accidents to speeders occur only in bad weather, or in heavy traffic, or on dangerous roads, but the weather is fine, there is no traffic, and the roads are in good condition. If you happen to be wrong about any of these suppositions (perhaps speed-accident correlation studies have controlled for these factors in their calculations, or speeders always assume that they're the exception), then it can't be correct that you *know* the reasons. You are ignorant about important details. Conversely, if you do know the reasons and yet speed, then you interpret the rule "Don't speed!" as simply shorthand for "Don't speed so long as the following conditions apply ...," none of which in fact apply in your case. If this is your situation, then you aren't in fact violating the rule, nor are you unmotivated by the reasons, since your reasons for speeding are not in discord with the reasons against speeding. Either way, it wouldn't be correct to say that you fit in option (b).

Something similar may be said about the prudential appeal to your own self-interest in telling you not to cause harm to another. Let's say that you know that you ought not to harm Billy, and you know that the reason has something to do with Billy's not liking that. You can still be indifferent to that reason. You might say it is precisely the fact that Billy doesn't like being harmed that motivates you to harm him. That you want to harm him entails that you don't want him to like it. That's partly the point. As put, you seem to be in situation (b). But is the reason not to harm Billy merely that Billy will be harmed and not like it? Most moral theories would say that's only a piece of the reason.[13] A continuing piece of the reason is that, precisely because Billy will not like being harmed, he will likely retaliate, now or later, with the help of others or with weapons, and his retaliation may be to cause the same degree or a worse degree of harm to you. If this is so, the short-term gain you get from harming Billy is outweighed by the long-term cost to you — either by being harmed in the end, or by expending energy to avoid being harmed by Billy, or by being boycotted from otherwise cooperative enterprises by others who now fear you. By this sort of calculation, it isn't that your selfishness prevents you from being moral, but, in Bishop Butler's terms, *you aren't being selfish enough!*[14] That is to say, you haven't worked things through fully. So here would be another case where, despite initial appearances, you aren't in case (b). You are rather in a state between (a) and (b), namely:

> (d) You know that X is immoral, you have a faulty or
>   incomplete knowledge of the reason for why X is
>   deemed immoral, and you are not moved by that faulty
>   or incomplete reason.

Despite my doubts about option (b) being a live option, the important point is that option (b) is not the kind of state that anyone would claim is innate, let alone option (d).

This leaves us with sense (a). But notice that sense (a) is a far cry from what we normally mean by moral agency (sense (c)). Even if we grant that moral knowledge of type (a) is innate, it is hardly sufficient to link innate knowledge to our thick sense of morality (c). An innate moral sense is more likely the thinner the moral sense is claimed to be. But the thinner the moral sense is claimed to be, the more useless the appeal to such a sense is. If both Hitler and Ghandi had the same God-given moral sense, *such* a moral sense would not be what we normally mean by a moral sense, and nor could it count as even a root of our moral sense.

Ignoring the above, innate knowledge of right and wrong — even in the thin sense (a) — is far from plausible. In clear-cut cases, like "Murder is wrong," articulate individuals are likely to agree. Although mere agreement is not sufficient for claiming innateness, there is far less agreement on the muddier cases: abortion, euthanasia, same-sex marriage, capital punishment, stem cell research, or whether one ought to rob the rich to pay the poor.

To recap, if there is any plausible account of the knowledge of right and wrong being innate, or writ on our souls by God, it cannot include the knowledge of *why* something is wrong or something is right. A child may have seen that the answer to question five on the exam is "17," and so responds "17" to question five, but few would say that the child therefore *knows* the answer to question five. If we really *know* the difference between right and wrong, we know the reasons. This returns us to the Euthyphro problem.

SIN AND MORAL INTUITION

Another problem with linking moral sense with a God-given innate trait concerns sin. If morality were innate in sense (c), explaining sin would be nigh impossible. It is much simpler to explain sin if morality is innate in sense (a). The easier it is to allow for sin, however, the more useless such an innate moral trait is. Two common rejoinders are typically offered. The first is that only some people are, by the grace of God, given the requisite moral sense. The second is that, although we all have a moral sense originally, some of us lose it along the way. A problem with the first option is that moral blame would be unjust. It would not be my fault to sin if I have not been graced by God with an internal instinct not to sin. Nor can my not being graced be explained by my sinning nature, since I wasn't graced to begin with. We don't say it is a deaf person's fault for failing to return your "Hello."

The problem with the second solution concerns why we would ever lose that initial sense of knowing right from wrong. Again, it can't be due to sin, for I wouldn't sin while I have the proper sense of right and wrong. Conversely, if my sense of right and wrong that I had originally was too weak to actually prevent me from going wrong, it could hardly count as being much help. This last worry is what Augustine tried to avoid, though poorly. God is supposed to be perfect, and so everything God creates should be perfect. An imperfect creation entails an imperfect creator. But humans sin. Sin is a sign of imperfection. It does no good to resolve the problem by saying, as Augustine did, that, "Well, sin is caused by humans, not God."[15] This doesn't work since humans are created by God — a supposedly perfect creator. But a creator of imperfect products cannot be a perfect creator.

Aquinas did slightly better by highlighting that humans are as perfect as they can be given that they have free will. But since they have free will, they may periodically choose wrongly: i.e., sin.[16] In this way, God remains a perfect creator, since humans are perfect, while sin is nevertheless possible. If we take the free will argument seriously, however, we cannot hope to imagine that God has embossed our souls with the concept of morality *as an instinctive action* without having to explain why we would so often veer from such action. Nor does it help if it is *knowledge* of right and wrong with which our souls are embossed, since such knowledge must be entirely insufficient. To avoid these charges, Aquinas claimed that it is not knowledge of right and wrong with which our souls are embossed, merely the capacity to learn right from wrong.[17] But saying this isn't saying much of anything. After all, we also have the capacity to murder, to debate on what even counts as right and wrong. Pointing out that we all have a capacity to be moral is as useless as saying that we all have the capacity to play the tuba.

To appeal to a knowledge of right and wrong, something other than "Do X!" is needed. The reason for doing X needs to be provided, and this reason needs to be endorsed by the agent. Presumably, the reason to be moral will have something to do with our recognition that some of our choices cause more suffering than others, and that we would do better in a world where we try to minimize the suffering. And if the rules that fall out of that consideration are roughly what we call morality, then adhering to a moral system is perhaps the best way that we have of achieving a reduction of suffering without undermining the free will God purportedly gave us. Morality, then, is a constraint on our freedom, but a constraint that we each (under normal conditions) have reason to endorse. If we didn't, the prospect of our being moral would be in serious doubt. Those reasons remain whether or not God exists. In other words, Aquinas's answer brings us back to the Euthyphro problem. The hope of avoiding the Euthyphro problem by appeal to some innate morality fails.

To say a trait, either skin colour or moral sense, is innate is to stop looking for an explanation. Why do we think murder wrong, and charity good? If "the belief is innate" is the best that you can do, you aren't even trying. This lack of trying, this absence of curiosity, is at the root of the Euthyphro problem. We might as well say, "Murder is intuitively wrong for those of us under conditions which lead us to so think."

STRATEGIC INTERACTION

At the outset of this chapter, I claimed that God is totally irrelevant to morality. In one sense, this may be false. It is common to claim of God that He is omniscient.[18] But knowing that a sock is in a box, or how many hairs you have is not really the kind of knowledge that matters to anyone. If omniscience can be applied to gods universally, it can only be a subset of omniscience: namely, *strategic* knowledge.[19] Strategic knowledge is the sort of knowledge that you have about other people's actions and thoughts and feelings. Thus, in a chess game, if I know that you like to move your queen out early, I can exploit that. If I know that you are trustworthy, I can rely on you to look after my child. If I know that you are a thief, I will not leave my jewels lying around in your presence. These are valuable bits of knowledge that I can have of you. But my knowing how many hairs are on your head is not.

It should not be surprising to recognize that morality is based on strategic information. By strategic, I don't mean to imply that morality is like bluffing in poker. Being strategic is not to be thought of as being "sly," for example. Morality is not a zero-sum competition, where every winner entails a loser. Quite the opposite is meant. Morality provides an opportunity for mutual benefit, an opportunity that selfish immoral sorts miss out on (generally, and over the long haul, but such odds are good enough to favour the continuance of morality over immorality or amorality). Strategic choice is to be contrasted with parametric choice. A parametric choice is one in which your actions directly determine your outcomes. A strategic choice occurs when your actions influence, but do not determine, outcomes. Instead, other people's actions play an integral part in your outcomes. Whenever people cooperate, are involved in an enterprise together, where individual actions can alter the cooperative dividend, their actions are strategic. This dynamic interaction is all that the term "strategic" means to invoke here.[20]

Let's say I have a reputation for being trustworthy. Therefore, you will more likely enter into some agreement with me, expecting me to uphold my end of the bargain. Cooperation can bring mutual benefit. Defection brings the defector greater benefit, mind you, but typically only in the short run. Defectors (generally) get a reputation for being defectors, and thereby lose out on future interactions that only cooperators are privy to. That we label people defector or cooperator is due to our not wanting to be cheated. Defectors gain at the expense of the cheated, and no one wants to be cheated. Since we each want to avoid being cheated, avoid being labelled a defector, and continue to reap the benefits of mutual cooperation, we learn to cooperate with cooperators and defect against defectors. That is, we become conditional (not unconditional) cooperators.[21] To be a conditional cooperator, we need to rely on strategic information (something that neither unconditional cooperators nor unconditional defectors require).

Since more people will cooperate with me if they think that I am a conditional cooperator, and cooperation yields long-term benefits when compared to defection, I do well broadcasting my cooperative disposition. Or conversely, if my being a cheater and defector gets known by others, I lose out on cooperative dividends. My short-term gain is offset by long-term losses. Thus, in order to be moral, we do better if we are as transparent as possible.[22] We wear our strategic information on our sleeves.[23]

Now, if you believe in a god who (i) knows all strategic information, and (ii) deals with you according to how well or badly you deal with others,[24] then you are more likely to behave morally with *everyone* than someone who disbelieves either (i) or (ii). So in this sense, we might be able to say, belief in God *increases* the chances of moral behaviour. Moreover, if I let you know that I believe in God, you'll more likely trust me. My adhering to religious practice can count as a signal to others that I'm a cooperator, that I'm a good bet for social interaction.[25] If so, we might expect to find a correlation between religious beliefs and morality. But such a correlation precludes the prospect that cheaters will come to exploit the correlation.[26] That is, if you will only cooperate with other theists, I may have a reason to pretend to be religious in order to interact with you. But saying this wouldn't mean I am religious, nor, for that matter, would it mean I'm a cooperator, since my ruse at being religious may be merely intended to exploit you. It is not uncommon for scam artists, criminals, and corrupt politicians to hide behind a veil of religiosity. But even if a positive correlation between morality and religious belief could be found (for example it's hard to consistently fake over time either my theism or my being a cooperator given my history of defection), correlation is not sufficient for causation. In fact, paying closer attention to the correlation shows that the causal pattern is probably the reverse. That is, morality is necessary for religion. Our coming to see the importance of morality for social agents is what makes religion a plausible (even if wrong-headed) extension.[27]

CONCLUSION

The worry that if we deny God, we deny morality as well, is ridiculously short-sighted.[28] Morality makes sense for social humans whether we believe in God or not, and whether God exists or not.

23

THE MEANING
OF LIFE

THE PROBLEM OF NIHILISM

Many lament that without God, there can be no meaning to life. God gives meaning to such people. To take away God is to take away the point of living. Without a meaning to life, what point would there be in continuing? A black hole of nihilism is all that awaits us should it prove the case that there is no God, no meaning to life. My goal in this chapter is to explain how meaning is not threatened by disbelief in God. That is, atheists need not be nihilists.

Let us distinguish between subjective and objective meanings of life. We'll call subjective meaning "S-meaning" and objective meaning "O-meaning." S-meaning is whatever meaning you derive from life. S-meaning will vary from person to person, from culture to culture, and from time to time. It will also vary for a given person over her life. S-meaning is relative to the person's beliefs, preferences, and desires, as well as her shifting culture. O-meaning, on the other hand, is invariable. It is possible that there are personal O-meanings (PO-meanings) as well as Universal O-meanings (UO-meanings). A UO-meaning is generally what people are looking for when they speak of the meaning of life. It is the meaning or purpose of our being here at all. It is the point of the whole enterprise. Whatever UO-meaning there is, it is the same for everyone. It is set prior to our arrival on earth, and its course will not be influenced by either our arrival or our departure. PO-meanings, on the other hand, may have some connection to individuals. Different people may have different PO-meanings. Moses had one PO-meaning and Judas another, perhaps. But even PO-meanings are invariable. Like UO-meanings (and unlike S-meanings) PO-meanings are insensitive to a person's particular preferences, beliefs, or desires. It is insensitive to cultural shifts. A PO-meaning is set at (or prior to) birth, and remains fixed. The only variability is whether or not a person satisfies, or even recognizes, her PO-meaning.

While people are generally aware of their S-meanings in life, one may never be aware of what one's PO-meaning is, let alone the UO-meaning. Perhaps I think that my PO-meaning is to count blades of grass, whereas it is really to set up a blood bank. Since I may never be aware of what my O-meaning is (whether PO- or UO-), we cannot say that O-meanings are necessarily the kind of meaning that motivate us. Only S-meanings psychologically move us. True, your S-meaning may perfectly overlap with your PO-meaning (and we hope PO-meanings conform to the UO-meaning) but no O-meaning can motivate you unless it is also your S-meaning.

I am of the view that there are no O-meanings, neither PO-meanings, nor UO-meanings. There are only S-meanings. Removing metaphysical agency also removes O-meanings, unless one's O-meaning is something like "pass on one's genes," which hardly fits very many, if any, S-meanings. The intricate connection between God and O-meaning is due to the following recognition. Unlike S-meanings, O-meanings do not derive from you. But from where are they derived? Somewhere else? But what kind of thing can provide such things? Only a supernatural agent. A hammer, for example has an O-meaning: to hammer nails. Where did this O-meaning come from? Not from the hammer. Therefore, if the hammer has an O-meaning, there is an intentional O-meaning granter that is different in kind than the hammer. That's us. But if *we* have an O-meaning in virtue of what it is to be human, then that O-meaning must be intentionally granted to us by something sufficiently different in kind from us in the way that we are different in kind from a hammer. What else can fit the bill but a god? That is why rejection of metaphysical agency also rejects O-meanings — both universal and personal (U and P).

But removing God does not remove S-meanings. For S-meanings are what *we* bring to life, not what life brings to us. Saying this, however, may seem insufficient for two reasons: (i) theists do believe in O-meanings; and (ii) some theists have S-meanings that are so integrally connected to their belief in God that yanking God out from under them would leave them in an abyss. Although I shall touch upon (i), my main focus in this chapter is to explain in what sense (ii) is overstated. To be sure, losing belief in God will impact *one* S-meaning in life, just as losing faith in communism, say, or losing a loved one can greatly impact one's life. Unlike O-meaning, however, S-meanings are essentially plural. Losing one S-meaning (in God or communism) is not to lose all S-meanings. There are other prospects in life. The fear of nihilism, therefore, is overstated. Moreover, loss of a loved one is loss of a real entity. If you've believed my arguments to this point in the *Primer*, loss of God is not.

REDUCTIO AD ABSURDUM

Some derive meaning from the belief that God has a purpose for them. For me, it is the reverse. Thinking that there may be a divine purpose to life is unsettling. Characters in a novel have a purpose, perhaps to be killed off by the hero. Pawns and slaves have a purpose. But are any of these purposes useful to pawns and slaves? Although slaves may well enhance the meaning of life for slave owners, the slaves find little meaning in that. Many theists accept this servitude nobly;[1] I resist it.

Further, if there is a grand O-meaning to life, then we are committed to finding that meaning not merely in the gratuitous circumstances favouring human survival or human entertainment, but also to find it in the most violent, despicable, and disastrous human deeds. If there really is a meaning to life that is furthered by torture, subjugation, and suffering, it is difficult to consider it worthy of our admiration.[2]

That I find the concept unsettling is of course no proof that the concept is mistaken. So instead, I invite you to consider this: if there is a grand O-meaning to life, then I may be mistaken about what gives my life meaning. If so, what gives my life meaning (my S-meaning) is for naught. But that possibility seems absurd to me. It seems patently false to assert that I do not, in fact, derive meaning from what I have psychologically derived meaning.

This is different from saying that the S-meaning I derive is commendable. It may not be commendable to you. It may not even be commendable to me if I reflect on matters a bit more deeply. But the brute fact that I presently do derive meaning from this — whatever this is — can't be ignored. Consider the prospect that much of the meaning in my life is derived from my love of my daughter and my wife. Why would that change suddenly on discovering that there really were no God? If one of the things that keeps me from the black hole of despair is my relations with others, why would I forfeit those relations if there were no God? To consider doing so is what seems absurd. If someone says, "I love you so long as there's money in the bank," most of us would not count that as love. The theist's claim ought to be similarly suspect: "I find meaning in my relation with you only so long as it is the case that God exists." Such considerations reveal a problem with the notion that the meaning of life can only be obtained through God.

THE ARGUMENT FROM CONSISTENCY

If there really is no God, it follows that there never was a god. If the meaning of life is contingent on God's existence, then it cannot be the case that life used to have meaning, but now it doesn't. Either there was always a meaning, or there never was a meaning. Since most of us believe that there is a meaning to life, that fact cannot be altered by a new discovery that God doesn't exist. Ergo, God and meaning have no necessary connection.

Some (Tillich, for example) may suggest that the term "God" be used to name the feature of the universe that is ultimately meaningful. Two questions arise: is this ultimate meaning an O-meaning or an S-meaning? If the latter, the term "God" would refer to wildly divergent S-meanings, rendering the notion "God" as empty as Wittgenstein's "beetle in a box" (see Chapter 2). If the former, the question then becomes whether that feature of the universe that is ultimately meaningful is, or is given to us by, a metaphysical agent. If not, "God" becomes too secularized to be of concern to atheists (see Chapter 17). And if the thing that is ultimately meaningful is a metaphysical agent, then we are back to saying that that metaphysical agent (God) is necessary for there being an O-meaning to life. My role at this stage of the *Primer* is not to rehash why belief in such a supernatural agent is misguided. My role in Part V is to highlight the consequences of abandoning belief in God. What I want to say in this chapter is that one needn't abandon one's conception of S-meaning. Moreover, S-meaning is all the meaning you've ever known. It is impossible that any O-meaning can matter to you unless it is also your S-meaning.

If you believed in God and you believed that life had meaning, and then you discovered that there is no God, you ought to still feel that life has meaning since nothing that is real in the world has changed. I'm assuming that for things to have effects the causes must be real. The effect that you find life meaningful must have a real cause. Whatever gave your life S-meaning still exists. Thus, the discovery that there is no such thing as a god cannot affect your belief about whether life has meaning. This is different if what gives you S-meaning in life is another person, and that person dies.

Let's say that you and your loved one enjoy a nice warm, sunny day with a cool drink and maybe a good book (perhaps *The Atheist's Primer*). What makes that enjoyable? The skin feels warm. The drink refreshes. The book stimulates. You are with the person you love. Would the sun no longer warm your skin, the drink no longer nourish your thirst, the book no longer stimulate your mind, your lover no longer inspire you if you happened not to believe in God? "Ah," but you might say, "I don't derive meaning from sensual stimuli. Meaning is greater, something beyond, something to do with purpose. I'm looking for O-meaning!"[3] But this is where I no longer understand you. What else is there but sensual stimuli? What's wrong with that? Why equate it with something base? For empiricists, at any rate, any noble idea that you can muster (*a priori* ideas excepted, of course) can be shown to be rooted in sensual stimuli.[4]

To think that empiricism is "bad" often appears to be due to confusing the empiricist dogma that all knowledge is rooted in sense impressions with the similar sounding term, "sensualism." Sensualism is the view that the best life is typified by wallowing in debauchery: the sensual delight in food, booze, sex, gambling, drugs. Sensualism was ridiculed by Dostoyevsky in his book, *The Brothers Karamazov*. Dostoyevsky describes the sensualist, Fyodor Pavlovich Karamazov (the father) as "worthless and depraved."[5] Dostoyevsky's intent was to show how shallow and misguided sensualism is, which is not hard to do. But being an empiricist is not the same as being a sensualist. The two are unrelated.

THE NON SEQUITUR

The reluctance to see that atheism does not deprive meaning to life stems, I believe, from a logical non sequitur. One can agree with the claim that without God there can be no O-meaning to life. Simply asking, "What is the meaning of life?" commits one to entertain the concept of a deity. As noted earlier, if there is an O-meaning to life, there is a purpose, and if there is a purpose, there is intent, and if there is intent, there is an intender. We call that intender "God." Such a derivation is why atheists squirm when asked whether there is a meaning to life. But they need not. Lawyers are supposed to object to these sorts of leading questions.

The objection ought to centre on the meaning of the little word, "the," embedded in the statement, "the meaning of life." The definite article points to O-meaning. We can ask about the S-meaning that caused you to do that, but to speak about *the* S-meaning makes no sense. But why assume that there is such a thing as an O-meaning? Why must we assume that the concept of meaning is objective? And why are we looking for only *one* meaning? Why must we assume that the meaning of my life is independent of my subjective goals and beliefs and desires? Why must we assume that there is one grand meaning and purpose to everything that is independent of personal and cultural influences? These presumptions force our hands. These presumptions illegitimately presume a god, and that is why the removal of God appears also to remove meaning. People think that reflecting on the purpose of life (O-meaning) points to God; whereas, it is the reverse: belief in God points to considerations of O-meaning. Removing God removes O-meaning, indeed, but not S-meaning.

As Sartre noted, "Existence precedes essence."[6] You find yourself existing. Now, it is up to you to define your essence, your meaning. In this sense, we *invent* our essence, we don't *discover* it. Shake off the chains of oppression caused by others telling you that there is a pre-defined purpose: a mould into which you must contort yourself. If your arms are too long for your standard-issue shirt sleeves, lop off your arms (as in Matt. 18:9). Nietzsche also dreaded becoming a slave to others' values.[7]

Admittedly, there are problems with the existentialist position. Should we follow existentialists' advice? If yes, are we letting them define our essence rather than us? Sartre has more of a problem with this than other existentialists, since he adopts a Kantian categorical imperative when he tells us how to choose. Choose as if you're doing so for all humankind, he tells us.[8] But if others are existentialists, too, they won't tolerate your choosing for them. And since you should know that, there is no credence in the dictate that that is how you should choose your actions, your goals, your values, your meaning. Another worry concerns Sartre's cajoling us to be "authentic." If you follow others' values, you are inauthentic. If you choose your own way and live by it, you are authentic. But what could "authentic" mean to an existentialist who rejects essences? Doesn't authenticity evoke real selves to which you must conform? Doesn't this put essence ahead of existence? One might say existential authenticity is simply adhering to whatever values that you chose for yourself. But if I am free to choose my own way, why should I be restricted by the way I happened to choose yesterday? Nietzsche has even more problems than Sartre, but my objections are not aimed at the root of existentialism. The root of existentialism is that meaning is a subjective affair. You need only the courage to go your own way. That is, despite certain weaknesses with Sartre and Nietzsche's arguments, I agree with them in rejecting O-meaning. There is no O-meaning to be found in life. The only meaning we've got is S-meaning. Meaning is what we bring to life, not what life brings to us. And nothing in this idea is hampered if we come to accept God's non-existence.

To put the existentialist message in self-help psychology terms, the "Meaning of Life" question ought to be understood as something personal. If it is viewed as something personal, there is no need to entertain the notion that there is one objective purpose of your life to which you must aspire, whether you know it or not. Rather, you are the creator of your own meaning. Failure to achieve your own set goals is what leads to dissatisfaction. Perhaps you are lazy, or perhaps the goals are unrealistic. The beauty of designing our own goals is that we are also able to modify or change them as we better understand our own natures and our social circumstances. At age five, my goal in life was to be a tractor driver. Circumstances changed and I changed my goals. This strikes me as a good thing. Since goal setting is both a subjective and social affair, so too is our understanding of the meaning of our lives.

As a result, there is no fear of existential angst should it be the case that God does not exist. We are by nature goal setters. Meaning derives from the goals we set. In this sense, meaning is inevitable, so long as we set goals. But belief in God is not inevitable.

DEATH

The worry about meaninglessness is often invoked by atheist conceptions of death. Atheists (of my ilk, at any rate) do not believe there is life after death. Some people find such a picture unbearably bleak. If this paltry life is it, it is difficult to imagine the point of existence at all. Even our S-meanings are going to evaporate. Such a fear about death — and not merely our personal death, but the eventual death of everyone that ever mattered to us, let alone the eventual extinction of our entire species — leaves many with a sick sort of feeling, an existential angst. Distaste of a situation does not render the situation false, however. Whether the S-meanings I have found useful to sustain my life are ultimately meaningless (in the sense that everyone will be dead in a million years and no trace of my petty life will survive), does not alter the impact of those S-meanings on my life now. That my hunger is sated by some fruits is not negated by telling me that in a day I will be hungry again. That I find joy in my daughter's accomplishments is not negated by telling me that my daughter will be dead in a hundred years. To think otherwise is to demand one's S-meanings are O-meanings, and that is the mistake. (For more on death, see the following chapter.)

REPHRASING THE QUESTION

The meaning of life, as atheists view it, is a personal and social matter, contingent on the individual's goals and abilities and cultural conditions.[9] Even atheists have personal goals, goals that are very meaningful to them. Therefore, ask not "What is the meaning of life?" Ask instead, "What gives your life meaning?" The latter question has no inevitable ties to God's existence.

24

DEATH

Concerning death, there are four views. (1) There is nothing after death. (2) There is something after death, and everyone goes there whether they like it or not. (3) There are two states after death. The enlightened go to a nice place, and the unenlightened go to a non-nice place. (4) There is something after death, and only the enlightened get to escape it. If atheism is built on the dismissal of supernatural claims, atheists can only accept view number 1.

One of the defining features of most religions is the belief that there's something after death. Or, to put the matter in reverse order, thinking about death seems to make thinking about religion almost inevitable.[1] We see a corpse but preserve the "spirit" of the person in our minds. The Judeo-Christian tradition is expressed by view 3 above. In this version, there are more death states than one. One is a bad place to be, and the other is a good place to be. Religious practice is claimed to offer the best hope of achieving the proper death state. For Buddhists, view 4 is believed. The ideal death state is to escape the continued cycle of life and death and rebirth. Process theologians advocate view 2. They think that God is still in the *process* of creating the world, and that everyone gets to heaven — believer, wrong believer, and non-believer alike.[2] If we doubt the possibility of a continued existence after death, we doubt one of the central foundations of most religions.

PLATONIC ARGUMENTS

Our empirical evidence doesn't seem to support continued existence after death. What we see is the decomposition of the body, not continued existence. One way around this brute fact is to complain that what we see is an illusion. This still popular tack can be traced back to Plato. Accordingly, *this* world — the world we live in, the world we perceive — is an illusion. The real world occurs elsewhere. This is best illustrated by Plato's analogy of the cave in *The Republic*. If we were chained in a cave, forced to stare at shadows of cut-out representations of objects, we would come to believe that those shadows were the objects themselves. How different are the three-dimensional representation of objects from our perceptions! And how different are those three-dimensional representation of objects from the objects they represent! The real world would be witnessed only once we remove our shackles and climb out of the cave into the sunlight. Similarly, the real world will be witnessed only once we pass out of this existence.[3] Of course, this is just an analogy, not an argument.

But Plato also gave an argument (of sorts) for life after death. In *Meno*, Socrates amuses his interlocutors by getting an uneducated slave boy to work out a geometry problem. The boy succeeds (with prodding).[4] Specifically, the slave boy is led to assert that when given a square with side S, so that its area is S^2, then a square of exactly $2S^2$ is formed by taking as its side the diagonal of the original square. Since the boy was uneducated, the demonstration (purportedly) showed that the boy knew at least some geometrical truths all along. But this is not possible (supposedly) unless the boy's soul existed in some earlier state. Socrates merely nudged the boy into recollecting something that he had forgotten. And this implies that the boy knew something (or everything) in his pre-existing state. Our souls commune with Truth in the death state (or the pre-life state, anyway). Such a view presupposes reincarnation. In any event, we know all in the non-life state, and merely forget once we are born. Our task while alive in this world, is to *recollect* as much as we can.

Now, so long as knowledge *is* recollecting what we knew in a previous world, and we have knowledge, then we must accept that we have existed in a previous world. And this leaves the door open for an existing world beyond our death. Alas, the notion that knowledge is merely recollection is itself dependent on the suspect claim that we have souls which communed with pure knowledge before our births.

GHOSTS IN THE MACHINE

Descartes notes a number of ways in which the soul and the body differ. For example, the body is extended, the soul is not. The body is known by empirical observation, the soul is not. You can falsely believe that you have a body. For all you know, the only body you have is a brain in a vat, and all your perceptions of your face, limbs, and torso are dream images. Despite not knowing about your body, however, you cannot falsely believe that you have a mind (since such a supposition would be disproved in the very act of believing it). From these differences in how we understand the mind and the body, Descartes concludes that the soul and body are completely different things. (This inference goes too fast, since lightning and electromagnetic energy can be understood differently, yet lightning is electromagnetic energy for all that.) Since the soul and body are completely different, the soul cannot depend on the body for its continued existence. (This too goes too fast, since a communicator and an audience are completely different things, but neither can exist without the other.) Since the soul does not depend on the body, the body's decay cannot have any effect on the soul.[5]

This line of reasoning was already prevalent in Plato's days. In *Phaedo*, the character Simmias complained that the argument doesn't hold. Although a lyre is completely different from the music it plays, we would not infer that the music is not dependent on the lyre. With the demise of the lyre, good luck finding the music.[6] Socrates rebuts the analogy. The lyre is always the dictator of the music, never the reverse, whereas the soul can dictate what the body does. For example, if my body wants to smoke, my soul needn't acquiesce, otherwise I could never quit smoking. If it can dictate what the body does, the soul is independent of the body in a way that the music is not independent of the lyre.[7] Socrates's answer highlights the standard description of the soul-body relation in terms of a driver-car relation. Once the car rusts out, it needn't mean that the driver is stranded. The driver can walk away and find another car.

Of course, this analogy works because both driver and car are corporeal objects. The "driver" has to be non-corporeal for the analogy to really hold, and this is where we begin to see the problem. We need a ghost in the machine metaphor to describe the soul in the body relation. Even if we could imagine a ghost in the driver's seat, further explanation is needed to explain how the incorporeal being moves the corporeal object.[8] If a ghost walks through walls, wouldn't it also be unable to step on a gas pedal, shift gears, or turn a steering wheel? But such an interaction problem is idle since we can't find the necessary analogue however hard we look. What other relation do we have evidence of in which a ghost operates a machine? Given the empty analogy, the better conclusion is that the soul is as fictitious an entity as any ghost.

BRAIN DAMAGE

Even if we wish to maintain that the "soul" is a real thing (let us call it the mind, or one's conscience, or something comparable), all evidence integrally links the soul to the body. Damage the brain, you damage consciousness. Damage the visual organs, you can no longer see. Damage the auditory organs, you can no longer hear. For example, persons suffering from spatial agnosia can't reproduce things occurring on the left side of figures.[9] A patient suffering from spatial agnosia is asked to reproduce the drawing he sees in Figure A. His result is shown in Figure B (see Table 24.1).

Table 24.1: Spatial Agnosia Imagery

FIGURE A	FIGURE B
⧋⧋⧋	⊦⧋

People who suffer from Alzheimer's disease lose their memory of cherished loved ones. Thus, memory, spatial recognition, and our entire sensory apparatuses, require normal functioning of the brain. But at death, the brain no longer functions at all. So, even if there were a place to continue existing after death, there is little hope that we would have any cognition of it. If Descartes were right, damage to the brain should have no impact on the soul. Since the evidence does not support Descartes's supposition, death to the brain will most likely result in death to the soul.

One might object with the following. A prisoner in a room has access to the world only through a small barred window. Block off that window and the prisoner will be unable to have access to the world outside his prison cell. And outsiders, looking in, would no longer be able to say whether the prisoner were still there or not, were alive or dead. But merely blocking the prisoner's access to the world outside his prison cell would not mean that the prisoner is dead. If the prison walls crumble, that doesn't mean that the prisoner disintegrates with them; quite the opposite: the prisoner is free.

But again, this picture works only because we suppose that the prisoner and the prison are corporeal objects. To suggest that brain damage does nothing to harm the dualist position, we need an example of how damage to a corporeal object does no damage to an incorporeal object. But where can we find such an analogue without simply begging the question about the existence of non-corporeal objects that have the necessary intimate connection with corporeal objects?

NEAR-DEATH EXPERIENCES

To say there is no empirical evidence in support of continued existence is, perhaps, too strong. Many cite the phenomena of Near-Death Experiences (NDEs). These are remembered events that have supposedly occurred *while* dead. The patients have died, usually on operating tables, and were then brought back to life. The account of their being dead is usually recorded by medical staff in terms of flat EEGs, or stoppage of the heart. Of the people who have gone through this experience, many report very similar things in a very similar sequence. First, there is a feeling of peace and contentment. Second, there is an out-of-body experience. They feel themselves lifted out of their body. Their body remains below; they are a floating presence above their body. In some cases, these floating presences are able to witness and later accurately recall the medical procedures done on their supine bodies.[10] Third, there is an entrance into a dark tunnel. To proceed at this point means that the person accepts her death. To reject death is to refrain from entering the tunnel. The finality of the choice has produced fear in many. Fourth, for those who entered the tunnel, a light is perceived at the end. The previously experienced fear dissolves at this point. The fifth stage, for those who have gone this far (and returned to tell about it) is the stage of entering the light. Previously felt presences are now seen. Often, these include loved ones who had died, and other welcoming presences.[11]

Since the pattern is the same in so many cases of people from varied backgrounds who have "died" and returned to life, many take this as empirical evidence of a life beyond the grave. Before we make such inferences, however, further reflections on the phenomenon are in order. I offer three basic worries.[12]

1. NDEs are not universal. This isn't a problem on its own. Theists can maintain that not everyone will get to experience the tunnel to heaven (assuming that's where the tunnel leads): only those deserving. (Good news for atheists who also have had good NDEs, since this entails that being an atheist does not discount one from getting to heaven.) Support for that notion is the evidence that some NDE accounts were nightmarish.[13] To be sure that the difference is sin, however, we would have to do more than assume that those who have the good NDEs are sin-free and those who have no NDEs or who have bad NDEs are sinful. A more obvious difference exists. NDEs are less likely to occur when brain structures have been damaged due to strokes or tumours than when the brain structures are not damaged.[14]

We know that opiates interact with specific receptors within the brain to produce their analgesic and intoxicating effects. We also know that endorphins have significant analgesic effects and react with the same brain sites that opiates do. Or, perhaps, more accurately, morphine and heroin act like endorphins. These drugs bind with endorphin receptors and make the nervous system believe that endorphins have been released. Endorphins are the body's natural painkillers and analgesics. They stimulate the pleasure centres of the brain to produce a sense of peace, contentment, and euphoria. Meanwhile, noradrenaline is a hormone released into the bloodstream as a stimulant. It increases the oxygen and glucose levels to the brain. The effect of noradrenaline in the brain is similar to adrenaline in sparking the "fight or flight" response system. It also increases focussed attention. This latter effect may explain the sensation of "time slowing down" often reported in accidents. Specific sites within the brain seem to be responsible both for the generation of endorphins and noradrenaline and for the analgesic effect caused by them.[15] For example, electrical stimulation of certain parts of the thalamus produces strong analgesic effects.[16] Both endorphins and noradrenaline are naturally released by the body, typically in times of stress and pain — as when a person is close to death. This leads one to suspect the NDE phenomenon to be a product of the brain releasing endorphins and/or noradrenaline.[17] In fact, similar experiences to the first stages of NDEs are reported by survivors of accidents. Time slows down. There is peace and contentment. Some report out-of-body experiences.[18] The causes and effects of noradrenaline and endorphins indicate that NDEs are simply a natural brain response to stressful events. Those whose brain functions are damaged or stopped will not be affected by any endorphin and/or noradrenaline in the bloodstream, and thus, would not likely experience NDEs. Specifically, functioning thalami and limbic lobes may well be necessary for NDEs.[19] In death, these are not functioning.[20] Such evidence means that NDEs cannot be used as evidence of an after-death experience when the brain is no longer functioning at all.

2. The notion that NDEs are caused by the brain is supposed to be countered by the fact that NDEs occur when the brain is dead. This counter has two worries. Surviving momentary heart stoppage is far more common than surviving momentary brain stoppage. So, the fact that the brain may still be reacting to endorphins while the heart has stopped is not ruled out.[21] And in cases of flat EEGs, the experience may not be during the death state, but prior to it, or alternatively, at the penumbra of waking out of the death state.[22] Dreams are often reported in their own time frame, whereas dream research indicates that dream images occur in a millisecond, and it is only upon waking when the brain, loathe to admit to chaos, organizes imagery into some random, vaguely coherent, vaguely linear whole.[23]

3. A third worry, related to the second, concerns the amount of interpretation that goes on both by witness testimony, and researchers happy to assemble the anecdotes into common themes. The earlier stages may well be the bare feelings related to the brain's defence mechanism. Similar brain functions would yield similar sensory experiences. The latter stages, however, may be more cultural interpretations induced by euphoria. Similarly, reports of LSD usage have common phenomenal elements, and the more personal journeys reported beyond these are deemed merely the individual's storyline. Dreams, too, are a universal phenomenon, but the content of dreams is culturally relative.

THE IDENTITY ARGUMENT

The last argument I shall discuss is aimed to debunk the notion of a continued existence after death. I avail myself of an illustration raised by Richard Brandt.[24] Suppose that you had a serious brain tumour and were told that, for a sizeable fee, an operation to save "your life" could be performed. The procedure would transplant someone else's brain into your body. Unfortunately, the result would be that your memory, preferences, and learned abilities would be wholly erased, and that the forming of memory brain traces would have to begin from scratch, as in a newborn baby. For that matter, perhaps you would have memories and preferences, but they would belong to the person whose brain was being donated to you. How large a fee would you be willing to spend for this operation? When I ask my students, at least, they tend to say, "Nothing at all!" For you, the operation is the same as your death. Continued existence without any memory traces of who you were is really not your continued existence. It's an existence, perhaps, but not *your* existence.

And this is the telling problem, since everything that means anything to us — memories, tastes, preferences, ideals, goals, aspirations, dreams, loves — all require a functioning brain.[25] If the brain dies, so too does our personal identity. That *something* may continue past death — for example, your nutrients join the food chain — is not really what is needed for religious notions of continued existence. As Bertrand Russell notes, the idea of after-death *experiences* is just the difficulty.[26] Whatever bits persist after your death, your ability to experience doesn't go with them. The supply of sensory stimuli is cut off. Being dead, there are no longer any operative sense organs or nervous system. Whatever survives, personal identity can't go with it.

H.H. Price objects. He notes that personal identity is preserved in dream states, without fuss. Likewise in the death state, if the death state is a state of continued mental imagings.[27] But dreams come from people with functioning brains. The death state does not have that luxury. Price complains that it is "just an empirical hypothesis" that all experiences require brain states.[28] He claims telepathy, telekinesis, prophecy, ghosts, etc., indicate otherwise. Of course, that some people experience phenomenal events that they interpret as ghosts or telekinesis doesn't establish the existence of ghosts and telekinesis. Moreover, any witness to these phenomenal experiences has a functioning brain state. Therefore, our admitting that persons sometimes experience these phenomenal states can't support claims of · what agents would experience absent brain states.

SUMMARY

The so-called empirical support of life-after-death just isn't there. NDEs can be explained without recourse to life after death hypotheses and cognitive science studies show too many cases where effects on the brain affect mental states and personality to take seriously the view that personal identity can continue past death of the brain.

———— ∞ ————

ERROR THEORY

RELIGION'S SUCCESS

But why do so many people believe in a god if it is a false belief?[1] This is an interesting question so long as it is not intended to be used as evidence for God's existence. Truth is not determined by jumping on a bandwagon. We don't assume that smoking is good for you merely because so many people smoke. Why do so many people believe in God is an interesting question only so long as we are confident that belief in God *is* a false belief. (Asking why a true belief has persisted over time and generations is not that interesting, but asking why a false belief is so persistent *is* interesting.) Theories for why false beliefs persist are called *error theories*.[2] Before I survey some of the error theories concerning religion, I want to first make clear that the answer to this question, let alone whether we find any satisfactory answer to it, is irrelevant to whether or not belief in God is a false belief. Accounting for why so many people believe in a God is an activity external to examining the epistemic warrant of belief in God.

PSYCHOLOGICAL AND SOCIOLOGICAL ACCOUNTS

Religion provides personal comfort, social cohesion, and answers to existential enigmas, and many commentators have thought that some or all of these psychological factors play a role in the persistence or *success* of religion. (We interpret "success" as the longevity of a belief.) Below, I briefly examine the plausible contenders. In the end, I suggest that none are sufficient taken by themselves, but taken together they do provide a wide enough net to account for the snaring of many an unwary mind.

Comfort
The role of comfort is well noted during funerals. Funeral services regularly try to provide comfort to grieving relatives and friends. The deceased

person is with God now, and who better to spend one's time with? That's all fine so long as the deceased person satisfied the requirements of getting into heaven. The worry that this person may not have so satisfied the requirements (she was human, after all, not a saint) shifts that worry to ourselves. Are we sinless enough? Have we done enough and the right kind of good deeds? The fear of hell and the constant reminder that everyone is a sinner tends to produce guilt and anxiety, not comfort.[3]

Fear

Is the persistence of belief in God induced by fear, then? The evolutionary biologist and atheist Richard Dawkins notes that at least two core messages of religion tend to be shared with effective persuasive advertising: (1) salvation is assured only so long as the consumer buys the specific product, and (2) the buyer is persuaded of the need for salvation.[4] Consider the marketing ploys for bad breath. You don't want your date to be ruined by bad breath do you? Well do you? Then buy (and use) Scope (or some similar product). Similarly, you don't want to go to hell, do you? Well, then, buy Catholicism (or some similar product). Such successful marketing relies heavily on fear. Effective advertising doesn't simply exploit our fear, but often *creates* it in us as well. The fear of bad breath, of going bald, of having "unsightly" facial hairs, of wearing passé clothing, of not fitting in, of bankruptcy, of home invasion, of identity theft, of disease, of cancer, of water contamination may all have legitimate roots in our general psyches — we want to fit in, we don't want bad things to happen to us — but the specific fears are often manufactured first; and then exploited. Since we are naturally moved by fear, many people will be moved by such advertising ploys — even so-called bright people who think that they know better. This is largely because appeals to our emotions are more powerful motivators than speculative reasoning.

Although you can get people to *do* stuff by threat, it seems less likely that you can get people to *believe* stuff by threat, especially unbelievable stuff. "Believe this rock is invisible or you'll be eaten by toads!"[5] And if the stuff you're asked to believe is believable independently of the threat, then neither threat nor fear explains its believability. And if the thing you're asked to believe is predicated on fear, and the fear is easily discounted, then the belief will not stick. For example, if you tell me that phones will give me cancer, I will have a reason to fear phones. But if I subsequently learn that phones cause cancer only if they're radiated, and no phone I've ever come across has ever been radiated, my fear of phones ought to relax. Of course, whether fears *ought* to relax is not the same as saying they *do* relax, and there's the rub. Especially when fears are coupled with long-standing traditions, the same fears your parents and your teachers have. Commonly held fears are resistant to ought reasoning. Using the longevity of religious belief may seem a bit unfair, since what we're trying to explain is the longevity itself. The first believers didn't believe because their ancestors believed. Still, the mere fact that religious belief was common *is* one part of the explanation for why it's still common.[6]

Another worry for the fear account, however, is that it is predicated on belief in hell. Not all religions have such a concept, and not even all Christian versions.[7] For those theists who do not believe in hell, perhaps the comfort offered by religious belief overrides the fear-mongering. If everyone gets to heaven, we can, after death, "see" our loved ones and our friends again, plus "meet" those people we've read about. I would love to chat with David Hume and Franz Kafka, for example. Wouldn't that be wonderful? If such thoughts quell our fear of death, our fear of meaninglessness, and such thoughts are predicated on religious belief, then religion holds a powerful sway over us.

Inadmissibility of Doubt

Apart from fear, Dawkins also suggests a third ploy that religions use that no advertisement has yet used. Advertisers can't chastise you for doubting whether their product works or not, or for doubting whether bad breath is really that common. But religion has an added weapon: the inadmissibility of doubt. Doubting the claims of religion is itself a sign of devilry, and since the devil can't be trusted, the act of doubting religious content is *a priori* untrustworthy. The doubter is *a priori* to be doubted. "He that trusteth in his own heart is a fool."[8] Dawkins applauds the move. This brilliant move is common among most, if not all, religions: the appeal to faith. "Just believe, dammit!" The combined tactics of (1) induced fear; (2) salvation from said fear by cultivating the religious story across cultures and generations; and, (3) the inadmissibility to doubt either (1) or (2) is said to account for religions' success. Such tactics would certainly make religious belief widespread and persistent.

On the other hand, it is noteworthy that the faith tactic isn't available for the marketing of other products. Presumably, this is because the appeal to faith works only for religion. If that is so, the tactic itself can't be blamed. Rather, it is something unique about the product which carries with it this ready-made marketing ploy. Consider an analogy offered by Brian Garvey.

> If you take this pill, you will live 10,000 years .... The pill costs five pounds.[9]

Garvey notes that he would keep his five pounds. Nor could we imagine convincing him otherwise merely by telling him that he ought to have faith. He wouldn't say, "Oh, sorry, I didn't know that I must have faith. Here are my five pounds." He would be just as dubious about this new claim. This shows that — contra Dawkins — there is something different going on in the case of religion than in normal marketing ploys. The concept of faith has to make sense for religion in a way that makes no sense for any other product. Religious concepts have to appear plausible to agents with minds like ours prior to someone's telling us that we are not allowed to doubt it.[10]

The pill argument says merely that an inadmissibility to doubt addendum can't work by itself: the belief has to be independently plausible. A pill that will make you live for ten thousand-years is not plausible given the average age of death. But religion does offer something plausible: comfort, social cohesion, an end to existential angst, and, besides, everyone else has taken the pill, too, including your parents and teachers and peers and they're doing fine. If all these fine people are saying "Take the pill," an inadmissibility to doubt isn't quite what's going on. Rather, it would be *odd* to doubt. For example, when my wife gave me some natural pills to take, I took them. I doubted their effectiveness, but I figured they wouldn't harm me. More importantly, if I resisted taking the pills, if I started into a discourse about non-scientific testing, my wife would have taken it as a personal affront. She wants to help me. Do I doubt her intentions? We often find ourselves accepting proffered pills simply to ease human relations. It is often easier to take the proffered pill, than to fight it. If "getting along" has more to do with the longevity of religion or religious belief, perhaps we should look at more sociological than psychological accounts.

Social Cohesion

Perhaps religion acts as social glue. Social cohesion is an important — perhaps necessary — aspect of human life. Any convention that helps social cohesion will be a strong contender for success.[11] We need not doubt that religion offers social cohesion. Still, there are many other activities that can build social cohesion as well, such as clubs, sports leagues, schools, and art communities, none of which rely on false beliefs or fear-mongering. True, other powerfully cohesive social groups do rely on false beliefs and fear-mongering, white supremacist groups, for example. Still, one could make the case that religion was the precursor of social networks. These competing social networks (good or bad) require a stable social network to begin with, and that is what religion provided. But such a tale would not explain why religion has not been abandoned for these other social networks.[12] Crawling may well have been a precursor to walking, but once we have mastered walking, we don't keep crawling around. Nor would it explain why religion, rather than any other social practice, was the common choice across so many cultures and times.[13]

Back to Freud

Freud offered an alternative error theory concerning religion.[14] Early childhood experience leaves lasting impressions; children go about the world under the ever watchful gaze of their parents. These parents are sometimes loving and sometimes wrathful. Through imprinting, we come to expect being watched, being judged, even after we grow out of childhood. We come to curse or thank or pray to this watcher, as the occasion warrants. When we are mindful, we know our folly: we know we are merely project-ing childhood echoes. But few of us are mindful, and even mindful ones are not mindful all the time. I still catch myself praying, or cursing, or thank-ing some supernatural entity. I do not think that such episodes are telling. It shows simply the lingering vestiges of childhood imprinting. That, and the fact that most of us, even staunch atheists, aren't that bright.

Problems with Freud's attachment theory are well publicized. For example, children five to six years of age can recognize that their par-ents may have false beliefs, but ascribe no such limitation to God.[15] The inference, then, is that God is not a simple anthropomorphization of one's parents. It is as if a god template is already lodged in children's brains, and through experience one learns that one's parents don't match up to it. Of course I agree that Freudianism as a general theory is horribly prob-lematic precisely for being non-falsifiable (see Chapter 20), but the simple message that one is heavily influenced by growing up under the watchful eyes of powerful figures who react to the actions you do (by rewards or punishments) — even behaviours that you didn't believe these superior agents witnessed — is notably similar to religious belief. Unfortunately for the Freudian account, however, understanding God as a Father figure in the sky is not a common understanding among all religions. It is so for only (some) monotheistic (single God) beliefs. This qualification seriously undermines the Freudian account. How can the internalization of parental authority explain the prevalence of religion when most religions have never conceived of gods as parental figures?

Explanation

Few people enjoy not knowing something. To avoid this state of nescience, people seem to prefer believing *something* rather than confessing not knowing anything at all. According to Barrett, attributing supernatural agency to ontological and cosmological questions makes sense, is natu-ral; whereas trying to come up with a natural explanation seems shaky, illogical, speculative, unlikely, non-natural.[16] As I discussed in Chapters 1, 6, and 7, this wildly overstates the case. And that's assuming that "God" *is* an explanation, as opposed to an attempt at removing the hope for an explanation entirely. Explanations normally make things simpler, whereas religious explanations more often complicate matters, if not make them downright opaque.[17] But even if "God" is deemed a permissible answer to many of our questions, "God" is replaced when we do find a natu-ral alternative. That is why we don't persist in calling thunder a case of God's being angry. Since naturalistic alternatives have been made available for every question where "God" might be an answer, the mere hatred of unknowing cannot itself account for the persistence of belief in God. It may have accounted for the origin of such a belief, but that's not sufficient for an error theory. And that's assuming that humans actually do have a hatred of not knowing — an assumption that may be false.[18]

What my brief review should highlight is that none of the psychological or sociological explanations are obviously wrong, but nor do any seem sufficient on their own. This suggest a pluralist account of the prevalence of religion. Religion succeeds because it casts a wide net, ensnaring many of our social and psychological needs. But saying this doesn't really say too much, given that these social and psychological needs can be met without religious belief, and the ones that can't are eradicable without loss. An alternative account appeals to evolution.

THE EVOLUTION OF BELIEF

More recent speculation on the origin and persistence of religion comes from evolution theorists. Richard Dawkins speculates that *memes* — cultural practices and beliefs — share the process of natural selection with genes. Genes are successful so long as they produce organisms carrying traits that enhance reproduction of those genes. Likewise, successful memes are those that can be fairly replicated across generations through learning or enculturation. What counts as "successful" will vary according to the cultural milieu and the nature of our cognitive faculties, just as what counts as a successful genetic trait will vary according to circumstances. In any event, the "success" of a meme needn't have anything to do with truth. One might assume, however, that a successful meme is one that confers adaptive benefits to meme owners. As Boyer notes, memes "that remain stable have some advantage."[19] And if we understand "familiar religious concepts [as being] just better-replicating memes than others,"[20] then we get the view that religion confers evolutionary advantage.[21] Then we are moved to speculate on plausible advantages, such as social cohesion, comfort, existential explanation, etc. The problem is not with the proposed advantages so much as assuming that a continuing trait necessarily confers advantage. Not everything that survives is an adaptation of natural selection.[22]

This may sound inconsistent with Darwinian evolutionary theory, but most evolutionary theorists suggest not.[23] Certain traits — so long as they are not harmful — may be passed on from generation to generation so long as they are somehow associated with adaptations. Adaptations are specifically selected. For example, everything else being equal, if greater speed enables the bearer of that trait to survive and reproduce better than her peers, natural selection will make that species increase in speed over time. But perhaps along with the increased muscle mass or longer leg bones, a by-product trait evolves: say, an altered pigmentation. The faster speed is an adaptation, but the altered pigmentation is not. It may become an adaptation, by the way, if the pigment colouration makes the bearer more camouflaged to its common predators, or to its common prey, or makes the bearer more sexually attractive. In such cases, we still don't say that the pigmentation is an adaptation: we say it is an *exaptation*.[24] An exaptation might *become* an adaptation so long as the gene gets selected *because* of that trait, as opposed to the gene being selected for some other trait, on which the exaptation piggybacks. So long as the pigmentation difference itself adds nothing for survivability or reproduction, however, we can say it is simply a by-product. Or, if you prefer, consider the Panda. Pandas have opposable "thumbs" both on their hands and their feet. The hand thumbs are clearly useful for eating bamboo and so are seen as adaptations, but the foot thumbs have no similar benefit, and are seen as simple by-products of whatever genetic modifications produced the hand thumbs.[25] Presumably, the genes regulating the growth of the pandas' wrists also regulate the growth of the ankles. As Gould notes, "It may be genetically more complex to enlarge a thumb and not to modify a big toe, than to increase both together."[26] The evolution of foot thumbs is not due to conferring fitness, but due merely to certain morphological constraints on genetic replication. Moreover, maladaptive traits may have adaptive origins. Take our overindulgence of sweets.[27]

It is conceivable, then, that religious belief is not an adaptation, but a by-product of an adaptation. That is to say, religious belief is predictable given some other adaptation of Homo sapiens.[28] One such account concerns a *hyperactive agent-detection device* (HADD).[29] The ability of humans to detect sentient creatures is a product of natural selection. The ability to distinguish a leaf falling from a predator or prey's footfall is important to survival. But as with many, if not all, detection devices, the ability to be flawlessly accurate requires apparatuses that are too unwieldy, that require extra resources to nourish despite no increase in available resources, etc. So, a common trick of nature is to tolerate errors. There are only two kinds of errors: false positives and false negatives. A false negative is when the system falsely reports the absence of any sentient creature. Saying "It's not a burglar in the house, it's just the furnace clicking on," when it is a burglar is an example of a false negative. A false positive is to falsely suppose the presence of a sentient creature when there isn't any sentient creature. Deducing the presence of a burglar in the house when the noise is simply the furnace clicking on is an example of a false positive. When it comes to detecting sentience, between the two kinds of errors, false negatives are more deadly.[30] Mistaking a grizzly bear for a babbling brook may cost you your life, whereas mistaking a babbling brook for a grizzly bear will be embarrassing at most, perhaps will give you needed exercise. We can, therefore, predict that sentient detection devices will tend to be overactive rather than underactive, because humans with underactive sentient detectors will be less likely to pass on their genes.

A by-product of HADD will be that we will tend to imagine sentient presences when there aren't any. And it is this tendency, this overextension of HADD, that accounts for the persistence of religious belief, as well as belief in ghosts, aliens, witches, etc. We feel some sentient presence, find no physical evidence for it, so we infer a non-physical sentient presence, rather than simply chalk it up to another false positive recording.

A problem exists. Normally, once we make a false positive concerning sentient presence, we are not thereafter doomed to persist in that belief. After not being burglarized, after not being attacked by a bear, I will readjust my sentient detection device. I will not come to believe that, since no physical bear is present, there must be a spiritual bear. I will not come to believe that, since there is no physical burglar present, a spiritual burglar must be present. To do so would be deemed insane. So why would we be able to make such inferences about a god? Yet the same hyperactive agent-detection device is employed in both. It might account for an initial gut reaction, but not the persistence of the belief after countervailing evidence.

True, we do persist in reacting to stimulus *as if* it's moved by some intentional agency, like cursing one's bad luck on a golf course, or cursing one's ill-behaving computer.[31] We commonly impute — or behave as if we impute — mental states to a wide range of things, including dots on computer screens.[32] As Hume famously noted, we have a tendency to see faces in the moon, armies in the clouds,[33] or in my case, Atlas in my linoleum. And the fact that we persist, despite our knowing our mistake in doing so, shows the *power* behind our mindlessly ascribing mental states in places where they don't belong. Moreover, the propensity to ascribe mental states to invisible objects starts early in life. Just watch a small child pour invisible tea into an invisible cup for her invisible friend.[34] HADDs may not tell us why religion persists, but it does tell us why religion is so natural.[35]

True enough, but there does seem an important difference between mis-ascribing mental states to inanimate or invisible things and ascribing mental states to a deity. In the former case, we *know* that we're just falsely ascribing mental states. But theists do not presume that they falsely ascribe mental states to their god.[36] The child does not *really* believe in her invisible friend, or invisible tea. The mad golfer does not *really* believe in a bad luck deity. We believe these things only at a visceral level, and they are *easily* and *readily* "corrected by experience and reflection."[37] But people's beliefs in gods are not. So, although HADDs may be part of the explanation for why religious belief is so rampant and persistent, it seems not to be the whole explanation. Barrett gets close to recognizing my worry here. He admits that people can turn off their HADDs for "noises that go bump in the night," but not for "crop circles" or God.[38] But why not? We can understand the workings of a light switch if it can be turned on and off, but not one that can be turned on and off every day except Wednesdays. That kind of a light switch requires an explanation beyond whatever explanation we give for light switches in general.

Perhaps I conflate what modern, primarily Western, atheists would say about imaginary friends and golf gods and computer demons, and ignore anthropological evidence that such (or such kinds of) beliefs are quite prevalent. That is, the rejection of such beliefs is decidedly modern and culture specific. Similarly, my rejection of HADDs as the explanation of the persistence of religion is no more than saying, "But it's epistemically uncalled for!" That it's uncalled for goes without saying. Its not having epistemic merit is irrelevant to its providing an evolutionary explanation, however.

If the HADD account is right, then, it is as if a god template is already lodged in our brains. But we mustn't overreact to this. We are not entitled to derive some evidence for God's existence from noting a propensity in the human brain to believe in a god. The capacity in the brain to infer a god is no more than the capacity in the brain to infer agency. A similar warning may be made of talk of a "God gene."[39] As Dennett observes, a god gene makes no more sense than a chocolate or a nicotine gene.[40] Our liking sweets has been selected. Our liking Swiss chocolate in particular has not been selected. Similarly, our overactive HADD has been selected. Our belief in God has not been selected.

CONCLUSION?

Have we found the right error theory yet? Are any naturalized accounts of religion's persistence correct? Should we expect only one error theory rather than a multitude? I confess that I do not know. Racism has been around for a long time, too, and we can speculate all we want about why it persists, but to think that discussion has anything to do with whether we think racism right or wrong is to miss the point. Such speculations are certainly worth pursuing, but, as I noted at the outset of this final chapter, the program is irrelevant to whether or not there is epistemic warrant for belief in a god. As to why religion persists despite lack of epistemic warrant, some kind of error theory — an account of why the error persists — will be needed, but whatever the correct error theory is — even if there is only one correct error theory rather than a multitude — won't make any difference to the question that this *Primer* addresses: Is belief in God epistemically warranted? The answer to *that* question is NO!

NOTES

PREFACE

1   See, for example Pascal Boyer, *Religion Explained: The Evolutionary Origins of Religious Thought* (New York: Basic Books, 2001) 155–58.

2   For other works on atheism, see, Julien Baggini, *Atheism: A Very Short Introduction* (New York: Oxford UP, 2003); Richard Carrier, *Sense and Goodness without God* (New York: Authorhouse, 2005); Christopher Hitchens (ed.), *The Portable Atheist: Essential Readings for the Nonbeliever* (Philadelphia: Da Capo Press, 2007); Michael Martin, *Atheism: A Philosophical Justification* (Philadelphia: Temple UP, 1990); Michael Martin (ed.), *The Cambridge Companion to Atheism* (Cambridge: Cambridge UP, 2007); Michael Martin and Ricki Monnier (eds.), *The Improbability of God* (Amherst, NY: Prometheus Books, 2006); Michael Martin and Ricki Monnier (eds.), *The Impossibility of God* (Amherst, NY: Prometheus Books, 2003); George Smith, *Atheism: The Case Against God* (Amherst, NY: Prometheus Books, 1989); and Victor Stenger, *The New Atheism: Taking a Stand for Science and Reason* (Amherst, NY: Prometheus Books, 2009). For a collection of modern arguments for the existence of God, not all of which I talk about in this primer, see William Lane Craig and J.P. Moreland (eds.), *The Blackwell Companion to Natural Theology* (Oxford: Blackwell, 2009); and Michael Martin and Ricki Monnier (eds.), *The Impossibility of God* (Amherst, NY: Prometheus Books, 2003).

3   For recent examples, see Sam Harris, *The End of Faith: Religion, Terror, and the Future of Reason* (New York: W.W. Norton, 2004); Christopher Hitchens, *God Is Not Great: How Religion Poisons Everything* (New York: Hachette Book Group, 2007); or Richard Dawkins, *The God Delusion* (New York: Houghton Mifflin, 2008).

4   David Hume, *The Natural History of Religion* (Stanford, CA: Stanford UP, 1956).

5   John Hick, "A Philosophy of Religious Pluralism," in John Hick (ed.), *Classical and Contemporary Readings in the Philosophy of Religion*, 3rd ed. (Englewood Cliffs, NJ: Prentice Hall, 1990) 418–32; or John Hick, *Philosophy of Religion* (Englewood Cliffs, NJ: Prentice-Hall, 1990) 109–19.

6   See also James Thrower, *A Short History of Western Atheism* (London: Pemberton Books, 1971); David Berman, *A History of Atheism in Britain: From Hobbes to Russell* (London: Routledge, 1988); Alister McGrath, *The Twilight of Atheism: The Rise and Fall of Disbelief in the Modern World* (New York: Doubleday, 2005); Michael Buckley, *At the Origins of Modern Atheism* (New Haven: Yale UP, 1987); and David Ramsey Steel, *Atheism Explained: From Folly to Philosophy* (Peru, IL: Open Court Press, 2008).

7   For those interested in such a catalogue, there are many good works out there. See, for example, Huston Smith, *The World's Religions* (San Francisco: HarperCollins, 1991); or Warren Matthews, *World Religions* (Belmont, CA: Wadsworth, 2006).

PART I. PRELIMINARIES

CHAPTER 1: WHY NOT AGNOSTICISM?

1   Some prefer the term, "agnosticism," to be applied, not to a fence-sitting position, but to the belief that God is so different from us, so beyond our ability to comprehend, that we simply can't say anything at all about God. This, for example, is Anthony Kenny's use. Anthony Kenny, *The Unknown God* (London: Continuum, 2004). Such a position, I treat as a kind of theism (a position I discuss in Chapter 17). It is deemed hubris to suppose that we can properly understand God, and so talk of God must be severely constrained. In this sense of agnosticism, God is totally other, totally unknown, totally ineffable. But this brand of agnosticism does not mean that God is not worshippable. Agnostic works in this theistic sense include *The Cloud of Unknowing*, a fourteenth-century anonymous work (Clitton Wolters [trans.] [Harmondsworth: Penguin, 1970]); or the works by St. Iraeneus of Lyon, *Against Heresies* (see John Hick, *Evil and the God of Love* [London: Macmillan, 1966], 217–21); and St. Anselm, *Proslogion*, in S.W. Deane (ed.), *Anselm's Basic Writings* (La Salle, IL: Open Court, 1962). As Anselm says, "God is greater than can be conceived." By this account, any conception that anyone has of God, cannot be accurate, since, by definition, God is greater than that. Anselmian agnosticism may be referred to as negative theism (*via negativa*). Supposedly, T.H. Huxley coined the term "agnosticism" as a reaction against gnosticism. Both gnostics and agnostics share the view that God is wholly removed from this world, but gnostics believe that we can fully know that other God through revelation. To confuse matters further, atheism is sometimes divided into two camps: positive and negative. Negative atheism refers to the absence of a belief in God *and* the absence of a belief that God doesn't exist. This captures agnosticism in the "I dunno" sense. For proponents of agnosticism as negative atheism, see Leslie Stephen, *An Agnostic's Apology: And Other Essays* (London: Smith and Elder, 1867); and Thomas Henry Huxley, *Collected Essays* (London: Macmillan, 1904). Positive atheism, on the other hand, is the belief that no God exists, or has ever existed. My meaning of agnosticism in this chapter is so-called negative atheism. Agnosticism in the Anselm sense I put under theism. What I mean by atheism in this primer is the so-called positive variety. The problem concerning what "theism" means I shall defer to the following two chapters.

2   Father F.C. Copleston and Bertrand Russell, *A Debate on the Argument from Contingency*. Broadcast in 1948 on the Third Program of the British Broadcasting Corporation. Reprinted in Bertrand Russell, *Why I Am Not a Christian* (London: George Allen & Unwin, 1957) 133–54.

3   For the suggestion that some proofs for the non-existence of God do work in the more general case — something I do not admit, but would not of course be opposed to — see Michael Martin and Ricki Monnier (eds.), *The Impossibility of God* (Amherst, NY: Prometheus Books, 2003).

4   This captures the point raised by Anthony Flew's 1950 "secret garden" parable. Anthony Flew, "Theology and Falsification," reprinted in Anthony Flew and Alasdair MacIntyre (eds.), *New Essays in Philosophical Theology* (New York: Macmillan, 1955) 96–99.

5   This was Anthony Flew's position. Anthony Flew, *The Presumption of Atheism* (New York: Barnes and Noble, 1976) 13–14. He thinks that such a presumption supports "negative atheism" rather than "positive atheism," however, which — in my terminology — would put him in the agnostics' camp. Now, evidently, Flew is

a theist, because he believes the universe hasn't been around long enough to be the result of mere chance. See Anthony Flew with Roy Abraham Varghese, *There is a God: How the World's Most Notorious Atheist Changed His Mind* (New York: HarperCollins, 2007).

6 Thanks to the Charles Pierce scholar, Don Roberts, for opening my eyes to this position while he beat me at speed chess.

7 For more on why common knowledge doesn't count for much, see Malcolm Murray and Nebojsa Kujundzic, *Critical Reflection* (Montreal: McGill-Queen's UP, 2005) 149–50.

8 Alston and Plantinga argue along these lines. See William Alston, "Religious Experience as a Ground of Religious Belief," in J. Runzo and C. Ihara (eds.), *Religious Experience and Religious Belief* (New York: UP of America, 1986) 31–51; William Alston, *Perceiving God: The Epistemology of Religious Experience* (Ithaca, NY: Cornell UP, 1993); William Alston, "Is Religious Belief Rational?" in S.M. Harrison and R.C. Taylor (eds.), *The Life of Religion* (Lanham, MD: UP of America, 1986) 1–15; and Alvin Plantinga, "On Taking Belief in God as Basic," in J. Runzo and C. Ihara (eds.), *Religious Experience and Religious Belief* (Lanham, MD: UP of America, 1986) 1–17. But the same argument was also made by Pascal. See Blaise Pascal, *Pensées*, W.F. Trotter (trans.) (New York: Random House, 1941 [1670]) ch. 7 "Morality and Doctrine," #434, 141–45.

9 To make this position credible, see G.E. Moore, "A Defense of Common Sense," in J.H. Muirhead (ed.), *Contemporary British Philosophy* (London: Allen and Unwin, 1925).

CHAPTER 2: WHICH GOD ARE YOU DENYING?

1 Pascal Boyer, *Religion Explained: The Evolutionary Origins of Religious Thought* (New York: Basic Books, 2001) 57.

2 For a discussion of what an intentional stance entails, see Daniel Dennett, *The Intentional Stance* (Cambridge, MA: MIT Press, 1989).

3 See, for example, Anthony Kenny, *The God of the Philosophers* (Oxford: Clarendon Press, 1979).

4 These "essential characteristics of God" accord with John Hick's list. For Hick, God is "the infinite, eternal, uncreated, personal reality, who has created all that exists and who is revealed in human creatures as holy and loving." John Hick, *Philosophy of Religion* (Englewood Cliffs, NJ: Prentice-Hall, 1990) 14. But see also St. Thomas Aquinas, *Summa Theologica*, in Anton C. Pegis (ed.), *Basic Writings of St. Thomas Aquinas* (New York: Random House, 1945) pt. I, ch. 1, questions 1–11. Are these testimonials too Western? The anthropologist Scott Atran offers a similar account. "In all religions, and thus in all societies, people believe that agents unseen have intentionally generated the world that we see. God created the world on purpose and knows what is true." Scott Atran, *In Gods We Trust: The Evolutionary Landscape of Religion* (Oxford: Oxford UP, 2002) 52.

5 For Boyer "a common feature of religion across the globe is a belief in invisible persons with a great interest in our behaviour" (Boyer, 18–19). The emphasis on "persons" is central. "That gods and spirits are construed very much like persons is probably one of the best known traits of religion" (Boyer, 142).

6 For medievalist views on creation in Judaism, Christianity, and Islam, see D.B. Burrell, *Freedom and Creation in Three Traditions* (Notre Dame: U of Notre Dame P, 1993).

7   See, for example, David Leeming, *A Dictionary of Creation Myths* (New York: Oxford UP, 1996); Barbara Sproul, *Primal Myths: Creation Myths Around the World* (New York: HarperOne, 1979); or Marie-Louise Von Franz, *Creation Myths* (Boston: Shambhala, 2001).

8   Paul Tillich, "Theism Transcended," in Paul Tillich, *The Courage to Be* (New Haven: Yale UP, 1952) 182–86.

9   Ludwig Wittgenstein, *Philosophical Investigations*, G.E.M. Anscombe (trans.) (Oxford: Blackwell, 1953) §293.

10   *The Cloud of Unknowing* is an anonymous work of the fourteenth century. See, for example, Clitton Wolters (trans.) (Harmondsworth: Penguin, 1970). As noted in Chapter 1, this view is sometimes referred to as agnosticism. See, for example, Anthony Kenny, *The Unknown God* (London: Continuum, 2004).

11   Thomas Aquinas, *Summa Theologica*, Q. 95, art. 1

12   Kai Nielsen explicitly makes this case. See Kai Nielsen, *Scepticism* (London: Macmillan Press, 1973).

13   David Hume made this point. "When two *species* of objects have always been observed to be conjoined together, I can *infer*, by custom, the existence of one wherever I *see* the existence of the other: And this I call the argument from experience. But how this argument can have place, where the objects, as in the present case, are single, individual, without parallel, or specific resemblance, may be difficult to explain. And will any man tell me with a serious countenance, that an orderly universe must arise from some thought and art, like the human; because we have experience of it? To ascertain this reasoning, it were requisite, that we had experience of the origin of worlds." David Hume, *Dialogues Concerning Natural Religion*, Norman Kemp Smith (ed.) (New York: Macmillan, 1987 [1779]) pt. II, 149–50.

14   Alfred North Whitehead, *Process and Reality: An Essay in Cosmology* (New York: Free Press, 1978 [1929]); Alfred North Whitehead, *Religion in the Making* (New York: Fordham UP, 1997 [1926]); Charles Hartshorne, *The Divine Relativity: A Social Conception of God* (New Haven: Yale UP, 1948); Charles Hartshorne, *A Natural Theology for Our Time* (La Salle, IL: Open Court, 1967).

15   See Ludwig Wittgenstein, *Philosophical Investigations*, G.E.M. Anscombe (trans.) (Oxford: Blackwell, 1953) 1–2.

16   Paul Tillich makes such a case. See Paul Tillich, *Dynamics of Faith* (New York: Harper and Row, 1957) 58; or Paul Tillich, *Systematic Theology*, vol. 1 (Chicago: U of Chicago P, 1951) pt. 2, ch. 1, 163–210. For my account of Tillich's position, see Chapter 17.

17   I am not saying anything new here. See, for example, David Hume, *A Treatise of Human Nature*, L.A. Selby-Bigge and P.H. Nidditch (eds.) (Oxford: Oxford UP, 1978); Paul Edwards, "Russell's Doubts about Induction," *Mind* 68 (1949): 141–63; Nelson Goodman, *Fact, Fiction and Forecast* (Indianapolis: Hackett, 1979); Wesley Salmon, "Inductive Inference," in B. Baumrin (ed.), *Philosophy of Science* (New York: Interscience, 1963) 353–70; and P.F. Strawson, *Introduction to Logical Theory* (New York: John Wiley & Sons, 1952) ch. 9.

18   According to Alan Watts, Mao-Tsu was the first to answer questions about Zen Buddhism by hitting the questioner. Alan Watts, *The Way of Zen* (New York: Vintage Books, 1957) 97. The idea that "searching" is already evidence of having gone astray is echoed in Buber. "[I]n truth, there is no god-seeking because there is nothing where one could not find him." Martin Buber, *I and Thou*, Walter Kaufmann (trans.) (New York: Charles Scribner's Sons, 1970) 128.

19 Other Buddhist schools find nature to be the thing to escape, not the thing to embrace.

20 Perhaps. The Judeo-Christian myth about the Garden of Eden may indicate something similar. Prior to sin, we were in tune with nature, and hence with God as well. But sin severed the link. The claim is that we do not define God as nature, but that being properly attuned to nature is *ipso facto* to be properly attuned to God. But if Adam and Eve were so attuned, the concept of original sin makes no sense. Sin caused us to veer from nature, but we could not veer from nature until we sinned.

21 In polytheistic religions, the set of gods is a unique set. Although not all of these gods are necessarily the creators of anything, let alone the universe, nor are those who are the creators of the universe necessarily the top gods, or even good gods, the creation of the world or universe is still attributed to one of these gods, even if merely a demigod.

CHAPTER 3: RELIGION WITHOUT GOD?

1 Paul Ricœur "Religion, Atheism, and Faith," in Alasdair MacIntyre and Paul Ricœur, *The Religious Significance of Atheism* (New York: Columbia UP, 1969) 59.

2 John Robinson, *Honest to God* (Philadelphia: Westminster Press, 1963); Thomas J.J. Altizer, *The Gospel of Christian Atheism* (Philadelphia: Westminster Press, 1966); Alistair Kee, *The Way of Transcendence: Christian Faith Without Belief in God* (New York: Penguin, 1993); Karen Armstrong, *History of God* (New York: Ballantine, 1993); A.N. Wilson, *God's Funeral* (London: John Murray, 1998); Don Cupitt, *After God* (New York: Basic Books, 1997); and Ray Billington, *Religion Without God* (New York: Routledge, 2002).

3 Altizer, 62. Similarly, Rabbi Rubenstein asks: "How can Jews believe in an omnipotent, beneficial God after Auschwitz?" Richard Rubenstein, *After Auschwitz: Radical Theology and Contemporary Judaism* (Indianapolis: Bobbs-Merril, 1966) 153.

4 See for example, Billington, 17.

5 Altizer, 24.

6 "Some people seem impervious to religious ritual and all other manifestations of religion, whereas others — like me — are deeply moved by the ceremonies, the music, and the art — but utterly unpersuaded by the doctrines." Daniel Dennett, *Breaking the Spell: Religion as a Natural Phenomenon* (New York: Penguin, 2006) 318.

7 Or as Stark and Finke put it, "Religion without God is like buying a ticket to see a soccer game without a ball." Rodney Stark and Roger Finke, *Acts of Faith: Explaining the Human Side of Religion* (Berkeley: U of California P, 2000) 146.

8 Bonhoeffer, for example, is annoyed with religions that make practitioners dependent on God. He calls it "religious exploitation." Dietrich Bonhoeffer, *Letters and Papers from Prison*, R. Fuller (trans.) (London: S.C.M. Press, 1967) 154. But he's not against religion *tout court*. Religions that foster autonomy are good, particularly "through participation in the being of Jesus" (210).

9 Billington, 17.

10 Billington, 17.

11 Billington, 130.

12 See Billington: the holy (93), music (94), Wordsworth (101), and Blake (100).

13 Billington, 5–6.

14 Lubac, 7 and vii. See also Miceli: "[A]theism induces man to fall down before himself in narcissistic adoration." Vincent Miceli, *The Gods of Atheism* (New Rochelle, NY: Arlington House, 1971) xvi. In stark contrast is Nietzsche's sentiment: Christianity is built on *ressentiment* (grudge-laden resentment). Friedrich Nietzsche, "'Good and Evil' 'Good and Bad'" in *Genealogy of Morals* (Oxford: Oxford UP, 1996) §10.

15 As perhaps we should call Nietzsche insane, who asks, "Must we ourselves not become gods simply to appear worthy of [having killed God]?" Nietzsche, *The Gay Science*, Section 125, Walter Kaufmann (trans.) (New York: Random House, 1974).

16 Billington, 130–31.

17 I am quoting one of my reviewers, who adds, "... indeed, there is reason to suppose that *all* non-matter is non-spiritual."

18 Billington, 130, 131.

19 Robinson, 47, 53.

20 Ricœur, 88.

21 Altizer, 103.

22 Altizer, 62.

23 Altizer, 107.

24 Martin Buber, *I and Thou*, Walter Kaufmann (trans.) (New York: Charles Scribner's Sons, 1970).

25 Ludwig Wittgenstein, *Tractatus Logico-Philosophicus*, D.F. Pears and B.F. McGuinness (London: Routledge & Kegan Paul, 1972) §7.

26 See Anthony Kenny, *The Unknown God* (London: Continuum, 2004) 35.

27 *Via negativa* is to show God by way of negation.

28 See for example, S. Paul Schilling, *God in an Age of Atheism* (Nashville: Abingdon Press, 1969) 161.

29 Alasdair MacIntyre, "The Debate about God: Victorian Relevance and Contemporary Irrelevance" in MacIntyre and Ricœur, 26–7.

CHAPTER 4: METAPHOR AND SACRED TEXTS

1 I owe this irreverent idea to one of Roz Chast's cartoons in *The New Yorker*.

2 For how religious stories are memorable for being "minimally counterintuitive," see Pascal Boyer, *Religion Explained: The Human Instincts that Fashion Gods, Spirits and Ancestors* (London: Heinemann, 2001) 61–71; and Scott Atran, *In Gods We Trust: The Evolutionary Landscape of Religion* (Oxford: Oxford UP, 2002) 100–07.

3 A nice collection of facts and arguments against the divine inspiration of the Bible may be found in John Loftus (ed.), *The Christian Delusion: Why Faith Fails* (Amherst, NY: Prometheus Books, 2010).

4 For a credible defence of literalist interpretation of — not so much the Bible but God talk in general — see, William Alston, *Divine Nature and Human Language* (Ithaca, NY: Cornell UP, 1989). In brief, he suggests that phrases like, "God loves us," or "God created the universe," can still be attributed to a non-corporeal being, since intentional corporeal actions are always preceded by intentional states that are not themselves exhibited by corporeal action. Such a position would work better if we were dualists: that is, if we were assured that the mind is something totally different than the body. Then our (or God's) having intentional states needn't be tied to limited mortal bodies. Unfortunately for Alston, being a dualist is (quite likely) positively

correlated with being a theist. For the non-dualist position, see, for example, Daniel Dennett, *Consciousness Explained* (New York: Penguin, 1993).

5   For a defence of understanding God talk as an analogy, see Thomas Aquinas, *Summa Theologica*, I, Q.13, A.5; or his *Summa Contra Gentiles*, bk. 1, chs. 28–34, both in Anton C. Pegis (ed.), *Basic Writings of St. Thomas Aquinas* (New York: Random House, 1945). See also James F. Ross, "Analogy as a Rule of Meaning for Religious Language," *International Philosophical Quarterly* 1,30 (1961): 468–502. For a defence of understanding God talk symbolically, see Paul Tillich, *The Dynamics of Faith* (New York: Harper and Row, 1957) 41–54. For metaphorical readings, see Paul Ricœur, "Biblical Hermeneutics," in J.D. Crossan (ed.), *Semeia 4* (Missoula, MT: Scholars Press, 1975); and Sallie McFague, *Metaphorical Theology: Models of God in Religious Language* (Philadelphia: Fortress Press, 1982).

6   This consideration drives Van Buren to recognize that reference to God can't be a reference to any real thing at all. Paul Van Buren, *Edges of Language* (New York: Macmillan, 1972) 134–37.

7   Ricœur, "Biblical Hermeneutics," 76.

8   Paul Ricœur, *Interpretation Theory: Discourse on the Subject of Meaning* (Fort Worth, TX: Texas Christian UP, 1976); and Paul Ricœur, *The Road to Metaphor: Multi-Disciplinary Studies of the Creation of Meaning in Language* (London: Routledge, 1978).

9   Donald Davidson, "What Metaphors Mean," in S. Sachs (ed.), *On Metaphor* (Chicago: U of Chicago P, 1979) 29–45.

10 H.P. Grice, "Logic and Conversation," in *Studies in the Way of Words* (Cambridge, MA: Harvard UP, 1989) 22–40.

PART II. "PROOFS"

CHAPTER 5: ONTOLOGIC ILLOGIC

1   St. Anselm, *Proslogion*, in S.W. Deane (ed.), *Anselm's Basic Writings* (La Salle, IL: Open Court, 1962).

2   Paul Tillich, "Theism Transcended," from *The Courage to Be* (New Haven: Yale UP, 1952).

3   See, for example, St. Anselm, *Monologion and Proslogion, with the Replies of Gaunilo and Anselm*, Thomas Williams (trans.) (Indianapolis: Hackett, 1995).

4   The proof that "God is greater than anything that can be conceived" is logically equivalent to "If God exists, then God is greater than anything that can be conceived," is as follows. Assign the first proposition as "G" and the second as "$E > G$." Then:

1. G p.

2. $G \lor \sim E$ 1, add.

3. $\sim G > \sim E$ 2, imp.

4. $E > G$ 3, trans.

That is, the first line is given to us (p stands for premise). The second is a valid inference from the first line using the rule of addition. (If A is true, A or B is true.) The third line is a valid inference from the second line using the rule of implication. (If A or B is true, then if it isn't A, it must be B.) The fourth line is a valid inference from the third line using the rule of transposition. (If A necessarily gives us B, then the absence of B entails the absence of A.)

5   For a much lengthier discussion, see Bertrand Russell's battle with the proposition, "The King of France is bald." Bertrand Russell, "On Denoting," in Robert Marsh (ed.), *Logic and Knowledge* (London: Allen and Unwin, 1956) 41–56.

6   Immanuel Kant, "The Impossibility of an Ontological Proof of the Existence of God," in his *Critique of Pure Reason*, Norman Kemp Smith (trans.) (London: St. Martin's Press, 1969) 504 (AK598).

7   William Rowe suggests that the claim, "existence is not a predicate," cannot mean that any mention of an attribute entails the existence of the subject. For we can sensibly speak of Dr. Doolittle's love of animals without supposing Dr. Doolittle is an existing being. William Rowe, *Philosophy of Religion* (Belmont, CA: Wadsworth, 1978) 36. Fair enough, but nor would our saying "Dr. Doolittle exists" confirm Dr. Doolittle's existence. The statement is true or false and cannot be ascertained by navel-gazing at the statement itself. We have to go outside into the world to see. *That's* Kant's point.

8   Thanks to one of my students, Sarah MacDonald, for raising this objection.

9   Norman Malcolm, "Anselm's Ontological Arguments," *Philosophical Review* 69,1 (1960): 41–62. For a modal argument, see Alvin Plantinga, *God, Freedom, and Evil* (New York: Harper & Row, 1974) 108. See also Peter Loptson's brief remarks in *Reality: Fundamental Topics in Metaphysics* (Toronto: U of Toronto P, 2001) 68.

CHAPTER 6: WHY IS THERE SOMETHING RATHER THAN NOTHING?

1   The cosmological argument is credited to Aquinas, and is typically understood as covering Aquinas's first three arguments for the existence of God. St. Thomas Aquinas, "Whether God Exists?" in his *Summa Theologica*, Question 2, Article 3, in Anton C. Pegis (ed.), *Basic Writings of St. Thomas Aquinas* (New York: Random House, 1945) 21–23.

2   The question is imprecise, of course. The Big Bang created the gases: they weren't in existence prior to the Big Bang. Even the bits that formed the gases, the quarks, occurred moments after the Big Bang. Still, something "exploded" and we aren't sure what.

3   Augustine believed that time was created by God and therefore it is inapt to speak of a time before creation, let alone a time before God — a possibility that we'll explore in more depth in Chapter 13.

4   Aquinas, 22. Samuel Clarke, *A Demonstration of the Being and Attributes of God* (Cambridge: Cambridge UP, 1998 [1705]).

5   This is Father F.C. Copleston's response to Bertrand Russell in the BBC radio broadcast of their debate. Reprinted in Bertrand Russell, *Why I Am Not a Christian* (London: George Allen & Unwin, 1957) 133–54.

6   Paul Edwards, "A Critique of the Cosmological Argument," in Hector Hawton (ed.), *The Rationalist Annual* (London: Pemberton Publishing Co., 1959) 63–77. See also Richard Swinburne, "Whole and Part in Cosmological Arguments," *Philosophy* 44,170 (1969): 339–40.

7   Edwards referred to five "Eskimos."

8   Explaining the original cause would be to explain the cause *in fieri*. To explain the sustenance of the group is to explain the cause *in esse*. This was deemed to be an important distinction by cosmological argument defenders. It fails to make any difference here.

9 William Rowe makes a similar case. William Rowe, *Philosophy of Religion* (Belmont, CA: Wadsworth, 1978) 16–29.

10 See Jeffrey S. Rosenthal's delightful book, *Struck By Lightning: The Curious World of Probabilities* (Toronto: HarperCollins, 2005).

11 When we speak of the cause of the chain of contingent beings, we can think in terms of efficient or final causes. An efficient cause of X details how X came about (a carpenter built it, say). A final cause of X explains why X came about (someone wanted to sit, say). "God made it," would count as an efficient explanation, whereas an account of why God made it would get at the final cause. Some hold such a distinction to be important. It isn't. If X has a final cause, this presupposes the efficient cause of X is an intentional agent. Moreover, and more to the point, an efficient cause of an infinite series presupposes that the series isn't infinite.

12 Couldn't the series have always existed yet be created by God so long as God Himself always existed? In this sense, when God created Himself, couldn't He at the same time have created the infinite series of contingent beings? Refer back to the section on inconsistency for the reply.

13 William Lane Craig, *The Kalām Cosmological Argument* (Eugene, OR: Wipf and Stock Publishers, 1979). *Kalām* is an Arabic term roughly capturing what we mean by natural theology, offering empirical arguments for God's existence. Craig follows the ninth-century Arabic philosopher al-Ghāzāli. For more on the *Kalām Argument*, see Allen Stairs and Christopher Bernard, *A Thinker's Guide to the Philosophy of Religion* (New York: Pearson Longman, 2007) 60–66.

14 This is what Kant means when he says, "existence is not a predicate." Immanuel Kant, "The Impossibility of an Ontological Proof of the Existence of God," in his *Critique of Pure Reason*, Norman Kemp Smith (trans.) (London: St. Martin's Press, 1969) 504 (AK598).

15 Technically, I should say that existence cannot be inserted at the level of an *intensional* definition. It may well be proper to speak of existence for *extensional* definitions. Will this make the concept of a necessary being plausible? No. Intensional definitions define the set, or spell out the criteria for what gets included in the particular set. Extensional definitions detail all or some existing members of that set. Perhaps you've never heard of a rucksack. To enlighten you, I may point at a rucksack and say, "That's a rucksack." My ostensive pointing is a form of an extensional definition. I've singled out one of the existing members of the intensional set of things that are rucksacks. Alternatively, I may have said that a rucksack is another name for a knapsack, i.e., the kinds of bags you carry on your back. This offers you an intensional definition. Mere intensional definitions can't include the concept of existence, since that would presuppose that null sets are impossible. It should be fairly obvious that when someone defines God as a necessary being or as a being greater than anything else, he is offering an intensional definition of God, not an extensional definition. To offer an (ostensive) extensional definition of God, we'd have to actually point at God and say, that's God (or that represents the entire set of things that are identical with God). Good luck.

16 Rowe, 19–22.

17 For a more detailed account of why a necessary being is incoherent, see J.N. Findlay, "Can God's Existence Be Disproved?" *Mind* 57 (1948) reprinted in William Rowe and William Wainwright (eds.), *Philosophy of Religion: Selected Readings*, 3rd ed. (Oxford: Oxford UP, 1988) 19–23.

18 G.W. Leibniz, *The Monadology and Other Writings*, R. Latta (trans.) (Oxford: Oxford UP, 1925) §32. William Rowe, *The Cosmological Argument* (Princeton, NJ: Princeton UP, 1971).

CHAPTER 7: DESIGN OR EVOLUTION?

1   Proponents of the Design Argument include St. Thomas Aquinas, "Whether God Exists?" in his *Summa Theologica*, Question 2, Article 3, "The Fifth Way" in Anton C. Pegis (ed.), *Basic Writings of St. Thomas Aquinas* (New York: Random House, 1945) 23; William Paley, *Natural Theology* (Edinburgh: William and Robert Chambers Publishers, 1849); and A.C. Ewing, "The Argument from Design," in his *The Fundamental Questions of Philosophy* (London: Routledge & Kegan Paul, 1951) 225–31.

2   Aquinas, 23.

3   Paley, 11–18.

4   The story about the moon's importance to life on earth I got from a visit to the Royal Ontario Museum in Toronto a number of years ago. Whether the axial tilt or spin rate is due precisely to the size or number of moons, however, may be questioned. That is to say, other factors may play a pivotal role. I hope the general idea suffices: that our earth currently enjoys life and altering a number of significant factors would greatly alter that condition, whether the factors I mentioned per se are the significant ones or not.

5   Astronomically low, in fact. See John Leslie, *Universes* (London: Routledge, 1989). For how this fact is used in favour of the design argument, see the *fine tuning* argument in Chapter 8.

6   Brian Garvey gives the analogy of tinkering with your car engine. Without knowing what you are doing, a small tinkering might make the car work better, whereas a large tinker will much more likely make the engine stop working all together. Brian Garvey, *Philosophy of Biology* (Montreal: McGill-Queen's UP, 2007) 11.

7   "Evolution is the process by which rare alleles become common, possibly universal, and universally distributed alleles become totally eliminated." David Hull, "On Human Nature," in David Hull and Michael Ruse (eds.), *The Philosophy of Biology* (Oxford: Oxford UP, 1998) 392.

8   There is more to the story of evolutionary development, including controversies about some of the details. A good account of the key concepts and debates can be found in Garvey's *Philosophy of Biology*.

9   Peter Van Inwagen, *Metaphysics* (Boulder, CO: Westview Press, 1993) 135.

10   Van Inwagen uses drawing straws in his example, and the odds of being successful (and hence alive) are far far lower than 0.03, but the point is the same.

11   Van Inwagen, 144.

12   For how much you stand to lose on average playing various casino games, see Jeffrey S. Rosenthal, *Struck By Lightning: The Curious World of Probabilities* (Toronto: HarperCollins, 2005) 40.

13   The odds of a coin coming up heads five times in a row are calculated by multiplying the odds of heads coming up in a single throw (½) five times (.5 x .5 x .5 x .5 x .5), i.e., .03. The odds of getting five heads at least once in one hundred five coin tosses are considerably higher, since the number of instances in which success is possible is increased. It's easier to work out the probability of this not happening. Since in any one of the 100 trials you have a .03 chance of getting five heads in a row, that means that you have a .97 chance of not getting five heads in a row in any one of the single throws. So, 97% of the time the first trial does not yield five heads. Since the trials are independent of each other, the odds of the second trial not yielding five heads will be 97% of 97% = about 94%. That is, the odds that the first trial won't yield five heads are 97%, while the odds that neither of the first two trials will yield five heads are 94%. Then you just keep multiplying by 97% until you've done it 100

times to get the probability of none of the 100 trials yielding five heads. The result of calculating .97 to the power of 100 is 0.0417995, or about .04. So the probability of getting five heads in at least one of the 100 trials is about 1 - 0.04 = .96.

14 For a nice account of the theories competing with Darwin's, see Ernst Mayr, *The Growth of Biological Thought* (Cambridge, MA: Harvard UP, 1982).

15 Nor did Darwin know anything about genetics, but at least his theory was consistent with what we now know about genetics.

16 Richard Dawkins, *The Blind Watchmaker* (New York: W.W. Norton, 1986).

17 Michael Behe, *Darwin's Black Box* (New York: Free Press, 1996).

18 Apart from Behe, see also Alvin Plantinga, "When Faith and Reason Clash: Evolution and the Bible," *Christian Scholar's Review* 21 (1991): 8–32.

19 Stephen Jay Gould and Elizabeth Vrba, "Exaptation: A Missing Term in the Science of Form," *Paleobiology* 8,1 (1982): 4–15. See also Stephen Jay Gould, "Exaptation: A Crucial Tool for Evolutionary Psychology," *Journal of Social Issues* 47 (1991): 43–65.

20 J.H. Ostrom, "Archaeopteryx and the Origin of Flight," *Quarterly Review of Biology* 49 (1974): 27–47; J.H. Ostrom, "Bird Flight: How Did it Begin?" *American Scientist*, 67 (1979): 46–56.

21 See, for example, K. Miller, "The Flagellum Unspun: The Collapse of Irreducible Complexity," in M. Ruse and W. Dembeski (eds.), *Debating Design: From Darwin to DNA* (Cambridge: Cambridge UP, 2004) 81–97.

CHAPTER 8: FINE TUNING AND ANALOGY

1 See Chapter 7, note 1 for references.

2 For example, Richard Swinburne, *The Existence of God* (Oxford: Clarendon Press, 1979) 171; and John Leslie, *Universes* (London: Routledge, 1989) 13–14, 107–08. See also Peter Van Inwagen, *Metaphysics* (Boulder, CO: Westview Press, 1993) 135, 144.

3 This is the number Rundle gives, anyway. Bede Rundle, *Why There Is Something Rather Than Nothing* (Oxford: Clarendon Press, 2004) 30.

4 The odds would be even lower if we could also imagine dials for the various ingredients. One for flour, one for eggs, one for sugar, one for butter, one for vanilla, one for baking powder, one for salt, and one for milk. If each of those dials had twenty five settings, and if altering any one setting on any dial would wreck the cake (think of what two cups of salt would do to the cake, for example), then, including the temperature and time dials, the odds the cake would come out fine by chance would be 1 in 25^{10}.

5 What number theorists arrive at varies. For a nice overview of the wide range of numbers on offer, see Richard Carrier, "The Argument from Biogenesis: Probabilities Against a Natural Origin of Life," *Biology and Philosophy* 14 (2004): 739–64.

6 For a more detailed argument along these lines, see Elliot Sober, "The Design Argument," in William Mann (ed.), *The Blackwell Guide to the Philosophy of Religion* (Oxford: Blackwell, 2005) 117–47. See also Michael Ikeda and Bill Jeffreys, "The Anthropic Principle Does Not Support Supernaturalism," in Michael Martin and Ricki Monnier (eds.), *The Improbability of God* (Amherst, NY: Prometheus Books, 2006) 155–66.

7 For an extensive examination of the history of miscalculating such a number, see Carrier, 749–52.

8   David Hume, *Dialogues Concerning Natural Religion*, Norman Kemp Smith (ed.) (New York: Macmillan, 1987 [1779]) pt. II, 149–50.

9   A softening of the assumption is possible. If you conceive of the universe as absolutely everything, then perhaps our cosmos is one infinitesimally tiny component of a much larger universe containing many, perhaps an infinite number of, big bangs, etc.

10   This example of a good analogical argument form comes from James Freeman, *Thinking Logically: Basic Steps for Reasoning* (Englewood Cliffs, NJ: Prentice Hall, 1988) 320.

11   For more on analogical arguments, see Malcolm Murray and Nebojsa Kujundzic, *Critical Reflection* (Montreal: McGill-Queen's UP, 2005) 365–88.

12   Paley, 11–18.

13   Hume, pt. VII, 180.

14   Hume, pt. V, 168.

CHAPTER 9: THE MORAL ARGUMENT

1   The phrase "everything would be permitted" occurs in the mouth of Ivan Karamazov in Fyodor Dostoyevsky's *The Brothers Karamazov*, David Magarshack (trans.) (New York: Penguin Books, 1982 [1880]), pt. 1, bk. 2, ch. 6, 77, but is not preceded by "If God were dead," although that antecedent is consistent with Ivan's point. Sartre is the one who actually utters it, although he claimed the phrase came from Dostoyevsky. See Jean-Paul Sartre, *Existentialism and Humanism* (London: Metheun, 1965) 27. In any event, the idea is also found in Friedrich Nietzsche, *Beyond Good and Evil*, J. Hollingdale (trans.) (London: Penguin, 1990) sec. 259–60, 193–94; and Friedrich Nietzsche, *The Genealogy of Morals*, H.B. Samuel (trans.) (New York: The Modern Library, [1887]) sec. 1–13, e.g., 1–29. The "God is dead" phrase comes from Friedrich Nietzsche's famous statement in *The Gay Science*, sec. 125, "The Madman," Walter Kaufmann (trans.) (New York: Random House, 1974) 181.

2   For my view on morality, see Malcolm Murray, *The Moral Wager: Evolution and Contract* (Dordrecht: Springer, 2007).

3   This is Aquinas's 4th argument. St. Thomas Aquinas, "Whether God Exists?" in his *Summa Theologica*, Question 2, Article 3, in Anton C. Pegis (ed.), *Basic Writings of St. Thomas Aquinas* (New York: Random House, 1945) 22–23.

4   Plato's theory of forms is discussed in a number of his dialogues, including, *The Republic* (Book VI, 509d–511c, Book VII, 514a–517c), *Phaedo* (72e–77a, 95a–107b), *Parmenides* (129a–130b, 132b–135c), and *Timaeus* (51c–52c). See Edith Hamilton and Huntington Cairns (eds.), *Plato: The Collected Dialogues* (Princeton: Princeton UP, 1961). Page numbers refer to the numbers in margins of most editions of Plato (derived from the pagination and page subdivisions of the 1578 Henri Estienne [Stephanus] edition).

5   For the fact-value distinction related to burning cats, see Gilbert Harman, *The Nature of Morality* (New York: Oxford UP, 1977) 4–5.

6   Immanuel Kant, "The Existence of God as a Postulate of Pure Practical Reason," ch. 2, sec. 5 in Kant's *Critique of Practical Reason*, Thomas Kingsmill Abbott (trans.) (London: Longmans, Green and Co., 1963) 221.

7   Kant, "Of Belief from a Requirement of Pure Reason," ch. 2, sec. 8, in Kant's *Critique of Practical Reason*, 241.

8   Kant, *Critique of Practical Reason*, ch. 2, sec. 5, 221–22.

9   Kant is careful not to call this a proof. Rather, it is a "practical postulate."

10   Kant, *Critique of Practical Reason*, ch. 2, sec. 5, 227–28.

11   J.L. Mackie, *Ethics: Inventing Right and Wrong* (Harmondsworth: Penguin, 1977) 38–42.

12   Kant, *Critique of Practical Reason*, ch. 2, sec. 8, 241.

13   J.L. Mackie, *The Miracle of Theism* (Oxford: Oxford UP, 1982) 109.

14   Whether the supererogatory really is exemplary is one thing that Susan Wolf, for example, doubts. See Susan Wolf, "Moral Saints," *The Journal of Philosophy*, 79,8 (1982): 419–39.

15   A few disagree. See, for example Peter Singer, "Famine, Affliction, and Morality," *Philosophy & Public Affairs* 1,3 (1972): 229–43; or Peter Unger, *Living High and Letting Die: Our Illusion of Innocence* (New York: Oxford UP, 1996).

16   To see the incoherence, ask yourself, who shaves the barber? I am not certain who dreamt up this riddle, but Bertrand Russell uses it in his "The Philosophy of Logical Atomism," reprinted in John Slater (ed.) *The Collected Papers of Bertrand Russell*, 1914–19, vol. 8 (London: Routledge, 1986) 228.

PART III. ATTRIBUTES

CHAPTER 10: THE PROBLEM OF SUFFERING

1   The character, Ivan Karamazov, gives a case about a general who lets his dogs attack a child. See Fyodor Dostoyevsky, *The Brothers Karamazov*, David Magarshack (trans.) (New York: Penguin Books, 1982 [1880]) pt. 2, bk. 5, ch. 4, 284.

2   Hume, attributing the argument to Epicurus, puts the matter this way: "Is [God] willing to prevent evil, but not able? then he is impotent. Is he able but not willing? then he is malevolent. Is he both able and willing? whence then is evil?" David Hume, *Dialogues Concerning Natural Religion*, Norman Kemp Smith (ed.) (New York: Macmillan, 1987 [1779]) bk. X, 198. See also William Rowe, "The Problem of Evil and Some Varieties of Atheism," reprinted in William Rowe and William Wainwright (eds.), *Philosophy of Religion: Selected Readings*, 3rd ed. (Oxford: Oxford UP, 1988) 242–50.

3   Not all theisms define God this way. There is no problem, if at least one of these features is dropped from the characteristics of God. If God weren't altogether good, or weren't capable of doing much, or didn't know anything about us, then there is no logical problem. Kushner, for example, argues that since God is good, yet there is evil, God must not have the power to stop all evil. Harold Kushner, *When Bad Things Happen to Good People* (New York: Avon, 1981). Proponents of *process theology* also avoid the problem of suffering by dropping the omnipotence attribute. See, for example, Alfred North Whitehead, *Process and Reality: An Essay in Cosmology* (New York: Free Press, 1978 [1929]); Alfred North Whitehead, *Religion in the Making* (New York: Fordham UP, 1997 [1926]); Charles Hartshorne. *The Divine Relativity: A Social Conception of God* (New Haven: Yale UP, 1948); and Charles Hartshorne, *A Natural Theology for Our Time* (La Salle, IL: Open Court, 1967). Other problems may ensue from such revamping: namely, whether such a creature is deserving of worship.

4   St. Anselm, *Proslogion*, in S.W. Deane (ed.), *Anselm's Basic Writings* (La Salle, IL: Open Court, 1962).

5   "Why is there misery at all in the world? Not by chance surely. For some reason then. Is it from the intention of a Deity? But he is perfectly benevolent. Is it contrary to his intention? But he is almighty. Nothing can shake the solidity of that reasoning,

so short, so clear, so decisive; *except we assert, that these subjects exceed all human capacity, and that our common measures of truth and falsehood are not applicable to them.*" David Hume, *Dialogues Concerning Natural Religion*, bk. X, 201. My emphasis.

6   Stephen Wykstra, "The Humean Obstacle to Evidential Arguments from Suffering: On Avoiding the Evils of 'Appearance'." *International Journal for Philosophy of Religion* 16 (1984): 73–93. Stephen Wykstra, "Rowe's Noseeum Arguments from Evil," in D. Howard-Snyder (ed.), *The Evidential Argument from Evil* (Bloomingdale, IN: Indiana UP, 1996) 126–50.

7   See, for example, Augustine, *Confessions* (Harmondsworth: Penguin Classics, 1961) bk. VII, chs. 12 and 13, 148–49; and Alvin Plantinga, *God, Freedom, and Evil* (New York: Harper & Row, 1974) 29–34.

8   See also Hume, *Dialogues*, bk. X, 205–06.

9   For a chilling reaction to such enormity of sin, see Elie Wiesel, *Night*, Marion Wiesel (trans.) (New York: Hill and Way, 2006).

10 See also Rom. 8:20–22. The idea that all sufferers are sinners is inconsistent, however, with other passages in the Bible, notably the New Testament. See, for example, the tale of the Good Samaritan (Luke 10:30–37 and John 9:1–3).

11 See Melvin Lerner and D.J. Miller, "Just World Research and the Attribution Process: Looking Back and Ahead," *Psychological Bulletin* 85,5 (1978): 1030–51.

12 Hume, *Dialogues Concerning Natural Religion*, bk. X, 199.

13 Fyodor Dostoyevsky, *The Brothers Karamazov*, bk. V, ch. 4, 287.

14 See, for example, Augustine *City of God* (New York: The Modern Library, 1950) bk. XI, sec. 9, 352–54, and *Confessions* (Harmondsworth: Penguin Classics, 1961) VII, 7, 18, or Gottfried Wilhelm Leibniz, *Theodicy*, Diogenes Allen (ed.), E.M. Huggard (trans.) (Don Mills, ON: J.M. Dent & Sons, 1966) 603.

15 Hume, *Dialogues*, bk. XI, 203–04.

16 See, for example, John Hick, "An Irenaean Theodicy," in John Hick (ed.), *Classical and Contemporary Readings in the Philosophy of Religion*, 3rd ed. (Englewood Cliffs, NJ: Prentice Hall, 1990) 391–405.

17 This was the prevailing view of Plato and Aristotle, and was not seriously doubted until Hobbes.

18 Hume makes this point. See David Hume, *Enquiries Concerning the Principles of Morals*, L.A. Selby-Bigge (ed.) (Oxford: Clarendon Press, 1989 [1777]) sec. III, pt. 1, 183–92.

19 Apart from virtue theorists, who emphasize the psychological well-being of virtuous agents (and who thereby emphasize the intrinsic value of moral behaviour along with morality's instrumental effects), Kantians would also object to my purely instrumentalist account of morality. For Kant, moral duty is a dictate of reason that overrides any instrumental benefit to individuals. For virtue theorists, see Aristotle, *Nicomachean Ethics*, in Richard McKeon (ed.), *The Basic Works of Aristotle* (New York: Random House, 1941); and Alasdair MacIntyre, *After Virtue* (Notre Dame: U of Notre Dame P, 1984). For Kantians, see Immanuel Kant, *Grounding for the Metaphysics of Morals*, James W. Ellington (trans.) (Indianapolis: Hackett, 1986); Thomas Hill, Jr., *Dignity and Practical Reason in Kant's Moral Theory* (Ithaca, NY: Cornell UP, 1992); and Christine Korsgaard, *The Sources of Normativity* (Cambridge: Cambridge UP, 1998). For arguments more in line with the instrumental view, see Thomas Hobbes, *The Leviathan* (Buffalo: Prometheus Books, 1988 [1651]); Philippa Foot, "Morality as a System of Hypothetical Imperatives," *Philosophical Review* 71 (1972): 305–16; Gilbert Harman, *The Nature of Morality* (New York: Oxford UP,

1977); J.L. Mackie, *Ethics: Inventing Right and Wrong* (Harmondsworth: Penguin, 1977); David Gauthier, *Morals By Agreement* (Oxford: Oxford UP, 1986); Brian Skyrms, *Evolution of the Social Contract* (Cambridge: Cambridge UP, 1996); or my book, *The Moral Wager* (Dordrecht: Springer, 2007).

20 At least we remove the need for all negative duties, like don't cause suffering, since suffering is impossible. Perhaps, however, one might think positive moral rules are useful, like helping someone feel better. Of course, it can't be the case that they are feeling bad, which might give us a reason to help them feel better, because feeling bad would be a kind of suffering. But the bare prospect of someone's feeling better is unlimited. Thus, for you to think morality still useful in a world without suffering, you would have to imagine a world where everyone has some kind of moral obligation to help make others (and not just some, presumably, but all others) happier, while at the same time recognizing that such a (supererogatory) duty is impossible to fulfill. I am not of the view that such a liberty-restricting world is ideal. Of course nothing prevents us from making others happier, but thinking this would be a moral requirement would seem to speak too loosely.

21 Perhaps other arguments exist. For example, if God wants us to relieve suffering in order for us to be good, then being good is partly defined by relief of suffering, but God doesn't relieve suffering: he lets us do it. Perhaps, then relief of suffering is not what's good: it's letting others relieve suffering that is good. But then we should all stand back and do nothing. For other sorts of responses to the problem of evil, see Richard Carrier, *Sense and Goodness without God* (New York: Authorhouse, 2005).

CHAPTER 11: OMNIPOTENCE

1 A notable exception is *process theology*. See, for example, Alfred North Whitehead, *Process and Reality: An Essay in Cosmology* (New York: Free Press, 1978 [1929]); Alfred North Whitehead, *Religion in the Making* (New York: Fordham UP, 1997 [1926]); Charles Hartshorne, *The Divine Relativity: A Social Conception of God* (New Haven: Yale UP, 1948); Charles Hartshorne, *A Natural Theology for Our Time* (La Salle, IL: Open Court, 1967); and Charles Hartshorne, *Omnipotence and Other Theological Mistakes* (New York: State U of New York P, 1983).

2 This version of the paradox of the stone can be found in George Mavrodes, "Some Puzzles Concerning Omnipotence," *The Philosophical Review* 72 (1963): 221–23; G. Wade Savage, "The Paradox of the Stone," *The Philosophical Review* 76 (1967): 74–79; and P.T. Geach, "Omnipotence," *Philosophy* 48 (1973): 7–20. A variant of the paradox of the stone made an appearance on the television show, *The Simpsons*. While on medicinal marijuana for his eyes — pecked at by his "murder of crows" — Homer asks Flanders whether God could create a burrito too hot for God to eat.

3 Thomas Aquinas, *Summa Theologica*, pt. I, Question 25 in Anton C. Pegis (ed.), *Basic Writings of St. Thomas Aquinas* (New York: Random House, 1945) 262–64.

4 Rowe, for example, makes this argument explicit. "*[C]reating a stone so heavy that God cannot lift it* is doing something inconsistent with one of God's essential attributes — the attribute of omnipotence." William Rowe, *Philosophy of Religion: An Introduction* (Belmont, CA: Wadsworth, 2001) 7.

5 Frankfurt gives this rendition. Harry Frankfurt, "The Logic of Omnipotence," *The Philosophical Review* 73 (1964): 262–63.

CHAPTER 12: OMNISCIENCE AND FREE WILL

1   Pascal Boyer, *Religion Explained: The Evolutionary Origins of Religious Thought* (New York: Basic Books, 2001) 155–58.

2   Luke 12:7.

3   Prior to the age of five. After that, they no longer think that their parents are omniscient, but they do think that God is omniscient. Justin Barrett, *Why Would Anyone Believe in God?* (Lanham, MD: Altamira Press, 2004) 78–79.

4   I should say "at least." Kane says there are five ways of understanding free will which cut across the compatibilist and libertarian distinctions. Robert Kane, *A Contemporary Introduction to Free Will* (Oxford: Oxford UP, 2005).

5   See Richard Taylor, *Metaphysics* (Upper Saddle River, NJ: Pearson, 1992), or, more guardedly, Thomas Nagel, *The View from Nowhere* (Oxford: Oxford UP, 1985) 113–20.

6   This hope is non-falsifiable. Let's say I chose pear at time 1 (T_1) in circumstance 1 (C_1). To prove I could have done otherwise, I chose peach at T_2 in C_2. How can my choosing peach at T_2 in C_2 prove that I could have chosen peach at T_1 in C_1?

7   See Paul-Henri Thiry, Baron d'Holbach, *The System of Nature*, H.D. Robinson (trans.) (Boston: J.P. Mendum, 1889 [1770]) 166–92; or John Hospers, "What Means This Freedom?" in Sidney Hook (ed.), *Determinism and Freedom in the Age of Modern Science* (New York: New York UP, 1958) 113–32.

8   See Walter Stace, *Religion and the Modern Mind* (Philadelphia: J.P. Lippincott, 1952) 248–58; and Daniel Dennett, "I Could Not Have Done Otherwise: So What?" *Journal of Philosophy* 81,10 (1984): 553–65.

9   Classical compatibilists tend to focus on external constraints. They had less to say about internal constraints like addictions, obsessions, neuroses, and compulsions, but this is not to say compatibilists cannot call such internal constraints cases of free will interference. See, for example, Harry Frankfurt, "Freedom of the Will and the Concept of a Person," in H. Frankfurt, *The Importance of What We Care About* (Cambridge: Cambridge UP, 1998) 11–25; Gary Watson, "Free Agency," *Journal of Philosophy* 8 (1975): 205–20; and Susan Wolf, *Freedom Within Reason* (Oxford: Oxford UP, 1990).

10 Nelson Pike, "Divine Omniscience and Voluntary Action," *The Philosophical Review* 74 (1965): 27–46. But see also Anthony Kenny, "Divine Foreknowledge and Human Freedom," in Anthony Kenny, *Aquinas: A Collection of Critical Essays* (Notre Dame: U of Notre Dame P, 1969); and Norman Kretzmann, "Omniscience and Immutability," *The Journal of Philosophy* 63,14 (1966): 409–21.

11 Augustine, "Divine Foreknowledge and Human Free Will," in Caroll Mason Sparrow (trans.), *St. Augustine on Free Will* (Richmond, VA: The Dietz Press, 1947) bk. 3, ch. 4.

12 To think all knowledge is like prediction to the extent that all knowledge could be wrong is to reject the standard definition of knowledge as justified true belief. Instead, we would think knowledge is simply justified belief. One may prefer this weaker definition of knowledge because our ability to determine what's "true" may be hopelessly mired in what we *believe* to be true. But the problem of how we know what's true is conceptually — if not practically — different from what is true.

13 This is also true of predicting future events of things. That my clock will tick tomorrow is a prediction, not a knowledge claim. For it is conditional upon, among other things, its battery not dying tonight, something I cannot know now. I can know that my clock *is* ticking. I can know that ticking clocks will continue to click so long as the battery is not dead. If I knew more about the inside of batteries (as God would

know), I might be able to know that my clock will tick tomorrow. Notice that saying this does not mean it is unreasonable for me to nevertheless predict that my clock will tick tomorrow. If knowledge is understood strictly, omniscience and L-free will collide.

14 If compatibilists do want to say one is not free to make a past true fact false, they would, presumably, understand the past as counting as an external constraint. This opens the door for saying omniscience conflicts even with compatibilist free will (C-free will), since to God, all your actions are, so to speak, already past. Thus omniscience interferes with even C-free will. But perhaps compatibilists will say that time does not count as an external constraint. If so, then one can be C-free whether or not an action is in the future, present, or past, and hence omniscience does not rule out C-free will. But if time does not count as an external constraint, then compatibilists would have to say that Jones is C-free today to mow the grass last week, which seems a weird thing to say. Since I cannot now decide which is weirder — time counting or not counting as an external constraint — I shall not explore this possibility here.

15 Of course the term "now" is a temporal term, but given that we are stuck in time, this is the best that we can do to capture the sense of an atemporal being's knowing. Conversely, we simply admit that an atemporal being cannot know anything: that knowledge is itself a temporal concept — which is roughly the point that will be raised below.

16 Boethius, *The Consolation of Philosophy*, Richard Green (trans.) (New York: MacMillan, 1962).

17 Gottfried Wilhelm Leibniz, "Essays on the Justice of God, and the Freedom of Man in the Origin of Evil," in his *Theodicy*, Diogenes Allen (ed.), E.M. Huggard (trans.) (Don Mills, ON: J.M. Dent & Sons, 1966) pt. 1, sec. 37, 47.

18 See Alvin Plantinga, *God, Freedom, and Evil* (New York: Harper & Row, 1974) 66–72.

CHAPTER 13: TIME AND IMMUTABILITY

1 Aquinas, "The Simplicity and Immutability of God," pt. I, Question 9, Article 1, in *Summa Theologica* in Anton C. Pegis (ed.), *Basic Writings of St. Thomas Aquinas* (New York: Random House, 1945) 70–71; Anselm, *Proslogion*, in S.W. Deane (ed.), *Anselm's Basic Writings* (La Salle, IL: Open Court, 1962) ch. 19.

2 The Neo-Platonists conceive of God as the sun, warming us all who do not cower in caves. Those who do not come out of the caves of ignorance do so at their own risk; it has nothing to do with God's lack of love. See, for example, Plotinus (c. CE 205–66), *Enneads*, A.H. Armstrong (trans.) (Cambridge, MA: Harvard UP, 1988). But this only works if we anthropomorphize the sun into thinking it shines on us because it loves us, as opposed to its shining regardless. Moreover, sometimes we fail to get sunlight because we cower in shade (for fear of skin cancer, probably) but at other times because it's night, or cloudy.

3 True, we can look simultaneously at three individual photographs of a child, a teenager, and an adult and nevertheless understand them to all be the same person at different times. We see the temporal relation while outside that time frame, so why can't God do likewise? But our understanding time is due to our being temporal beings. That is why we can see the temporal relations between the photographs. But given God's atemporality, God cannot understand that temporal relation.

4 See Brian Greene, *The Fabric of the Cosmos: Space, Time, and the Texture of Reality* (New York: Penguin, 2005).

5 Charles Hartshorne, *The Divine Relativity* (New Haven: Yale UP, 1948) ch. 3.

6   Anselm, *Proslogion*, ch. 8.

7   Hartshorne's position, referred to as *process theology*, better maps onto non-academic views of religion. As Boyer observes, a common feature of diverse religions across the globe is a belief in invisible persons with a great interest in our behaviour. Pascal Boyer, *Religion Explained: The Evolutionary Origins of Religious Thought* (New York: Basic Books, 2001) 18–19.

8   See also John Hick, *Philosophy of Religion* (Englewood Cliffs, NJ: Prentice-Hall, 1990) 14.

9   Hugh McCann, "The God Beyond Time," in Louis Pojman (ed.), *Philosophy of Religion* (Belmont, CA: Thomson Wadsworth, 2003) 213–30. For opposing views, see also Richard Swinburne, *The Coherence of Theism* (Oxford: Clarendon Press, 1977) 217; and Stephen Davis, "Temporal Eternity," in his *Logic and the Nature of God* (Grand Rapids, MI: Eerdmans, 1983) 16–22.

CHAPTER 14: IS GOD LOVE?

1   A CEGEP (see-jĕp) is a post-secondary, but pre-university, education institution in Québec, Canada, corresponding to grades 12 and 13 elsewhere. CEGEP is a French acronym for Collège d'enseignement général et professionnel, or "College of General and Vocational Education."

2   See for example: C.S. Lewis, *The Four Loves* (San Diego, CA: Harcourt Brace Jovanovich, 1988); John Templeton, *Agape Love: A Tradition Found in Eight World Religions* (Philadelphia: Templeton Foundation Press, 1999); Augustine, *Confessions* (Harmondsworth: Penguin Classics, 1961); Gene Outka, *Agape: An Ethical Analysis* (New Haven: Yale UP, 1978); Karl Barth, *Church Dogmatics*, vol. 4, *The Doctrine of Reconciliation* (Edinburgh: T & T Clark, 1976); Iris Murdoch, *Metaphysics as a Guide to Morals* (New York: Penguin, 1993); and Anders Nygren, *Agape and Eros*, P.S. Watson (trans.) (Philadelphia: The Westminster Press, 1953) 75–80.

PART IV. FAITH

CHAPTER 15: FAITH AND REASON

1   For the "that/how" distinction, see Gilbert Ryle, *The Concept of the Mind* (London: Penguin, 1990) 28–32.

2   This is roughly Plantinga's position: "[Atheists] may disagree, but how is that relevant? Must my criteria, or those of the Christian community, conform to their examples? Surely not. The Christian community is responsible to *its* set of examples, not to theirs." Alvin Plantinga, "On Taking Belief in God as Basic," in John Hick (ed.), *Classical and Contemporary Readings in the Philosophy of Religion*, 3rd ed. (Englewood Cliffs, NJ: Prentice Hall, 1990) 498–99.

3   For more on this, see Russell's distinction between *knowledge by acquaintance* and *knowledge by description*. Bertrand Russell, *The Problems of Philosophy* (Buffalo, NY: Prometheus Books, 1988) ch. 5, 46–59. I will return to this distinction in Chapter 21.

4   See, for example, William James, "The Will to Believe," in William James, *The Will to Believe and Other Essays* (Cambridge, MA: Harvard UP, 1979) 13–34.

5   See William Alston, "Religious Experience as a Ground of Religious Belief," in J. Runzo and C. Ihara (eds.), *Religious Experience and Religious Belief* (New York: UP of America, 1986) 31–51; William Alston, *Perceiving God: The Epistemology of Religious Experience* (Ithaca, NY: Cornell UP, 1993); William Alston, "Is Religious Belief Rational?" In S.M. Harrison and R.C. Taylor (eds.), *The Life of*

Religion (Lanham, MD: UP of America, 1986) 1–15; Alvin Plantinga, "On Taking Belief in God as Basic." But the same argument was also made by Pascal. Blaise Pascal, *Pensées*, W.F. Trotter (trans.) (New York: Random House, 1941 [1670]) ch. 7 "Morality and Doctrine," #434, 141–45.

6 As William James notes, *"Do you like me or not? ...* Whether you do or not depends ... on whether I meet you half-way, am willing to assume that you must like me, and show you trust and expectation. The previous faith on my part in your liking's existence is in such cases what makes your liking come. But if I stand aloof, and refuse to budge an inch until I have objective evidence ... ten to one your liking never comes" (James, "The Will to Believe," IX, 28).

7 For example, see Alvin Plantinga, *God and Other Minds: A Study of the Rational Justification of Belief in God* (Ithaca, NY: Cornell UP, 1990). Barrett, too, places heavy emphasis on the other minds analogy. "[H]ow ordinary people come to believe in God and other minds is strikingly similar." Justin Barrett, *Why Would Anyone Believe in God?* (Lanham, MD: Altamira Press, 2004) 98.

8 William James, "The Sentiment of Rationality," in William James, *The Will to Believe and Other Essays*, 80.

9 James, "The Sentiment of Rationality," 78.

10 William Kingdon Clifford, "The Ethics of Belief," in *The Ethics of Belief and Other Essays* (New York: Prometheus Books, 1999) 70–96.

11 There may be other examples, like reliance on memory, or belief in the existence of the past, but the examples in the text suffice to make the general point: some secular faiths are reasonable.

12 By "experience with God," I do not mean the bandwagoning appeal of people telling you about God, although Barrett evidently counts that as "experience" (Barrett, 41). People tell us about ghosts and aliens and trolls, but few would count that as constituting personal experience with these things.

13 For behavioural accounts of mind, see Gilbert Ryle, *The Concept of the Mind* (London: Penguin Books, 1990). For functional accounts, see Hilary Putnam, "The Nature of Mental States," in *Mind, Language, and Reality: Philosophical Papers*, vol. 2 (Cambridge: Cambridge UP, 1975) 429–44; or Jerry Fodor, *Psychological Explanation* (New York: Random House, 1968). For eliminativist accounts, see Paul Churchland, *Matter and Consciousness* (Cambridge, MA: MIT Press, 1984); or Daniel Dennett, *Consciousness Explained* (New York: Penguin, 1993).

14 Barrett, 99–100.

15 Just as we distinguish faulty sense recordings from acceptable sense recordings based on our other senses and prior probabilities, we also distinguish faulty memories from reliable memories. I remember getting lost returning from kindergarten. Part of the memory was spurned on by my parents re-telling the tale over the years, but I also had the distinct recollection of arriving at a bridge with the letters "E R I E" printed on its side and knowing then that I must be lost. Only much later did I doubt the accuracy of this recollection. It dawned on me that my train set (received much later in life) came with a bridge with the word "Erie" written on its side. In hindsight, I also surmised three other problems with my memory. For one, a kindergartener could not see over the particular bridge to see what was written on its side. For two, apart from graffiti, most bridges do not have "E R I E" written on them. For three, many years later I returned and found nothing written on it. Reflecting on these facts led me to suspect that, despite the vividness of my memory about getting lost, it was more probable that my memory was corrupt. I juxtaposed one memory onto another. If belief in God is like belief in one's memory being reliable, this won't help theists. The reliable memories are consistent with prior probabilities and current facts. Unreliable memories are not.

Lacking any prior probability for supernatural agency, belief in God should be similar to my Erie memory — a belief to discard, not to treat as basic.

16 For this sort of argument, see O.K. Bouwsma, "Descartes' Evil Genius," in *Philosophical Essays* (Lincoln, NE: U of Nebraska P, 1965) 85–98. Originally published in *The Philosophical Review* 58,2 (1949): 141–51.

17 Solipsism is the view that only you exist: everything else — including other people — is simply an image of your mind. The worry about your being merely a brain in a vat with mental images being fed into you intravenously typifies solipsism — although something feeding you the images contaminates the picture a bit.

18 Hume made this point in his discussion of natural beliefs. See David Hume, *A Treatise of Human Nature*, L.A. Selby-Bigge and P.H. Nidditch (eds.) (Oxford: Oxford UP, 1978) 119, 214–15. See also Norman Kemp Smith, *The Philosophy of David Hume* (London: Palgrave, 2005) 455–58.

19 For an account of the different ways of viewing faith, see T.J. Mawson, *Belief in God* (Oxford: Oxford UP, 2005) 219–33.

20 Aquinas, "On the Truth of the Catholic Faith," in *Summa Contra Gentiles*, in Anton C. Pegis (ed.), *Basic Writings of St. Thomas Aquinas* (New York: Random House, 1945) bk. 1.

CHAPTER 16: FIDEISM

1 According to Peterson, et al., fideism is "the view that religious belief systems are not subject to rational evaluation." Michael Peterson, William Hasker, Bruce Reichenbach, and David Basinger, *Reason and Religious Belief*, 3rd ed. (New York: Oxford UP, 2003) 45. Later in the book, however, they define fideism as "the view that faith is immune to external critique" (231). The two definitions are not equivalent. The first captures the Kierkegaardian account, the second the Wittgensteinian account. For a nice discussion of Kierkegaard's influence on Wittgenstein, however, see Charles L. Creegan, *Wittgenstein and Kierkegaard: Religion, Individuality and Philosophical Method* (London: Routledge, 1989).

2 Søren Kierkegaard, *Fear and Trembling*, Sylvia Walsh (trans.) (Cambridge: Cambridge UP, 2006 [1843]).

3 Søren Kierkegaard, "The Subjectivity of Truth; Inwardness; Truth is Subjective," in *Concluding Unscientific Postscript*, David T. Swensen (trans.) (Princeton: Princeton UP, 1941) bk. 2, pt. 2, ch. 2, 171. See also Martin Buber, *I and Thou*, Walter Kaufmann (trans.) (New York: Charles Scribner's Sons, 1970); William James, "Will to Believe" in *Will to Believe and Other Essays* (Cambridge, MA: Harvard UP, 1979) X, 31; and John Hick, *The Philosophy of Religion* (Englewood Cliffs, NJ: Prentice-Hall, 1990) 10–11.

4 "If I am capable of grasping God objectively, I do not believe, but precisely because I cannot do this I must believe." Kierkegaard, "Subjectivity of Truth," 182.

5 Such placebo accounts of religion capture William James's pragmatic appeal to religion. See James, "Will to Believe" 19, 30. See also William James, *Pragmatism* (New York: Longmans, Green, 1970) 75–78, 198–209, 218–23.

6 Kiekergaard also said that faith is not an act of will, but a "miracle." Søren Kierkegaard, *Philosophical Fragments* (Princeton: Princeton UP, 1985) 295. He was agreeing with Hume, who meant it sarcastically. See David Hume, "On Miracles," in his *Enquiry Concerning Human Understanding*, L.A. Selby-Bigge (ed.) (Oxford: Clarendon Press, 1989) 114–16.

7 Ludwig Wittgenstein, *Philosophical Investigations*, G.E.M. Anscombe (trans.) (Oxford: Blackwell, 1953) §454 (132e). See also, Ludwig Wittgenstein, *The Blue and Brown Books* (or *Preliminary Studies for "The Philosophical Investigations"*) (New York: Harper & Row, 1964) 33–34.

8 Ludwig Wittgenstein, "Lectures on Religious Belief," in Cyril Barrett (ed.), *Wittgenstein: Lectures and Conversations* (Berkeley, CA: U of California P, 1966) 53–54.

9 See also Kai Nielsen, "A Critique of Wittgensteinian Fideism," in William Rowe and William Wainwright (eds.), *Philosophy of Religion*, 3rd ed. (Oxford: Oxford UP, 1998) 312. As well, see Kai Nielsen, *Scepticism* (London: Macmillan, 1973) 61–67.

10 D.Z. Phillips, "Philosophy, Theology, and the Reality of God," *The Philosophical Quarterly* 13 (1963): 344–50; or D.Z. Phillips, "Faith, Scepticism and Religious Understanding," in D.Z. Phillips (ed.), *Religion and Understanding* (Oxford: Blackwell, 1967) 63–79. See also Norman Malcolm, "The Groundlessness of Belief," in Stuart C. Brown (ed.), *Reason and Religion* (Ithaca, NY: Cornell UP, 1997) 145–57.

CHAPTER 17: ULTIMATE CONCERN

1 Paul Tillich, *Dynamics of Faith* (New York: Harper and Row, 1957) 1–41; Paul Tillich, *Systematic Theology*, vol. 1 (Chicago: U of Chicago P, 1951) 211–15.

2 Pantheism is the view that God and the universe together with everything in the universe are identical.

3 Tillich, 31.

4 "The being of God is being-itself." Paul Tillich, *Systematic Theology*, vol. 1, 235.

5 Paul Tillich, "Two Types of Philosophy of Religion," *Union Seminary Quarterly Review* (1964) 3–13, reprinted in John Hick (ed.), *Classical and Contemporary Readings in the Philosophy of Religion*, 3rd ed. (Englewood Cliffs, NJ: Prentice Hall, 1990) 259.

6 "God does not exist. He is being-itself beyond essence and existence." Tillich, *Systematic Theology*, vol. 1, 205. "It is as atheistic to affirm the existence of God as it is to deny it. God is being-itself, not *a* being." Tillich, *Systematic Theology*, vol. 1, 237.

7 Paul Tillich, *The Courage to Be* (New Haven: Yale UP, 1966) 184–85.

8 Tillich, "Two Types of Philosophy of Religion," 254.

9 Tillich, "Two Types of Philosophy of Religion," 263.

10 "The term 'ultimate concern' unites the subjective and the objective side of the act of faith." Tillich, *Dynamics of Faith*, 10.

11 Martin Buber, *I and Thou*, Walter Kaufmann (trans.) (New York: Charles Scribner's Sons, 1970); Tillich, *The Courage to Be*, 160–63. Tillich, *Systematic Theology*, vol. 1, 271.

12 A fourth possibility is to treat the verb objectively and the noun subjectively. Although I believe that I'm in a state of being ultimately concerned, I'm not (objective verb), but what I believe I have an ultimate concern in is an ultimate concern due to my being ultimately concerned in it (subjective noun). Such a possibility is incoherent.

13 Tillich, *Systematic Theology*, vol. 1, 13; Tillich, "Two Types of Philosophy of Religion," 263.

14 "[A]ll modern philosophy is Christian, even if it is humanistic, atheistic, and intentionally anti-Christian," (Tillich, *Systematic Theology*, vol. 1, 27). "[E]verything finite participates in being-itself and in its infinity. Otherwise it would not have the power of being" (Tillich, *Systematic Theology*, vol. 1, 237). "The protest of atheism against such a highest person is correct. There is no evidence for his existence, nor is he a matter of ultimate concern.... [Rather,] [t]he divine life participates in every life as its ground and aim. God participates in everything that is" (Tillich, *Systematic Theology*, vol. 1, 245). Buber's sentiments are the same: "But whoever abhors the name and fancies that he is godless — when he addresses with his whole devoted being the You of his life that cannot be restricted by any other, he addresses God" (Buber, 124).

15 Perhaps "never" is too strong for all atheists. For me, it is apt. I don't believe in any non-natural properties, religious or non-religious, but some atheists may believe in some non-religious non-natural properties. Take, for example, Moore's belief that good is a non-natural, non-reducible property. G.E. Moore, *Principia Ethica* (Cambridge: Cambridge UP, 1986 [1903]).

CHAPTER 18: PO-MO THEO

1   Martin Heidegger, *Identity and Difference*, Joan Stambaugh (trans.) (New York: Harper & Row, 1969); Jacques Derrida, *Speech and Phenomena and Other Essays on Husserl's Theory of Signs*, D. Allison (trans.) (Evanston, IL: Northwestern UP, 1973); and Jean-Luc Marion, *God Without Being*, T.A. Carlson (trans.) (Chicago, IL: U of Chicago P, 1982). Good secondary sources include J.D. Caputo, *The Mystical Element in Heidegger's Thought* (New York: Fordham UP, 1986); and K. Hart, *The Trespass of the Sign: Deconstruction, Theology and Philosophy* (Cambridge: Cambridge UP, 1989).

2   Martin Buber, *I and Thou*, Walter Kaufmann (trans.) (New York: Charles Scribner's Sons, 1970). As does Tillich: Paul Tillich, *Systematic Theology*, vol. 1 (Chicago: U of Chicago P, 1951) 271. And James: William James, "Will to Believe" in *Will to Believe and Other Essays* (Cambridge, MA: Harvard UP, 1979) X, 31.

3   Anonymous, *The Cloud of Unknowing*, Clitton Wolters (trans.) (Harmondsworth: Penguin, 1970).

4   As note 1 in Chapter 1 indicates, there are two meanings given to "agnosticism": the general sense and the technical sense. Under the technical "God is unknowable" sense, *The Cloud of Unknowing* approach is agnostic. Under the general "fence-sitting" position, however, *The Cloud of Unknowing* approach is not agnostic. My use of "agnosticism" here follows the general sense.

5   G.W.F. Hegel, *Phenomenology of Spirit*, A. Miller (trans.) (Oxford: Clarendon Press, 1977 [1807]) 479–93.

6   Jacques Derrida, "Différance," in Alan Bass (trans.) *Margins of Philosophy* (Chicago, IL: Chicago UP, 1982) 1–28.

7   For more on the distinction between *a priori* and *a posteriori* claims, see Chapter 5.

8   For an accessible introduction to Zen Buddhism, see Alan Watts, *The Way of Zen* (New York: Vintage Books, 1957).

9   Or Sufism, perhaps. See Ian Almond, *Sufism and Deconstruction: A Comparative Study of Derrida and Ibn 'Arabia* (London: Routledge, 2004).

10 Meister Eckhart, *Selected Writings*, Oliver Davies (trans.) (Harmondsworth: Penguin Classics 1995); Rudolf Otto, *Mysticism of East and West*, B. Bracey and R. Payne (trans.) (New York: Macmillan, 1960).

11 Marion, *God Without Being*, 7–24.

12 Wittgenstein imagines a situation where everyone has a box that no one else could see into and whatever was in each person's box was called a "beetle." In such a case, the word "beetle" wouldn't be the name of a thing. The thing in the box would have "no place in the language-game at all; not even as a *something*: for the box might even be empty." Ludwig Wittgenstein, *Philosophical Investigations*, G.E.M. Anscombe (trans.) (Oxford: Blackwell, 1953) §293.

CHAPTER 19: PASCAL'S WAGER

1 Blaise Pascal, *Pensées*, W.F. Trotter (trans.) (New York: Random House, 1941 [1670]) "Of the Necessity of the Wager," ch. 3, #233, 81–84.

2 This presupposes the traditional line that atheists can't get to heaven. John Hick, among others, denies this. On his view, a form of *process theology*, everyone gets to heaven eventually. Hell is a myth. John Hick, *Evil and the God of Love* (New York: Macmillan, 1966) 377–81. I ignore this possibility in what follows. ·

3 For a modern take on Pascal's wager, see Stark and Finke's economic analysis of religious faith. Rodney Stark and Roger Finke, *Acts of Faith: Explaining the Human Side of Religion* (Berkeley: U of California P, 2000).

4 Pascal published his polemical attack against the Jesuits, *The Provincial Letters*, under a pseudonym, presumably to avoid excommunication. See Richard Popkin, "Blaise Pascal," in Paul Edwards (ed.), *The Enclyopedia of Philosophy* (New York: Macmillan and Free Press, 1967) vol. 6, 52.

5 Pascal, *Pensées*, #233, 83.

6 "[L]egislators make the citizens good by forming habits in them." Aristotle, *Nichomaechean Ethics*, Richard Mckeon (ed.), *The Basic Works of Aristotle* (New York: Random House, 1941) bk. II, sec. 1 (1103b) 952. See, also secs. 1–4 (1103b–1105b) 952–56.

7 If Pascal's audience were agnostics, his argument would succeed so long as agnostics are those who agree that God's existence has a 50–50 chance. Pascal's rebuttal, then, would give another reason — apart from those discussed in Chapter 1 — for why agnosticism is untenable.

8 See William James, *Pragmatism* (New York: Longmans, Green, 1970) 75–78, 198–209, 218–23. For James, since one's life goes psychologically better believing in God than not, one should believe in God — *whether or not God exists in fact*. "[W]e are better off even now if we believe [religious affirmations] to be true." William James, "Will to Believe" in *Will to Believe and Other Essays* (Cambridge, MA: Harvard UP, 1979) X, 30. Whether it is true that one's life goes psychologically better believing in God is contentious. But even if it is true for some people, it cannot count as favourable to theism. Theists would never admit that their belief in God is merely a placebo for an unsatisfactory life. One should have a reason to believe in God irrespective of whether such a belief would make one's life psychologically go better.

9 Pascal, *Pensées*, #233, 82.

CHAPTER 20: NON-FALSIFIABILITY

1 Anthony Flew, "Theology and Falsification," in Anthony Flew and Alasdair MacIntyre (eds.), *New Essays in Philosophical Theology* (New York: Macmillan, 1955) 96–99. For his further discussion on the short paper, see Anthony Flew, *The Presumption of Atheism* (New York: Harper & Row, 1976) 71–80. The original parable is derived from John Wisdom, "Gods," *Proceedings of the Aristotlean Society* (1944) reprinted in John Wisdom, *Philosophy and Psycho-Analysis* (Oxford: Blackwell, 1953) 149–68.

2   Sennett and Yandell suggest that theism can be falsified by imagining counterfactual worlds — worlds that would clearly entail the non-existence of God. Yandell admits some holdouts may maintain their beliefs anyway, but such would be a matter of "uncommon stubborness," not that faith is inherently non-falsifiable. Keith Yandell, "A Reply to Nielsen's Comments," in Keith Yandell (ed.), *God, Men, and Religion: Readings in the Philosophy of Religion* (New York: McGraw-Hill, 1973) 242; James Sennett, "Theism and Other Minds: On the Falsifiability of Non-Theories," *Topoi* 14 (1995): 149–60. But maintaining faith given the current factual world is already uncommonly stubborn.

3   See, for example, A.J. Ayer, *Language, Truth, and Logic* (New York: Dover, 1952); Rudolph Carnap, *The Logical Structure of the World and Pseudo Problems in Philosophy*, Rolf George (trans.) (Berkeley, CA: U of California P, 1969); Carl Hempel, "On the Logical Positivists' Theory of Truth," *Analysis* 2 (1934–35): 49–59.

4   Karl Popper, *The Logic of Scientific Discovery* (New York: Basic Books, 1959) 40–42.

5   Part of Popper's reason to focus so heavily on falsification concerned his worry that we cannot technically *verify* a theory. We cannot conclusively prove a general law true from even a million observations that cohere with the theory. All that we can "verify" are the observations that we have seen. But these observations are insufficient to warrant the inference that it will *always* be so, or that it is a *law* that it is so, as David Hume articulated (David Hume, *Enquiry Concerning Human Understanding*, L.A. Selby-Bigge [ed.] [Oxford: Clarendon Press, 1989 (1777)] sec. VII, 60–79). The worry revolves around treating "verify" too narrowly, however. It is true that our hypothesis that the sun will come up tomorrow, say, is not deductively valid, but scientific method concerns itself with inductive generalizations.

6   Hick, *Philosophy of Religion*, 103–05.

7   Depending on translation, the quote is, "Where we are, death is not; where death is, we are not." Epicurus, *Letter to Menoeceus* ¶ 3. See for example, Eugene O'Connor (trans.) *The Essential Epicurus* (Amherst, NY: Prometheus Books, 1993).

8   For example, Alvin Plantinga, *God and Other Minds* (Ithaca, NY: Cornell UP, 1990) 156–85. See also Richard Swinburne, *The Coherence of Theism* (Oxford: Oxford UP, 1977) 22–29. Even some atheists reject the non-falsifiability criteria, for example, J.L. Mackie, *The Miracle of Theism* (Oxford: Clarendon Press, 1982) 1–3.

9   John Hick, "Theology and Verification," *Theology Today* 17 (1960): 260–61. See also John Hick, *Faith and Knowledge* (New York: Macmillan, 1966) ch. 8.

10 This example comes from John Hick, *Philosophy of Religion* (Englewood Cliffs, NJ: Prentice Hall, 1990) 104.

11 See Keith Stanovich, *How to Think Straight about Psychology* (Glenview, IL: Scott, Foresman and Company, 1986) 18–19, 120–21.

12 For a great example of this, see Anne Fausto-Sterling, *Myths of Gender: Biological Theories about Women and Men* (New York: Basic Books, 1985) 32. For a defence of science in general, see Malcolm Murray and Nebojsa Kujundzic, *Critical Reflection* (Montreal: McGill-Queen's UP, 2005) 340–64.

13 A "fair coin" is defined as one that has an equal chance of landing on any one side of a two sided coin. Perhaps an expert coin flipper, like an expert knife thrower, can nevertheless tilt the odds in favour of one side over another.

PART V. IMPLICATIONS

CHAPTER 21: MYSTICISM

1   The Brights network suggests that to reject the supernatural is also to reject mystical experiences. ("A bright is a person who has a naturalistic worldview, free of supernatural and mystical elements." July 2008 bulletin. <http://www.the-brights.net/>.) This would be so only if mysticism is interpreted as a supernatural experience. It is this identification that I reject. Mystical states are simply replicable brain states.

2   For seminal accounts, see William James, *Varieties of Religious Experience* (London, Collier Books, 1969) 299–336; Rudolph Otto, *Mysticisms East and West*, B. Bracey and R. Payne (trans.) (New York: Macmillan, 1960); Walter Stace, *Mysticism and Philosophy* (New York: Macmillan, 1961); R.C. Zaehner, *Mysticism: Sacred and Profane* (Oxford: Oxford UP, 1973); Ninian Smart, "Numinous Experience and Mystical Experience," in his *Dialogues of Religions* (London: SMC Press, 1960); Philip C. Almond, *Mystical Experience and Religious Doctrine: An Investigation of the Study of Mysticism in World Religions* (Berlin: Moulin, 1982); Evelyn Underhill, *Mysticism* (New York: Dutton, 1961); William Wainwright, *Mysticism* (Brighton: Harvester Press, 1981); C.B. Martin, *Religious Belief* (Ithaca, NY: Cornell UP, 1962); and C.D. Broad, "The Appeal to Religious Experience," in his *Religion, Philosophy and Psychical Research* (London: Routledge, 2000). For a critique, see Kai Nielsen, *Scepticism* (London: Macmillan, 1973) 67–73. For modern takes, see Charles Taylor, *Varieties of Religion Today: William James Revisited* (Cambridge, MA: Harvard UP, 2003); John Horgan, *Rational Mysticism: Dispatches from the Border between Science and Spirituality* (New York: Houghton Mifflin, 2003); and Andrew Newberg, Eugene D'Aquili, and Vince Rause, *Why God Won't Go Away: Brain Sciences and the Biology of Belief* (New York: Random House, 2002) 98–127.

3   Martin Buber, *I and Thou*, Walter Kaufmann (trans.) (New York: Charles Scribner's Sons, 1970) 160.

4   Buber, 158.

5   See, for example, William James, *Varieties of Religious Experience*, lecture XVI.

6   Daniel Carr, "Endorphins at the Approach of Death," *Lancet* 8269,14 (1981): 390; Russell Noyes, Jr., "The Encounter with Life-Threatening Danger: Its Nature and Impact," *Essence* 5,1 (1981): 21–32.

7   But "God" would not be the right term; rather "Nothingness."

8   Buber, 127.

9   See, for example, Steven Katz "Mysticism and the Interpretation of Sacred Scripture," in Steven Katz (ed.), *Mysticism and Sacred Scripture* (Oxford: Oxford UP, 2000) 7–66.

10 See, for example, Huston Smith, "Do Drugs have Religious Import?" *Journal of Philosophy* 71,18 (1964): 517–30.

11 Father F.C. Copleston in his radio debate with Bertrand Russell, broadcast in 1948 on the Third Program of the British Broadcasting Corporation. Reprinted in Bertrand Russell, *Why I Am Not a Christian* (London: George Allen & Unwin, 1957) 143.

12 Joe Novack, in conversation, supplied me with the magic eye poster analogy. He used it as an analogy to faith. You need faith that a three-dimensional image is present in order to go through the various procedures to see the three-dimensional image. Without prior belief that anything is there to be seen beyond the squiggly lines, you won't bother with the necessary steps. Thus, you won't ever see the three-

dimensional image, which, of course, would seem to confirm your disbelief. I like the analogy, though it fails for the same reasons as those outlined in Chapter 15.

13 Copleston, 143.

14 Bertrand Russell, *The Problems of Philosophy* (Buffalo, NY: Prometheus Books, 1988) ch. 5, 46–59.

15 James, *Varieties of Religious Experience*, 335.

16 Copleston, 144.

17 I use "veridical" here rather than "true" or "real," not because I'm pompous (or not merely because I'm pompous) but because the latter terms create an ambiguity. We can say that the *experience* is real, or true. That means that it is true that they had the experience, or that the experience is a real phenomenon. But whether that subjective experience gives an accurate picture of objective reality is another matter entirely.

18 I am one of those who profess to have had mystical experiences. Yet, I remain an atheist.

CHAPTER 22: GOD AND MORALITY

1 For a recent (but by no means simplistic) view, see Charles Taylor, *The Secular Age* (Cambridge, MA: Harvard UP, 2007).

2 For an account of the origin of the phrase, see Chapter 9, note 1.

3 Kant's moral theory, by the way, is unaffiliated with Kant's moral argument for God's existence. His moral theory involves the categorical imperative and does not rely on the *summum bonum*.

4 See my extended argument in Malcolm Murray, *The Moral Wager: Evolution and Contract* (Dordrecht: Springer, 2007).

5 Especially not doing *harm* to others, but some of your actions may not harm me, yet I'd still call it immoral, like your spiking my drink with a tasteless, non-toxic additive merely for your amusement, or your spying on me even though you don't do anything with the information gleaned and I never find out about it.

6 Plato, *Euthyphro*, in Edith Hamilton and Huntington Cairns (eds.), *Plato: The Collected Dialogues* (Princeton: Princeton UP, 1987) 170–85.

7 Plato, *Euthyphro*, 7a.

8 Jan Narveson was fond of making this point in his moral theory lectures at the University of Waterloo, Waterloo, Ontario. See also, Jan Narveson, *The Libertarian Idea* (Philadelphia: Temple UP, 1988).

9 This is Bishop Butler's position, for example. "Every man finds within himself the rules of right, and any obligations to follow it." Joseph Butler, *Fifteen Sermons Preached at the Rolls Chapel* (London, 1726) Sermon II, 32.

10 Brian Garvey, *The Philosophy of Biology* (Montreal: McGill-Queen's UP, 2007) 98–99.

11 Garvey, 99.

12 Garvey, 94–107. See also Paul Griffiths, "What is Innateness?" *The Monist* 85 (2002): 70–85.

13 Some moral theories (or some interpretations of some moral theories) might say that you ought not to harm Billy even if Billy likes being so harmed, but this seems misconceived. Let's say that Billy asks you to pull out his impacted tooth even if it harms him. A moral theory that says bluntly, "No, don't harm ever, even if the harm

is desired by the harmed!" collapses into senseless rule-following. Although harm is normally a bad thing, consent is the morally crucial factor.

14 Butler's example concerns a trap. Despite your love of cheese, say, you wouldn't snatch the cheese if it were in a trap. Being properly selfish, you would avoid the temptation. Butler, Sermon II, 38.

15 Augustine, *Confessions* (Harmondsworth: Penguin Classics, 1961) bk. 7, chs. 12 & 13, 148–49. See also Augustine, "Divine Foreknowledge and Human Free Will," in Caroll Mason Sparrow (trans.) *St. Augustine on Free Will* (Richmond, VA: The Dietz Press, 1947) bk. 3, ch. 4.

16 "In those, however, who have use of free will — and they alone are capable of committing venial sin — the infusion of grace never occurs without an actual exercise of free will towards God and against sin." St. Thomas Aquinas, *Summa Theologica*, in Anton C. Pegis (ed.), *Basic Writings of St. Thomas Aquinas* (New York: Random House, 1945) Q87, art. 2. See also Q113, art. 5.

17 Aquinas, Q95, art. 1.

18 Scott Atran *In Gods We Trust: The Evolutionary Landscape of Religion* (Oxford: Oxford UP, 2002) 73; Justin Barrett, *Why Would Anyone Believe in God?* (Lanham, MD: Altamira Press, 2004) 78–79. See also J. Piaget, *The Child's Conception of the World* (New York: Harcourt Brace, 1929).

19 Pascal Boyer, *Religion Explained: The Evolutionary Origins of Religious Thought* (New York: Basic Books, 2001) 151–58.

20 David Gauthier, *Morals By Agreement* (Oxford: Oxford UP, 1986) 21.

21 See Murray, *The Moral Wager*, 95–99, 147–51.

22 See Gauthier, 174–77.

23 This way of describing morality fits contractarian and evolutionary models. Other theories would put the matter differently. Most theories also keep God out of their picture of morality, however, and that's the main message in this chapter. Mill claimed that utilitarianism is the principle that God would use to determine morality. John Stuart Mill, *Utilitarianism* (Buffalo, NY: Prometheus Books, 1987 [1863]) 41. He says this to avoid the charge that he left God out of his account of morality. Kant's version of morality is founded on the categorical imperative: "Act only on that maxim by which you can will to be a universal law." Immanuel Kant, *Grounding for the Metaphysics of Morals*, James W. Ellington (trans.) (Indianapolis: Hackett, 1986) Ak. 414. By this formula, moral obligations are deductive calculations based on self-consistency. No talk of God is required. (I happen to think that this logic works only so long as we invoke the more basic principle of consent, but for that discussion, see my *Moral Wager*, 46–47.) Only virtue theory (and of course brazen theistic accounts) lends itself to talk of God, but not necessarily so. Virtue theorists emphasize well-being as the motive for adopting moral dispositions, but religion does not have a monopoly on theories of well-being. (I also happen to think that it is not helpful to collapse theories of morality into theories of well-being [see my *Moral Wager*, 28–31], but that disagreement is also not germane to the topic here.)

24 See Rodney Stark and Roger Finke, *Acts of Faith: Explaining the Human Side of Religion* (Berkeley: U of California P, 2000) 103; or Rodney Stark, *One True God: Historical Consequences of Monotheism* (Princeton: Princeton UP, 2001) 12–15.

25 Boyer, 167.

26 See, for example, Phil Zuckerman, *Society Without God* (New York: New York UP, 2008), and Gregory Paul, "The Chronic Dependence of Popular Religiosity upon Dysfunctional Psychosocial Conditions," *Evolutionary Psychology* 7,3 (2009): 398–41.

27 Boyer, 170.

28 For more against equating morality with religion, see J.L. Mackie, *The Miracle of Theism* (Oxford: Clarendon Press, 1982) 102–18.

CHAPTER 23: THE MEANING OF LIFE

1   The word "Islam" means submission, for example.

2   This is Ivan Karamazov's point in Fyodor Dostoyevsky, *The Brothers Karamazov*, David Magarshack (trans.) (New York: Penguin Books, 1982 [1880]) pt. 1, bk. 2, ch. 6, 77; and bk. 5, ch. 4, 287. Sartre also takes up the theme. See Jean-Paul Sartre, *Existentialism and Humanism* (London: Methuen, 1965) 27.

3   As perhaps Charles Taylor would say. For him, life does not have meaning without God. Living merely for the good points of family, career, security, and such is insufficient for Taylor. Charles Taylor, *The Secular Age* (Cambridge, MA: Harvard UP, 2007).

4   See David Hume, "Of the Origin of Ideas" in *Enquiries Concerning Human Understanding*, L.A. Selby-Bigge (ed.) (Oxford: Clarendon Press, 1989 [1777]) sec. II, 17–22.

5   Dostoyevsky, pt. 1, bk. 1, ch. 1, 3.

6   Sartre, 26.

7   See for example, Friedrich Nietzsche, *Beyond Good and Evil*, J. Hollingdale (trans.) (London: Penguin, 1990) §260, 197; §261, 199.

8   Sartre, 29.

9   I am happy to discover that this is also Einstein's answer to the question, "What is the meaning of life?" Albert Einstein, *The World As I See It* (New York: Philosophical Library, 1949) 1.

CHAPTER 24: DEATH

1   Pascal Boyer, *Religion Explained: The Human Instincts that Fashion Gods, Spirits and Ancestors* (London: Heinemann, 2001) 203–28; Justin Barrett, *Why Would Anyone Believe in God?* (Lanham, MD: Altamira Press, 2004) 56–58; Daniel Dennett, *Breaking the Spell: Religion as a Natural Phenomenon* (New York: Penguin, 2006) 112–13.

2   See, for example, John Hick, *Evil and the God of Love* (New York: Macmillan, 1966) 377–81.

3   Plato, *The Republic*, in Edith Hamilton and Huntington Cairns (eds.), *Plato: The Collected Dialogues* (Princeton: Princeton UP, 1961) bk. VII, 514a–517c.

4   Plato, *Meno*, in Hamilton and Cairns (eds.), 82b–86b.

5   René Descartes, *Meditations on First Philosophy*, Laurence J. Lafleur (trans.) (New York: Macmillan, 1951) Meditations II and III.

6   Plato, *Phaedo*, in Hamilton and Cairns (eds.), 85e3–86d4.

7   Plato's rebuttal is specious. The musician may be following sheet music, which tells him how to play the lyre, just as the "soul" follows health standards in telling the "body" not to smoke.

8   This is one of the problems Gilbert Ryle noted in *The Concept of the Mind* (London: Penguin, 1990) 17. Descartes, evidently aware of the problem, suggested that the interaction between mind and body occurred in the pineal gland. René Descartes, *Passions of the Soul*, Stephen Voss (trans.) (Indianapolis: Hackett, 1989) 37, n. 35

and 36. This is like dealing with cat faeces by moving them from the living room to the bedroom.

9 Technically, unilateral spatial agnosia. See J.M. Heaton, *The Eye: Phenomenology and Psychology of Function and Disorder* (London: Tavistock, 1938); and E.A. Weinstein, M. Cole, M.S. Mitchell, and O.G. Lyerly, "Anosognosia and Aphasia," *Archives of Neurology* 10 (1964): 376–86. My limited knowledge comes from Coren Porac Ward, *Sensation and Perception* (Orlando, FL: Academic Press, 1984) 504. Table 24.1 is my own rendition modelled after the figure shown in Ward.

10 I am uncertain if only *some* recollections have been accurate, or *all* recollections have been accurate. Nor am I clear on what counts as "accurate." Nor am I convinced that experimenter effects have been ruled out. Someone sharing my doubts is Keith Augustine. See his "Does Paranormal Perception Occur in Near-Death Experiences?" *Journal of Near-Death Studies* 25,4 (2007): 203–36; "Near-Death Experiences with Hallucinatory Features," *Journal of Near-Death Studies* 26,1 (2007): 3–31; and "Psychophysiological and Cultural Correlates Undermining as Survivalist Interpretation of Near-Death Experiences," *Journal of Near-Death Studies* 26,2 (2007): 89–125.

11 Raymond Moody, Jr., *Life after Life: The Investigations of a Phenomenon–Survival of Bodily Death* (Harrisburg, PA: Stackpole Books, 1976); Stanislav Grof and Christina Grof, *Beyond Death: The Gates of Consciousness* (London: Thames, 1980); Kenneth Ring, *Life at Death: A Scientific Investigation of the Near-Death Experience* (New York: Coward, McCann & Geoghegan, 1980).

12 Apart from Augustine's articles noted above, these worries are also echoed in Susan Blackmore's *Dying to Live: Near-Death Experiences* (Amherst, NY: Prometheus Books, 1993), and G.M. Woerlee's *Mortal Minds: The Biology of Near Death Experiences* (Amherst, NY: Prometheus Books, 2005).

13 Maurice Rawlings, *Beyond Death's Door* (Nashville, TN: Thomas Nelson, 1978). Maurice Rawlings, *Before Death Comes* (Nashville, TN: Thomas Nelson, 1980).

14 Daniel Carr, "Endorphins at the Approach of Death," *Lancet* 8269,14 (1981): 390; Daniel Carr, "Pathophysiology of Stress-Induced Limbic Lobe Dysfunction: A Hypothesis Relevant to Near-Death Experiences," *Anabiosis* 2,1 (1982): 75–89; Bruce Greyson, "Near-Death Experiences and Attempted Suicide," *Suicide and Life-Threatening Behavior* 11,1 (1981): 10–16; Russell Noyes, Jr., "Near-Death Experiences: Their Interpretation and Significance," in Robert Kastenbaum (ed.), *Between Life and Death* (New York: Springer, 1979) 73–88.

15 See, for example, Shimon Amir, Zavie Brown, and Zalman Amit, "The Role of Endorphins in Stress: Evidence and Speculations," *Neuroscience and Behavioural Reviews* 4 (1980): 27–86, or S. Clare, "Adrenaline and Noradrenaline: Introduction," *Encyclopedia of Life Sciences* (London: John Wiley & Sons, 2006).

16 H. Akil and S.J. Watson, "The Role of Endogenous Opiates in Pain Control," in H.W. Kosterlitz and L.Y. Terenius (eds.), *Pain and Society* (Weinheim: Verlag Chemie, 1980) 201–22.

17 For effects on the amygdala to explain NDEs, see Scott Atran *In Gods We Trust: The Evolutionary Landscape of Religion* (Oxford: Oxford UP, 2002) 188–90.

18 Carr, "Endorphins at the Approach of Death." Russell Noyes, Jr., "The Encounter with Life-Threatening Danger: Its Nature and Impact," *Essence* 5,1 (1981): 21–32.

19 At any rate, no evidence that NDEs can occur without these physiological structures has been given.

20 Thanks to Dr. Michael Lantz for helping me make as much sense of the brain as I could muster here.

21 Russell Noyes, Jr., "Is There Evidence for Life After Death?" *The Humanist* 37,1 (1977): 51–53.

22 Blackmore concludes that NDEs are likely a result of loss of oxygen to the brain. Susan Blackmore, *Beyond the Body: An Investigation of Out-of-the-Body Experience* (Chicago: Academy Chicago, 1989).

23 See, for example, Owen Flanagan, "Deconstructing Dreams: The Spandrels of Sleep," *The Journal of Philosophy* 92 (1995): 5–27; or Owen Flanagan, *Dreaming Souls: Sleep, Dreams, and the Evolution of the Conscious Mind* (New York: Oxford UP, 2000).

24 Richard Brandt, "The Morality of Abortion," *The Monist* 56 (1972): 504–26, reprinted and revised in R.L. Perkins (ed.), *Abortion: Pro and Con* (Cambridge, MA: Schenkman, 1974). See especially, 166–67.

25 How the brain stores memory, admittedly, has not been solved. It appears to involve the patterns of cell firings, not specific cells themselves. See, for example, Eric Kandel, *In Search of Memory: The Emergence of a New Science of Mind* (New York: W.W. Norton, 2006); or Leonard Stern, *The Structures and Strategies of Human Memory* (Homewood, IL: The Dorsey Press, 1985).

26 Bertrand Russell, *Why I am Not a Christian* (London: Unwin, 1979) 70–73.

27 H.H. Price, "Survival and the Idea of 'Another World'," *Proceedings of the Society for Psychical Research* 1,182 (1953): 1–25, reprinted in John Donnelly (ed.), *Language, Metaphysics, and Death* (New York: Fordham UP, 1978) 176–95. See also Terence Penhelum, *Survival and Disembodied Existence* (London: Routledge & Kegan Paul, 1970).

28 Price, 188.

CHAPTER 25: ERROR THEORY

1 Is religion so widespread? Steel thinks it really isn't. "[O]rdinary people believe in God in the same way that they believe their best friend's wife doesn't look her age." David Ramsey Steel, *Atheism Explained: From Folly to Philosophy* (Peru, IL: Open Court Press, 2008) 269.

2 For Hume's error theory concerning religion, see David Hume, *The Natural History of Religion* (Stanford, CA: Stanford UP, 1956).

3 See, for example, Pascal Boyer, *Religion Explained: The Human Instincts that Fashion Gods, Spirits and Ancestors* (London: Heinemann, 2001) 20.

4 Richard Dawkins, "Viruses of the Mind," in B. Dalbom (ed.), *Dennett and his Critics* (Oxford: Blackwell, 1993) 13–27.

5 See, for example, Justin Barrett, *Why Would Anyone Believe in God?* (Lanham, MD: Altamira Press, 2004) 120–21.

6 See, for example, Jack David Eller, *Introducing Anthropology of Religion* (New York: Routledge, 2007).

7 For example, John Hick, *Philosophy of Religion* (Englewood Cliffs, NJ: Prentice Hall, 1990) 124–25.

8 Proverbs 28:26.

9 Brian Garvey, *Philosophy of Biology* (Montreal: McGill-Queen's UP, 2007) 204.

10 "Religious concepts are probably influenced by the way the brain's inference systems produce explanations without our being aware of it" (Boyer, 18). "The mind it takes to have religion is the standard architecture that we all have by virtue of being members of the species" (Boyer, 135). "[R]eligious concepts are parasitic upon other mental capacities" (Boyer, 311).

11 David Sloan Wilson, *Darwin's Cathedral: Evolution, Religion, and the Nature of Society* (Chicago: U of Chicago P, 2002). See also Boyer, 20, 135, 155–58, 167.

12 Perhaps more societies than formalized religions would care to admit are abandoning religion in favour of other kinds of social networks. See Gregory Paul, "The Chronic Dependence of Popular Religiosity upon Dysfunctional Psychosocial conditions," *Evolutionary Psychology* 7,3 (2009): 398–441; and Phil Zuckerman, *Society Without God* (New York: New York UP, 2008).

13 See also Daniel Dennett, *Breaking the Spell: Religion as a Natural Phenomenon* (New York: Penguin, 2006) 188. Or more to Dennett's point: "The best that can be said for religion is that it helps some people achieve the level of citizenship and morality typically found in brights" (Dennett 55). A "bright" is one who rejects supernatural explanations. See <http://www.the-brights.net/>.

14 Sigmund Freud, *Totem and Taboo* (New York: Prometheus, 2000). See also Feuerbach, "God is the manifested inward nature of man." Ludwig Feuerbach, "The Essence of Religion Considered Generally," in *The Essence of Christianity*, George Eliot (trans.), 1854, ch. 1, §2, reprinted in John Hick, *Classical and Contemporary Readings in the Philosophy of Religion* (Englewood Cliffs, NJ: Prentice-Hall, 1990) 149.

15 Scott Atran, *In Gods We Trust: The Evolutionary Landcape of Religion* (Oxford: Oxford UP, 2002) 73; Barrett, 78–79. See also J. Piaget, *The Child's Conception of the World* (New York: Harcourt Brace, 1929).

16 Barrett, 34–6, 109.

17 Boyer, 14. Dennett believes that the "mists of incomprehension and failure of communication are not just annoying impediments to rigorous refutation; they are themselves design features of religions worth looking at closely on their own" (Dennett, 217).

18 See for example, Boyer, 134.

19 Boyer, 37. See also Dan Sperba *Explaining Culture: A Naturalistic Approach* (Oxford: Blackwell, 1996).

20 Boyer, 37.

21 For an in-depth exploration of the meme theory (in general, let alone applied to religion), see Susan Blackmore, *The Meme Machine* (Oxford: Oxford UP, 1999). For a more tainted view, see Darrell Ray, *The God Virus: How Religion Infects Our Lives and Culture* (Bonner Springs, KA: IPC Press, 2009).

22 See Stephen Jay Gould and Richard Lewontin, "The Spandrels of San Marco and the Panglossian Paradigm: A Critique of the Adaptationist Programme," *Proceedings of the Royal Society* B205 (1979): 581–98.

23 Gould and Lewontin's criticisms raised in "The Spandrels of San Marco," are internal. They are not objecting to Darwinian evolution itself. They merely note that the story is a bit more complex than typical accounts suggest. See also Stephen Jay Gould "Exaptation: A Crucial Tool for Evolutionary Psychology," *Journal of Social Issues* 47 (1991): 43–65. Jerry Fodor, on the other hand, thinks Gould fails to recognize how damaging his own critique is to Darwinian evolution on the whole. See Jerry Fodor, "What Darwin Got Wrong," paper presented at the Atlantic Region Philosophical Association Meeting, St. Francis Xavier University, Nova Scotia, Canada, Oct. 29, 2008. This will become a similarly named book co-written with Massimo Piattelli-Palmarini. But see also Jerry Fodor, "Why Pigs Don't Have Wings," *London Review of Books*, Oct. 18, 2007, 19–22; or Jerry Fodor, *The Mind Doesn't Work That Way* (Cambridge, MA: MIT Press, 2000) 79–100.

24 Stephen Jay Gould and Elizabeth Vrba, "Exaptation: A Missing Term in the Science of Form," *Paleobiology* 8,1 (1982): 4–15.

25 Stephen Jay Gould, *The Panda's Thumb: More Reflections in Natural History* (Harmondsworth: Penguin, 1980) 19–27.

26 Gould, *Panda's Thumb*, 24.

27 Dennett, 63–64.

28 Boyer, 18.

29 See Atran, 59–61. See also Barrett, 31–44; Boyer, 144–48; and Dennett, 112–16.

30 Or *more generally* deadly. In the case of the burglar, it might be better if I accept the false negative and go back to sleep, rather than the true positive and get up, confront the burglar, and be killed.

31 Dennett, 117.

32 Atran, 60.

33 Hume, 29.

34 Boyer, 130.

35 Boyer, 145. See also Dennett, 112.

36 This supposition has been challenged. According to George Rey, since the notion that God exists is so patently absurd, it isn't possible that so many people actually believe in God. More likely they are engaged in self-delusion, like ignoring the signs of infidelity in your spouse. Rey figures that our *wish* to believe trumps what we really know. George Rey, "Meta-Atheism: Religious Avowal as Self-Deception," in Louise Antony (ed.), *Philosophers Without Gods* (New York: Oxford UP, 2007) 243–65. See also Steele, 269.

37 Hume, 29. See also Atran: "Human minds appear to be programmed to look for, and readily countenance, agents as the causes of complex and uncertain happenings. Scientists intellectually wean people away from reliance on the psychological bias by encouraging withdrawal from it by degrees" (Atran, 49). For the view that science isn't very successful at weaning people of superstition, however, see David Vyse, *Believing in Magic: The Psychology of Superstition* (Oxford: Oxford UP, 1997).

38 Barrett, 38–39.

39 See Dean Hamer, *The God Gene: How Faith is Hardwired into Our Genes* (New York: Doubleday, 2004).

40 Dennett, 83. "Whenever you think of Jesus some parts of your brain are going to be more active than others, but whenever you think of *anything* this is going to be the case ... [Hence] using neuro-imaging to study religious beliefs is almost as hapless as using a voltmeter to study a chess-playing computer" (Dennett, 316). See also Boyer, 309.

BIBLIOGRAPHY

Akil, H. and S.J. Watson. "The Role of Endogenous Opiates in Pain Control." In H.W. Kosterlitz and L.Y. Terenius (eds.), *Pain and Society*, 201–22. Weinheim: Verlag Chemie, 1980.

Almond, Ian. *Sufism and Deconstruction: A Comparative Study of Derrida and Ibn 'Arabia*. London: Routledge, 2004.

Almond, Philip C. *Mystical Experience and Religious Doctrine: An Investigation of the Study of Mysticism in World Religions*. Berlin: Moulin, 1982.

Alston, William. *Divine Nature and Human Language*. Ithaca, NY: Cornell UP, 1989.

——. "Is Religious Belief Rational?" In S.M. Harrison and R.C. Taylor (eds.), *The Life of Religion*, 1–15. Lanham, MD: UP of America, 1986.

——. *Perceiving God: The Epistemology of Religious Experience*. Ithaca, NY: Cornell UP, 1993.

——. "Religious Experience as a Ground of Religious Belief." In J. Runzo and C. Ihara (eds.), *Religious Experience and Religious Belief*, 31–51. New York: UP of America, 1986.

Altizer, Thomas J.J. *The Gospel of Christian Atheism*. Philadelphia: Westminster Press, 1966.

Amir, Shimon, Zavie Brown, and Zalman Amit. "The Role of Endorphins in Stress: Evidence and Speculations." *Neuroscience and Behavioural Reviews* 4 (1980): 27–86.

Anonymous. *The Cloud of Unknowing*, Clitton Wolters (trans.). Harmondsworth: Penguin, 1970.

Anselm, St. *Monologion and Proslogion, with the Replies of Gaunilo and Anselm*, Thomas Williams (trans.). Indianapolis: Hackett, 1995.

——. *Proslogium*. In S.W. Deane (ed.), *Anselm's Basic Writings*. La Salle, IL: Open Court, 1962.

Antony, Louise (ed.). *Philosophers without Gods*. New York: Oxford UP, 2007.

Aquinas, St. Thomas. *Summa Contra Gentiles*. In Anton C. Pegis (ed.), *Basic Writings of St. Thomas Aquinas*. New York: Random House, 1945.

——. *Summa Theologica*. In Anton C. Pegis (ed.), *Basic Writings of St. Thomas Aquinas*. New York: Random House, 1945.

Aristotle. *Nichomaechean Ethics*. In Richard Mckeon (ed.), *The Basic Works of Aristotle*, 935–1112. New York: Random House, 1941.

Armstrong, Karen. *History of God*. New York: Ballantine Books, 1993.

Atran, Scott. *In Gods We Trust: The Evolutionary Landscape of Religion*. Oxford: Oxford UP, 2002.

Augustine. *City of God*. New York: The Modern Library, 1950.

——. *Confessions*. Harmondsworth: Penguin Classics, 1961.

——. "Divine Foreknowledge and Human Free Will." In Caroll Mason Sparrow (trans.), *St. Augustine on Free Will*. Richmond, VA: The Dietz Press, 1947.

Augustine, Keith. "Does Paranormal Perception Occur in Near-Death Experiences?" *Journal of Near-Death Studies* 25,4 (2007): 203–36.

——. "Near-Death Experiences with Hallucinatory Features." *Journal of Near-Death Studies* 26,1 (2007): 3–31.

——. "Psychophysiological and Cultural Correlates Undermining as Survivalist Interpretation of Near-Death Experiences." *Journal of Near-Death Studies* 26,2 (2007): 89–125.

Ayer, A.J. *Language, Truth, and Logic*. New York: Dover, 1952.

Baggini, Julien. *Atheism: A Very Short Introduction*. New York: Oxford UP, 2003.

Barrett, Justin. *Why Would Anyone Believe in God?* Lanham, MD: Altamira Press, 2004.

Barth, Karl. *Church Dogmatics*. Vol. 4, *The Doctrine of Reconciliation*. Edinburgh: T & T Clark, 1976.

Behe, Michael. *Darwin's Black Box*. New York: Free Press, 1996.

Berman, David. *A History of Atheism in Britain: From Hobbes to Russell*. London: Routledge, 1988.

Billington, Ray. *Religion Without God*. New York: Routledge, 2002.

Blackmore, Susan. *Beyond the Body: An Investigation of Out-of-the-Body Experience*. Chicago: Academy, 1989.

——. *Dying to Live: Near-Death Experiences*. Amherst, NY: Prometheus Books, 1993.

——. *The Meme Machine*. Oxford: Oxford UP, 1999.

Boethius, St. *The Consolation of Philosophy*, Richard Green (trans.). New York: Macmillan, 1962.

Bonhoeffer, Dietrich. *Letters and Papers from Prison*, R. Fuller (trans.). London: S.C.M. Press, 1967.

Bouwsma, O.K. "Descartes' Evil Genius." In *Philosophical Essays*, 85–98. Lincoln, NE: U of Nebraska P, 1965. Originally published in *The Philosophical Review* 58,2 (1949): 141–51.

Boyer, Pascal. *Religion Explained: The Human Instincts that Fashion Gods, Spirits and Ancestors*. London: Heinemann, 2001.

Brandt, Richard. "The Morality of Abortion." *The Monist* 56 (1972): 504–26. Reprinted and revised in R.L. Perkins (ed.), *Abortion: Pro and Con*, 151–69. Cambridge, MA: Schenkman, 1974.

Broad, C.D. *Religion, Philosophy and Psychical Research*. London: Routledge, 2000.

Buber, Martin. *I and Thou*, Walter Kaufmann (trans.). New York: Charles Scribner's Sons, 1970.

Buckley, Michael. *At the Origins of Modern Atheism*. New Haven: Yale UP, 1987.

Burrell, D.B. *Freedom and Creation in Three Traditions*. Notre Dame: U of Notre Dame P, 1993.

Butler, Joseph. *Fifteen Sermons Preached at the Rolls Chapel*. London, 1726.

Caputo, J.D. *The Mystical Element in Heidegger's Thought*. New York: Fordham UP, 1986.

Carnap, Rudolph. *The Logical Structure of the World and Pseudo Problems in Philosophy*, Rolf George (trans.). Berkeley, CA: U of California P, 1969.

Carr, Daniel. "Endorphins at the Approach of Death." *Lancet* 8269,14 (1981): 390.

——. "Pathophysiology of Stress-Induced Limbic Lobe Dysfunction: A Hypothesis Relevant to Near-Death Experiences." *Anabiosis* 2,1 (1982): 75–89.

Carrier, Richard. "The Argument from Biogenesis: Probabilities Against a Natural Origin of Life." *Biology and Philosophy* 14 (2004): 739–64.

——. *Sense and Goodness without God*. New York: Authorhouse, 2005.

Churchland, Paul. *Matter and Consciousness*. Cambridge, MA: MIT Press, 1984.

Clare, S. "Adrenaline and Noradrenaline: Introduction." *Encyclopedia of Life Sciences*. London: John Wiley & Sons, 2006.

Clarke, Samuel. *A Demonstration of the Being and Attributes of God*. Cambridge: Cambridge UP, 1998.

Clifford, William Kingdon. *The Ethics of Belief and Other Essays*. New York: Prometheus Books, 1999.

Copleston, Father F.C. and Bertrand Russell. *A Debate on the Argument from Contingency*. Broadcast in 1948 on the Third Program of the British Broadcasting Corporation. Reprinted in Bertrand Russell, *Why I Am Not a Christian*, 133–54. London: George Allen & Unwin, 1957.

Craig, William Lane. *The Kalām Cosmological Argument*. Eugene, OR: Wipf and Stock Publishers, 1979.

Craig, William Lane and J.P. Moreland (eds.). *The Blackwell Companion to Natural Theology*. Oxford: Blackwell, 2009.

Creegan, Charles L. *Wittgenstein and Kierkegaard: Religion, Individuality and Philosophical Method*. London: Routledge, 1989.

Cupitt, Don. *After God*. New York: Basic Books, 1997.

Darwin, Charles. *The Origin of Species*, W.J. Burrow (ed.). Harmondsworth: Penguin, 1968.

Davidson, Donald. "What Metaphors Mean." In S. Sachs (ed.), *On Metaphor*, 29–45. Chicago: U of Chicago P, 1979.

Davis, Stephen. *Logic and the Nature of God*. Grand Rapids, MI: Eerdmans, 1983.

——. "Temporal Eternity." *Logic and the Nature of God*, 16–22. Grand Rapids, MI: Eerdmans, 1983.

Dawkins, Richard. *The Blind Watchmaker*. New York: W.W. Norton, 1986.

——. *The God Delusion*. New York: Houghton Mifflin, 2008.

——. "Viruses of the Mind." In B. Dalbom (ed.), *Dennett and his Critics*, 13–27. Oxford: Blackwell, 1993.

Dennett, Daniel. *Breaking the Spell: Religion as a Natural Phenomenon*. Harmondsworth: Penguin, 2006.

——. *Consciousness Explained*. New York: Penguin, 1993.

——. "I Could Not Have Done Otherwise: So What?" *Journal of Philosophy* 81,10 (1984): 553–65.

——. *The Intentional Stance*. Cambridge, MA: MIT Press, 1989.

Derrida, Jacques. "Différance." In Alan Bass (trans.), *Margins of Philosophy*, 1–28. Chicago, IL: Chicago UP, 1982.

——. *Speech and Phenomena and Other Essays on Husserl's Theory of Signs*, D. Allison (trans.). Evanston, IL: Northwestern UP, 1973.

Descartes, René. *Meditations on First Philosophy*, Laurence J. Lafleur (trans.). New York: Macmillan, 1951.

——. *Passions of the Soul*, Stephen Voss (trans.). Indianapolis: Hackett, 1989.

Dostoyevsky, Fyodor. *The Brothers Karamazov*, David Magarshack (trans.). New York: Penguin Books, 1982.

Eckhart, Meister. *Selected Writings*, Oliver Davies (trans.). Harmondsworth: Penguin 1995.

Edwards, Paul. "A Critique of the Cosmological Argument." In Hector Hawton (ed.), *The Rationalist Annual*, 63–77. London: Pemberton Publishing Co., 1959.

——. "Russell's Doubts about Induction." *Mind* 68 (1949): 141–63.

Einstein, Albert. *The World As I See It*. New York: Philosophical Library, 1949.

Eller, Jack David. *Introducing Anthropology of Religion*. New York: Routledge, 2007.

Epicurus. *Letter to Menoeceus*. In Eugene O'Connor (trans.), *The Essential Epicurus*. Amherst, NY: Prometheus Books, 1993.

Ewing, A.C. "The Argument from Design." *The Fundamental Questions of Philosophy*, 225–31. London: Routledge & Kegan Paul, 1951.

Fausto-Sterling, Anne. *Myths of Gender: Biological Theories about Women and Men*. New York: Basic Books, 1985.

Feuerbach, Ludwig. "The Essence of Religion Considered Generally." Reprinted in John Hick, *Classical and Contemporary Readings in the Philosophy of Religion*, 149–63. Englewood Cliffs, NJ: Prentice-Hall, 1990.

Findlay, J.N. "Can God's Existence Be Disproved?" *Mind* 57 (1948). Reprinted in William Rowe and William Wainwright (eds.), *Philosophy of Religion: Selected Readings*, 3rd ed., 19–23. Oxford: Oxford UP, 1988.

Flanagan, Owen. "Deconstructing Dreams: The Spandrels of Sleep." *The Journal of Philosophy* 92 (1995): 5–27.

——. *Dreaming Souls: Sleep, Dreams, and the Evolution of the Conscious Mind*. New York: Oxford UP, 2000.

Flew, Anthony. *The Presumption of Atheism*. New York: Harper & Row, 1976.

——. "Theology and Falsification." In Anthony Flew and Alasdair MacIntyre (eds.), *New Essays in Philosophical Theology*, 96–99. New York: Macmillan, 1955.

Flew, Anthony with Roy Abraham Varghese. *There is a God: How the World's Most Notorious Atheist Changed His Mind*. New York: HarperCollins, 2007.

Fodor, Jerry. *The Mind Doesn't Work That Way*. Cambridge, MA: MIT Press, 2000.

——. *Psychological Explanation*. New York: Random House, 1968.

——. "Why Pigs Don't Have Wings." *London Review of Books* (Oct. 18, 2007) 19–22.

Fodor, Jerry, and Massimo Piattelli-Palmarini. "What Darwin Got Wrong." Paper presented at the Atlantic Region Philosophical Association Meeting, St. Francis Xavier University, Nova Scotia, Canada, Oct. 29, 2008.

Foot, Philippa. "Morality as a System of Hypothetical Imperatives." *Philosophical Review* 71 (1972): 305–16.

Frankfurt, Harry. "Freedom of the Will and the Concept of a Person." In H. Frankfurt, *The Importance of What We Care About*, 11–25. Cambridge: Cambridge UP, 1998.

——. "The Logic of Omnipotence." *The Philosophical Review* 73 (1964): 262–63.

Freeman, James. *Thinking Logically: Basic Steps for Reasoning*. Englewood Cliffs, NJ: Prentice Hall, 1988.

Freud, Sigmund. *Totem and Taboo*. New York: Prometheus, 2000.

Garvey, Brian. *Philosophy of Biology*. Montreal: McGill-Queen's UP, 2007.

Gauthier, David. *Morals By Agreement*. Oxford: Oxford UP, 1986.

Geach, P.T. "Omnipotence." *Philosophy* 48 (1973): 7–20.

Goodman, Nelson. *Fact, Fiction and Forecast*. Indianapolis: Hackett, 1979.

Gould, Stephen Jay. "Exaptation: A Crucial Tool for Evolutionary Psychology." *Journal of Social Issues* 47 (1991): 43–65.

——. *The Panda's Thumb: More Reflections in Natural History*. Harmondsworth: Penguin, 1980.

Gould, Stephen Jay and Richard Lewontin. "The Spandrels of San Marco and the Panglossian Paradigm: A Critique of the Adaptationist Programme." *Proceedings of the Royal Society* B205 (1979): 581–98.

Gould, Stephen Jay and Elizabeth Vrba. "Exaptation: A Missing Term in the Science of Form." *Paleobiology* 8,1 (1982): 4–15.

Greene, Brian. *The Fabric of the Cosmos: Space, Time, and the Texture of Reality*. New York: Penguin, 2005.

Greyson, Bruce. "Near-Death Experiences and Attempted Suicide." *Suicide and Life-Threatening Behavior* 11,1 (1981): 10–16.

Grice, H.P. "Logic and Conversation." In *Studies in the Way of Words*, 22–40. Cambridge, MA: Harvard UP, 1989.

Griffiths, Paul. "What is Innateness?" *The Monist* 85 (2002): 70–85.

Grof, Stanislav and Christina Grof. *Beyond Death: The Gates of Consciousness*. London: Thames, 1980.

Hamer, Dean. *The God Gene: How Faith is Hardwired into Our Genes*. New York: Doubleday, 2004.

Hamilton, William. "The Death of God Theologies Today" in Thomas Altizer and William Hamilton, *Radical Theology and the Death of God*. New York: Bobbs-Merrill, 1996.

Harman, Gilbert. *The Nature of Morality*. New York: Oxford UP, 1977.

Harris, Sam. *The End of Faith: Religion, Terror, and the Future of Reason*. New York: W.W. Norton, 2004.

Hart, K. *The Trespass of the Sign: Deconstruction, Theology and Philosophy*. Cambridge: Cambridge UP, 1989.

Hartshorne. Charles. *The Divine Relativity: A Social Conception of God*. New Haven: Yale UP, 1948.

——. *A Natural Theology for Our Time*. La Salle, IL: Open Court, 1967.

——. *Omnipotence and Other Theological Mistakes*. New York: State U of New York P, 1983.

Heaton, J.M. *The Eye: Phenomenology and Psychology of Function and Disorder.* London: Tavistock, 1938.

Hegel, G.W.F. *Phenomenology of Spirit,* A. Miller (trans.). Oxford: Clarendon Press, 1977.

Heidegger, Martin. *Identity and Difference,* Joan Stambaugh (trans.). New York: Harper & Row, 1969.

Hempel, Carl. "On the Logical Positivists' Theory of Truth." *Analysis* 2 (1934–35): 49–59.

Hick, John (ed.). *Classical and Contemporary Readings in the Philosophy of Religion,* 3rd ed. Englewood Cliffs, NJ: Prentice Hall, 1990.

——. *Evil and the God of Love.* London: Macmillan, 1966.

——. *Faith and Knowledge.* New York: Macmillan, 1966.

——. "An Irenaean Theodicy." In John Hick (ed.), *Classical and Contemporary Readings in the Philosophy of Religion,* 3rd ed., 391–405. Englewood Cliffs, NJ: Prentice Hall, 1990.

——. *Philosophy of Religion.* Englewood Cliffs, NJ: Prentice-Hall, 1990.

——. "A Philosophy of Religious Pluralism." In John Hick (ed.), *Classical and Contemporary Readings in the Philosophy of Religion,* 3rd ed., 418–32. Englewood Cliffs, NJ: Prentice Hall, 1990.

——. "Theology and Verification." *Theology Today* 17 (1960): 260–61.

Hill, Thomas Jr. *Dignity and Practical Reason in Kant's Moral Theory.* Ithaca, NY: Cornell UP, 1992.

Hitchens, Christopher. *God is not Great: How Religion Poisons Everything.* New York: Hachette Book Group, 2007.

Hitchens, Christopher (ed.). *The Portable Atheist: Essential Readings for the Nonbeliever.* Philadelphia: Da Capo Press, 2007.

Hobbes, Thomas. *The Leviathan.* Buffalo: Prometheus Books, 1988.

d'Holbach, Baron Paul-Henri Thiry. *The System of Nature,* H.D. Robinson (trans.). Boston: J.P. Mendum, 1889.

Horgan, John. *Rational Mysticism: Dispatches from the Border between Science and Spirituality.* New York: Houghton Mifflin, 2003.

Hospers, John. "What Means This Freedom?" In Sidney Hook (ed.), *Determinism and Freedom in the Age of Modern Science,* 113–32. New York: New York UP, 1958.

Hull, David. "On Human Nature." In David Hull and Michael Ruse (eds.), *The Philosophy of Biology.* Oxford: Oxford UP, 1998.

Hume, David. *Dialogues Concerning Natural Religion,* Norman Kemp Smith (ed.). New York: Macmillan, 1987.

——. *Enquiries Concerning Human Understanding and Concerning the Principles of Morals,* L.A. Selby-Bigge (ed.). Oxford: Clarendon Press, 1989.

——. *The Natural History of Religion.* Stanford, CA: Stanford UP, 1956.

——. *A Treatise of Human Nature,* L.A. Selby-Bigge and P.H. Nidditch (eds.). Oxford: Oxford UP, 1978.

Huxley, Thomas Henry. *Collected Essays.* London: Macmillan, 1904.

Ikeda, Michael and Bill Jeffreys. "The Anthropic Principle Does Not Support Supernaturalism." In Michael Martin and Ricki Monnier (eds.), *The Improbability of God,* 155–66. Amherst, NY: Prometheus Books, 2006.

Iraeneus, St. of Lyon. *Against Heresies*. Whitefish, MT: Kessinger Publishing, 2004.

James, William. *Pragmatism*. New York: Longmans, Green, 1970.

——. *Varieties of Religious Experience*. London: Collier Books, 1969.

——. *The Will to Believe and Other Essays*. Cambridge, MA: Harvard UP, 1979.

Kandel, Eric. *In Search of Memory: The Emergence of a New Science of Mind*. New York: W.W. Norton, 2006.

Kane, Robert. *A Contemporary Introduction to Free Will*. Oxford: Oxford UP, 2005.

Kant, Immanuel. *Critique of Practical Reason*, Thomas Kingsmill Abbott (trans.). London: Longmans, Green and Co., 1963.

——. *Critique of Pure Reason*, Norman Kemp Smith (trans.). London: St. Martin's Press, 1969.

——. *Grounding for the Metaphysics of Morals*, James W. Ellington (trans.). Indianapolis: Hackett, 1986.

Katz, Stephen. "Mysticism and the Interpretation of Sacred Scripture." In Steven Katz (ed.), *Mysticism and Sacred Scripture*, 7–66. Oxford: Oxford UP, 2000.

Kee, Alistair. *The Way of Transcendence: Christian Faith Without Belief in God*. New York: Penguin, 1993.

Kenny, Anthony. *Aquinas: A Collection of Critical Essays*. Notre Dame: U of Notre Dame P, 1969.

——. "Divine Foreknowledge and Human Freedom." In Anthony Kenny, *Aquinas: A Collection of Critical Essays*. Notre Dame: U of Notre Dame P, 1969.

——. *The God of the Philosophers*. Oxford: Clarendon Press, 1979.

——. *The Unknown God*. London: Continuum, 2004.

Kierkegaard, Søren. *Concluding Unscientific Postscript*, David T. Swensen (trans.). Princeton: Princeton UP, 1941.

——. *Fear and Trembling*, Sylvia Walsh (trans.). Cambridge: Cambridge UP, 2006.

——. *Philosophical Fragments*. Princeton: Princeton UP, 1985.

Korsgaard, Christine. *The Sources of Normativity*. Cambridge: Cambridge UP, 1998.

Kretzmann, Norman. "Omniscience and Immutability." *The Journal of Philosophy* 63,14 (1966): 409–21.

Kushner, Harold. *When Bad Things Happen to Good People*. New York: Avon, 1981.

Leeming, David. *A Dictionary of Creation Myths*. New York: Oxford UP, 1996.

Leibniz, Gottfried Wilhelm. *The Monadology and Other Writings*, R. Latta (trans.). Oxford: Oxford UP, 1925.

——. *Theodicy*, Diogenes Allen (ed.), E.M. Huggard (trans.). Don Mills, ON: J.M. Dent & Sons, 1966.

Lerner, Melvin and D.J. Miller. "Just World Research and the Attribution Process: Looking Back and Ahead." *Psychological Bulletin* 85,5 (1978): 1030–51.

Leslie, John. *Universes*. London: Routledge, 1989.

Lewis, C.S. *The Four Loves*. San Diego, CA: Harcourt Brace Jovanovich, 1988.

Loftus, John (ed.). *The Christian Delusion: Why Faith Fails*. Amherst, NY: Prometheus Books, 2010.

Loptson, Peter. *Reality: Fundamental Topics in Metaphysics*. Toronto: U of Toronto P, 2001.

Lubac, Henri de. *The Drama of Atheist Humanism*, Edith Riley (trans.) New York: World Publishing Co., 1966

MacIntyre, Alasdair. *After Virtue*. Notre Dame: U of Notre Dame P, 1984.

——. "The Debate about God: Victorian Relevance and Contemporary Irrelevance." In Alasdair MacIntyre and Paul Ricœur, *The Religious Significance of Atheism*, 26–27. New York: Columbia UP, 1969.

Mackie, J.L. *Ethics: Inventing Right and Wrong*. Harmondsworth: Penguin, 1977.

——. *The Miracle of Theism*. Oxford: Clarendon Press, 1982.

Malcolm, Norman. "Anselm's Ontological Arguments." *Philosophical Review* 69,1 (1960): 41–62.

——. "The Groundlessness of Belief." In Stuart C. Brown (ed.), *Reason and Religion*, 145–57. Ithaca, NY: Cornell UP, 1997.

Marion, Jean-Luc. *God Without Being*, T.A. Carlson (trans.). Chicago, IL: U of Chicago P, 1982.

Martin, C.B. *Religious Belief*. Ithaca, NY: Cornell UP, 1962.

Martin, Michael. *Atheism: A Philosophical Justification*. Philadelphia: Temple UP, 1990.

—— (ed.). *The Cambridge Companion to Atheism*. Cambridge: Cambridge UP, 2007.

Martin, Michael and Ricki Monnier (eds.). *The Impossibility of God*. Amherst, NY: Prometheus Books, 2003.

—— (eds.). *The Improbability of God*. Amherst, NY: Prometheus Books, 2006.

Matthews, Warren. *World Religions*. Belmont, CA: Wadsworth, 2006.

Mavrodes, George. "Some Puzzles Concerning Omnipotence." *The Philosophical Review* 72 (1963): 221–23.

Mawson, T.J. *Belief in God*. Oxford: Oxford UP, 2005.

Mayr, Ernst. *The Growth of Biological Thought*. Cambridge, MA: Harvard UP, 1982.

McCann, Hugh. "The God Beyond Time." In Louis Pojman (ed.), *Philosophy of Religion*, 213–30. Belmont, CA: Thomson Wadsworth, 2003.

McFague, Sallie. *Metaphorical Theology: Models of God in Religious Language*. Philadelphia: Fortress Press, 1982.

McGrath, Alister. *The Twilight of Atheism: The Rise and Fall of Disbelief in the Modern World*. New York: Doubleday, 2005.

Miceli, Vincent. *The Gods of Atheism*. New Rochelle, NY: Arlington House, 1971.

Mill, John Stuart. *Utilitarianism*. Buffalo, NY: Prometheus Books, 1987.

Miller, K. "The Flagellum Unspun: The Collapse of Irreducible Complexity." In M. Ruse and W. Dembeski (eds.), *Debating Design: From Darwin to DNA*, 81–97. Cambridge: Cambridge UP, 2004.

Moody, Raymond Jr. *Life after Life: The Investigations of a Phenomenon–Survival of Bodily Death*. Harrisburg, PA: Stackpole Books, 1976.

Moore, G.E. *Principia Ethica*. Cambridge: Cambridge UP, 1986.

——. "Proof of an External World." In G.E. Moore, *Philosophical Papers*, 32–59. London: Allen & Unwin, 1959.

Murdoch, Iris. *Metaphysics as a Guide to Morals*. New York: Penguin, 1993.

Murray, Malcolm. *The Moral Wager: Evolution and Contract*. Dordrecht: Springer, 2007.

Murray, Malcolm and Nebojsa Kujundzic. *Critical Reflection.* Montreal: McGill-Queen's UP, 2005.

Nagel, Thomas. *The View from Nowhere.* Oxford: Oxford UP, 1985.

Narveson, Jan. *The Libertarian Idea.* Philadelphia: Temple UP, 1988.

Newberg, Andrew, Eugene D'Aquili, and Vince Rause. *Why God Won't Go Away: Brain Sciences and the Biology of Belief,* 98–127. New York: Random House, 2002.

Nielsen, Kai. "A Critique of Wittgensteinian Fideism." In William Rowe and William Wainwright (eds.), *Philosophy of Religion,* 3rd ed., 304–12. Oxford: Oxford UP, 1998.

——. *Scepticism.* London: Macmillan Press, 1973.

Nietzsche, Friedrich. *Beyond Good and Evil,* J. Hollingdale (trans.). London: Penguin, 1990.

——. *The Gay Science,* Walter Kaufmann (trans.). New York: Random House, 1974.

——. *The Genealogy of Morals,* Douglas Smith (trans.). Oxford: Oxford UP, 1996.

Noyes, Russell, Jr. "The Encounter with Life-Threatening Danger: Its Nature and Impact." *Essence* 5,1 (1981): 21–32.

——. "Is There Evidence for Life After Death?" *The Humanist* 37,1 (1977): 51–53.

——. "Near-Death Experiences: Their Interpretation and Significance." In Robert Kastenbaum (ed.), *Between Life and Death,* 73–88. New York: Springer, 1979.

Nygren, Anders. *Agape and Eros,* P.S. Watson (trans.). Philadelphia: The Westminster Press, 1953.

Ostrom, J.H. "Archaeopteryx and the Origin of Flight." *Quarterly Review of Biology* 49 (1974): 27–47.

——. "Bird Flight: How Did it Begin?" *American Scientist* 67 (1979): 46–56.

Otto, Rudolph. *Mysticisms East and West,* B. Bracey and R. Payne (trans.). New York: Macmillan, 1960.

Outka, Gene. *Agape: An Ethical Analysis.* New Haven: Yale UP, 1978.

Paley, William. *Natural Theology.* Edinburgh: William and Robert Chambers Publishers, 1849.

Pascal, Blaise. *Pensées,* W.F. Trotter (trans.). New York: Random House, 1941.

Paul, Gregory. "The Chronic Dependence of Popular Religiosity upon Dysfunctional Psychosocial Conditions." *Evolutionary Psychology* 7,3 (2009): 398–441.

Penhelum, Terence. *Survival and Disembodied Existence.* London: Routledge & Kegan Paul, 1970.

Peterson, Michael, William Hasker, Bruce Reichenbach, and David Basinger. *Reason and Religious Belief,* 3rd ed. New York: Oxford UP, 2003.

Phillips, D.Z. "Faith, Scepticism and Religious Understanding." In D.Z. Phillips (ed.), *Religion and Understanding,* 63–79. Oxford: Blackwell, 1967.

——. "Philosophy, Theology, and the Reality of God." *The Philosophical Quarterly* 13 (1963): 344–50.

Piaget, J. *The Child's Conception of the World.* New York: Harcourt Brace, 1929.

Pike, Nelson. "Divine Omniscience and Voluntary Action." *The Philosophical Review* 74 (1965): 27–46.

Plantinga, Alvin. *God, Freedom, and Evil.* New York: Harper & Row, 1974.

——. *God and Other Minds.* Ithaca, NY: Cornell UP, 1990.

——. "On Taking Belief in God as Basic." In J. Runzo and C. Ihara (eds.), *Religious Experience and Religious Belief*, 1–17. Lanham, MD: UP of America, 1986. Reprinted in John Hick (ed.), *Classical and Contemporary Readings in the Philosophy of Religion*, 3rd ed., 484–99. Englewood Cliffs, NJ: Prentice Hall, 1990.

——. "When Faith and Reason Clash: Evolution and the Bible." *Christian Scholar's Review* 21 (1991): 8–32.

Plato. *Euthyphro*. In Edith Hamilton and Huntington Cairns (eds.), *Plato: The Collected Dialogues*, 169–85. Princeton: Princeton UP, 1961.

——. *Meno*. In Edith Hamilton and Huntington Cairns (eds.), *Plato: The Collected Dialogues*, 353–84. Princeton: Princeton UP, 1961.

——. *Parmenides*. In Edith Hamilton and Huntington Cairns (eds.), *Plato: The Collected Dialogues*, 920–56. Princeton: Princeton UP, 1961.

——. *Phaedo*. In Edith Hamilton and Huntington Cairns (eds.), *Plato: The Collected Dialogues*, 40–98. Princeton: Princeton UP, 1961.

——. *The Republic*. In Edith Hamilton and Huntington Cairns (eds.), *Plato: The Collected Dialogues*, 575–844. Princeton: Princeton UP, 1961.

——. *Timaeus*. In Edith Hamilton and Huntington Cairns (eds.), *Plato: The Collected Dialogues*, 1151–211. Princeton: Princeton UP, 1961.

Plotinus. *Enneads*, A.H. Armstrong (trans.). Cambridge, MA: Harvard UP, 1988.

Popkin, Richard. "Blaise Pascal." In Paul Edwards (ed.), *The Enclyopedia of Philosophy*, vol. 6, 51–55. New York: Macmillan, 1967.

Popper, Karl. *The Logic of Scientific Discovery*. New York: Basic Books, 1959.

Price, H.H. "Survival and the Idea of 'Another World'." *Proceedings of the Society for Psychical Research* 1,182 (1953): 1–25. Reprinted in John Donnelly (ed.), *Language, Metaphysics, and Death*, 176–95. New York: Fordham UP, 1978.

Putnam, Hilary. "The Nature of Mental States." In *Mind, Language, and Reality: Philosophical Papers*, vol. 2, 429–44. Cambridge: Cambridge UP, 1975.

Rawlings, Maurice. *Before Death Comes*. Nashville, TN: Thomas Nelson, 1980.

——. *Beyond Death's Door*. Nashville, TN: Thomas Nelson, 1978.

Ray, Darrell. *The God Virus: How Religion Infects our Lives and Culture*. Bonner Springs, KA: IPC Press, 2009.

Rey, George. "Meta-Atheism: Religious Avowal as Self-Deception." In Louise Antony (ed.), *Philosophers without Gods*, 243–65. New York: Oxford UP, 2007.

Ricœur, Paul. "Biblical Hermeneutics." In J.D. Crossan (ed.), *Semeia 4*. Missoula, MT: Scholars Press, 1975.

——. *Interpretation Theory: Discourse on the Subject of Meaning*. Fort Worth, TX: Texas Christian UP, 1976.

——. "Religion, Atheism, and Faith." In Alasdair MacIntyre and Paul Ricœur, *The Religious Significance of Atheism*, 57–98. New York: Columbia UP, 1969.

——. *The Road to Metaphor: Multi-Disciplinary Studies of the Creation of Meaning in Language*. London: Routledge, 1978.

Ring, Kenneth. *Life at Death: A Scientific Investigation of the Near-Death Experience*. New York: Coward, McCann & Geoghegan, 1980.

Robinson, John. *Honest to God*. Philadelphia: Westminster Press, 1963.

Rosenthal, Jeffrey S. *Struck By Lightning: The Curious World of Probabilities*. Toronto: HarperCollins, 2005.

Ross, James F. "Analogy as a Rule of Meaning for Religious Language." *International Philosophical Quarterly* 1,30 (1961): 468–502.

Rowe, William. *The Cosmological Argument*. Princeton, NJ: UP, 1971.

——. *Philosophy of Religion*. Belmont, CA: Wadsworth, 1978.

——. "The Problem of Evil and Some Varieties of Atheism." Reprinted in William Rowe and William Wainwright (eds.), *Philosophy of Religion: Selected Readings*, 3rd ed., 242–50. Oxford: Oxford UP, 1988.

Rubenstein, Richard. *After Auschwitz: Radical Theology and Contemporary Judaism*. Indianapolis: Bobbs-Merril, 1966.

Rundle, Bede. *Why There Is Something Rather Than Nothing*. Oxford: Clarendon Press, 2004.

Russell, Bertrand. "On Denoting." In Robert Marsh (ed.), *Logic and Knowledge*, 41–56. London: Allen and Unwin, 1956.

——. "The Philosophy of Logical Atomism." Reprinted in John Slater (ed.), *The Collected Papers of Bertrand Russell, 1914–19*, vol. 8. London: Routledge, 1986.

——. *The Problems of Philosophy*. Buffalo, NY: Prometheus Books, 1988.

——. *Why I am Not a Christian*. London: Unwin, 1979.

Ryle, Gilbert. *The Concept of the Mind*. London: Penguin, 1990.

Salmon, Wesley. "Inductive Inference." In B. Baumrin (ed.), *Philosophy of Science*, 353–70. New York: Interscience Publishers, 1963.

Sartre, Jean-Paul. *Existentialism and Humanism*. London: Methuen, 1965.

Savage, G. Wade. "The Paradox of the Stone." *The Philosophical Review* 76 (1967): 74–79.

Schilling, S. Paul. *God in an Age of Atheism*. Nashville: Abingdon Press, 1969.

Sennett, James. "Theism and Other Minds: On the Falsifiability of Non-Theories." *Topoi* 14 (1995): 149–60.

Singer, Peter. "Famine, Affliction, and Morality." *Philosophy & Public Affairs* 1,3 (1972): 229–43.

Skyrms, Brian. *Evolution of the Social Contract*. Cambridge: Cambridge UP, 1996.

Smart, Ninian. "Numinous Experience and Mystical Experience." *Dialogues of Religions*. London: SMC Press, 1960.

Smith, George. *Atheism: The Case Against God*. Amherst, NY: Prometheus Books, 1989.

Smith, Huston. "Do Drugs Have Religious Import?" *Journal of Philosophy* 61,18 (1964): 517–30.

——. *The World's Religions*. San Francisco: HarperCollins, 1991.

Smith, Norman Kemp. *The Philosophy of David Hume*. London: Palgrave, 2005.

Sober, Elliot. "The Design Argument." In William Mann (ed.), *The Blackwell Guide to the Philosophy of Religion*, 117–47. Oxford: Blackwell, 2005.

Sperba, Dan. *Explaining Culture: A Naturalistic Approach*. Oxford: Blackwell, 1996.

Sproul, Barbara. *Primal Myths: Creation Myths Around the World*. New York: HarperOne, 1979.

Stace, Walter. *Mysticism and Philosophy*. New York: Macmillan, 1961.

——. *Religion and the Modern Mind*. Philadelphia: J.P. Lippincott, 1952.

Stairs, Allen and Christopher Bernard. *A Thinker's Guide to the Philosophy of Religion.* New York: Pearson Longman, 2007.

Stanovich, Keith. *How to Think Straight about Psychology.* Glenview, IL: Scott, Foresman and Company, 1986.

Stark, Rodney. *One True God: Historical Consequences of Monotheism.* Princeton: Princeton UP, 2001.

Stark, Rodney and Roger Finke. *Acts of Faith: Explaining the Human Side of Religion.* Berkeley: U of California P, 2000.

Steel, David Ramsey. *Atheism Explained: From Folly to Philosophy.* Peru, IL: Open Court Press, 2008.

Stenger, Victor. *The New Atheism: Taking a Stand for Science and Reason.* Amherst, NY: Prometheus Books, 2009.

Stephen, Leslie. *An Agnostic's Apology: and Other Essays.* London: Smith and Elder, 1867.

Stern, Leonard. *The Structures and Strategies of Human Memory.* Homewood, IL: The Dorsey Press, 1985.

Strawson, P.F. *Introduction to Logical Theory.* New York: John Wiley & Sons, 1952.

Swinburne, Richard. *The Coherence of Theism.* Oxford: Clarendon Press, 1977.

——. *The Existence of God.* Oxford: Clarendon Press, 1979.

——. "Whole and Part in Cosmological Arguments." *Philosophy* 44,170 (1969): 339–40.

——. *The Secular Age.* Cambridge, MA: Harvard UP, 2007.

Taylor, Charles. *Varieties of Religion Today: William James Revisited.* Cambridge, MA: Harvard UP, 2003.

Taylor, Richard. *Metaphysics.* Upper Saddle River, NJ: Pearson, 1992.

Templeton, John. *Agape Love: A Tradition Found in Eight World Religions.* Philadelphia: Templeton Foundation Press, 1999.

Thrower, James. *A Short History of Western Atheism.* London: Pemberton Books, 1971.

Tillich, Paul. *The Courage to Be.* New Haven: Yale UP, 1966.

——. *Dynamics of Faith.* New York: Harper and Row, 1957.

——. *Systematic Theology,* vol. 1. Chicago: U of Chicago P, 1951.

——. "Two Types of Philosophy of Religion." *Union Seminary Quarterly Review* (1964): 3–13.

Underhill, Evelyn. *Mysticism.* New York: Dutton, 1961.

Unger, Peter. *Living High and Letting Die: Our Illusion of Innocence.* New York: Oxford UP, 1996.

Van Buren, Paul. *Edges of Language.* New York: Macmillan, 1972.

Van Inwagen, Peter. *Metaphyics.* Boulder, CO: Westview Press, 1993.

Von Franz, Marie-Louise. *Creation Myths.* Boston: Shambhala, 2001.

Vyse, David. *Believing in Magic: The Psychology of Superstition.* Oxford: Oxford UP, 1997.

Wainwright, William. *Mysticism.* Brighton: Harvester Press, 1981.

Ward, Coren Porac. *Sensation and Perception.* Orlando, FL: Academic Press, 1984.

Watson, Gary. "Free Agency." *Journal of Philosophy* 8 (1975): 205–20.

Watts, Alan. *The Way of Zen*. New York: Vintage Books, 1957.

Weinstein, E.A., M. Cole, M.S. Mitchell, and O.G. Lyerly. "Anosognosia and Aphasia." *Archives of Neurology* 10 (1964): 376–86.

Whitehead, Alfred North. *Process and Reality: An Essay in Cosmology*. New York: Free Press, 1978.

——. *Religion in the Making*. New York: Fordham UP, 1997.

Wiesel, Elie. *Night*, Marion Wiesel (trans.). New York: Hill and Way, 2006.

Wilson, A.N. *God's Funeral*. London: John Murray Publishers, 1998.

Wilson, David Sloan. *Darwin's Cathedral: Evolution, Religion, and the Nature of Society*. Chicago: U of Chicago P, 2002.

Wisdom, John. "Gods." *Proceedings of the Aristotelean Society* (1944). Reprinted in John Wisdom, *Philosophy and Psycho-Analysis*, 149–68. Oxford: Blackwell, 1953.

Wittgenstein, Ludwig. *The Blue and Brown Books (or Preliminary Studies for "The Philosophical Investigations")*. New York: Harper & Row, 1964.

——. "Lectures on Religious Belief." In Cyril Barrett (ed.), *Wittgenstein: Lectures and Conversations*, 53–72. Berkeley, CA: U of California P, 1966.

——. *Philosophical Investigations*, G.E.M. Anscombe (trans.). Oxford: Blackwell, 1953.

——. *Tractatus Logico-Philosophicus*, D.F. Pears and B.F. McGuinness (trans.). London: Routledge & Kegan Paul, 1972.

Woerlee, G.M. *Mortal Minds: The Biology of Near Death Experiences*. Amherst, NY: Prometheus Books, 2005.

Wolf, Susan. *Freedom Within Reason*. Oxford: Oxford UP, 1990.

——. "Moral Saints." *The Journal of Philosophy* 79,8 (1982): 419–39.

Wykstra, Stephen, "The Humean Obstacle to Evidential Arguments from Suffering: On Avoiding the Evils of 'Appearance'." *International Journal for Philosophy of Religion* 16 (1984): 73–93.

——. "Rowe's Noseeum Arguments from Evil." In D. Howard-Snyder (ed.), *The Evidential Argument from Evil*, 126–50. Bloomingdale, IN: Indiana UP, 1996.

Yandell, Keith (ed.). *God, Men, and Religion: Readings in the Philosophy of Religion*. New York: McGraw-Hill, 1973.

Zaehner, R.C. *Mysticism: Sacred and Profane*. Oxford: Oxford UP, 1973.

Zuckerman, Phil. *Society Without God*. New York: New York UP, 2008.

AUTHOR INDEX